JEWISH LIBYA

MODERN JEWISH HISTORY

Henry Feingold, *Series Editor*

Jewish Libya

Memory and Identity
in Text and Image

◆ ◆ ◆

Edited by
Jacques Roumani, David Meghnagi,
and Judith Roumani

Syracuse University Press

Published with the support of family and friends of Jacques Roumani.

Syracuse University Press
Syracuse, New York 13244-5290

For a listing of books published and distributed by Syracuse University Press,
visit www.SyracuseUniversityPress.syr.edu.

ISBN: 978-0-8156-3562-8 (hardcover)   978-0-8156-3580-2 (paperback)
978-0-8156-5427-8 (e-book)

Library of Congress Cataloging-in-Publication Data
Names: Roumani, Jacques, editor. | Meghnagi, David, editor. | Roumani, Judith, editor.
Title: Jewish Libya : memory and identity in text and image / edited by Jacques Roumani,
    David Meghnagi, and Judith Roumani.
Description: First edition. | Syracuse, New York : Syracuse University Press, 2018. |
    Series: Modern Jewish history | Includes bibliographical references and index.
Identifiers: LCCN 2018012695 (print) | LCCN 2018017465 (ebook) |
    ISBN 9780815654278 (E-book) | ISBN 9780815635628 | ISBN 9780815635628
    (hardback : alk. paper) | ISBN 9780815635802 (pbk.: alk. paper)
Subjects: LCSH: Jews—Libya—History. | Jews—Libya—Civilization. | Jews—Libya—
    Social life and customs. | Jewish women—Libya. | Jews—Libya—Interviews.
Classification: LCC DS135.L44 (ebook) | LCC DS135.L44 J48 2018 (print) |
    DDC 961.2/004924—dc23
LC record available at https://lccn.loc.gov/2018012695

Manufactured in the United States of America

In Memory of Jacques
To Our Children, Elisa and David
and
Our Grandson, Ace

◆ ◆ ◆

Contents

Tables

◆ ◆ ◆

In Memoriam

Jacques Roumani z"l

A wound that cannot heal! That is the only way I can describe the untimely passing of my dear brother, Jacques. A few weeks after, and still my pen cannot describe him in the past tense!

Reading the extensive exchange of letters between us in 1960, he a teenager writing in Benghazi and I in the United States, does not leave room for the thought that these were of yesteryear. In these letters, he comes alive with his concerns about the family, about the future of our careers, and about Judaism. Already then, in 1960, he expressed an urgency to leave Libya, emphasizing the deteriorating situation of the Jews there.

His enrollment at the American High School in Benghazi, and the geographical distance that separated us, highlighted those concerns and strengthened his determination and urgency to register at any American university in order to live his dream of democracy and the values he had internalized, as he described, from Ralph Waldo Emerson's 1841 essay "Self-Reliance." He adopted American literature as his own and became fascinated by American history, cherishing the concepts of American democracy as expounded by the American Founding Fathers.

In 1961, Jacques landed in New York City and attended Yeshiva University. The geographical distance between us was now narrowed to the extent that I could go and visit him in New York from Boston almost every weekend. We spent time together enjoying our new freedom, anticipating the arrival of the family and paving the way for his transfer to Brandeis University. These visits brought us closer than ever before.

For Jacques, Yeshiva University served not only as a springboard to study in the United States but also as an introduction to a new Jewish world—the Yiddish world and its language—with words like *daven* and *tsholent* for which Jacques could not find a literary counterpart, as much as he tried, in the Jewish language of our country of origin.

Thus the subsequent year, 1962, marked Jacques' transfer to Brandeis University and the beginning of his rapid climb in the welcoming new world. From Brandeis he went to Princeton University, and from there to a Fulbright; the World Bank; projects in Asia, northern and southern Africa, and Latin America; and lately university teaching.

True to the spirit of the Protestant work ethic, as reflected in the American way of life, Jacques also found time to write and contribute his share on subjects dear to him, such as modern Libya and the Middle East. But it pains us all that he was unable to see the fruits of his latest endeavor in the form of this book on which he had labored untiringly.

Although a full-fledged product of American education, Jacques never abandoned his admiration for and practice of his heritage and continued to enrich it with the acquired knowledge resulting from his interaction with different environments.

The impressive dossier of the history of his life would have made other people vain and pretentious, but Jacques insisted on humility and shyness, warmth and consideration, exemplifying that part of his childhood and youth.

Not only the family but also his friends from near and far mourn his passing. It was too early. We would have wanted him to stay longer. And yet despite the pain, we all feel thankful and lucky to have had him pass through our lives and to have left us richer than before. He fits the proverb that says one should put life in years and not years in life. He managed successfully to put life in years!

May your legacy, dear brother, continue to shine on your family and brighten the horizon of our world.

Maurice M. Roumani, Jerusalem, January 2017

◆ ◆ ◆

Preface

This book was born originally from an idea of Jacques Roumani z″l, who intensely wanted it to come into being and got me involved through his passionate commitment to its concrete planning and realization.

Sad to say, Jacques has left us, just a little while before the book was ready for publishing. And while I write this, there rises up in my mind, in sorrow and affection, the memory of someone who was unique. And it's as if this person is present among us, with his gentleness, his reserved attitude, his kindness, and the critical acuity with which he used to share his thoughts, words, and emotions.

Jacques was a person of integrity, a man of culture, who loved the liturgical song of his community of origin and who put his best effort as a scholar into valorizing and preserving the memory of the culture of Jews of the Arab world.

After he moved from Benghazi to the United States, Jacques achieved important positions within the World Bank, which never affected the simplicity and generosity with which he would be open to new relationships. He was a political analyst and an expert on the Arab world, especially Libya, and published numerous articles that became classics on the subject. The idea behind this book had a different meaning, though. With hindsight, it can be read as a sort of living will. It is not only a book on the memory and history of a community, but it is also a project for revitalizing a community life that had never been completely snuffed out. It is an open book that throws a bridge between memory and research, traditions lived and recounted, and the reality of the historical and cultural changes that have taken place.

It is what one might call a "hybrid" book in which researchers and cultural operators are involved in various ways in interrogating each other about what has remained of an ancient tradition and how to transmit it to future generations.

David Meghnagi, Rome, February 2017

JEWISH LIBYA

Introduction

JACQUES ROUMANI

A fiftieth anniversary can be compared to middle age in the life of an individual. Metaphorically, one can also relate such an anniversary to the proverbial midlife crisis. In this case, I would not describe it as a full-blown crisis but a crisis of smaller dimensions. The members of the Libyan Jewish Community of Rome, by now well established, as well as Libyan Jewish communities that exist mainly in Israel, in other parts of Europe, and, to a far lesser extent, in the United States, can at last allow themselves to reflect on the meaning of their past. They can now ask themselves how to nourish and sustain their authentic religious and cultural patrimony so that it can become part of the identity of the descendants of this Community, which is truly unique within the panorama of the Jews of the Middle East and North Africa.

Taking up again the metaphor of midlife, we know that normally a person who is fifty years old decides either to keep on going full steam ahead, to go to town as one might say, or to slow down and take a siesta. We are well aware that many Libyan Jews have chosen to go ahead at full speed in various sectors in Israel (e.g., minister Moshe Kahlon, business tycoon Yitzhak Tshuva) and also in Italy and other parts of the world (e.g., Moisés Naím, former minister of Venezuela and later scholar and editor of an influential journal, *Foreign Policy*, in Washington; Walter Arbib of Canada, founder of SkyLink Aviation, a search and rescue company).

The aim of this book is to capture the essence of the Libyan Jewish cultural heritage in order to reawaken and preserve memory and to contribute to maintaining this very special identity within the framework of the Italian Jewish community and other Jewish communities.

I would like to emphasize that within this book memory is based on history but it is not history. Fortunately, the history of the Jews of Libya is well documented. It has been neatly summarized in one of our chapters, the one by Vivienne Roumani-Denn, from which I quote:

> Jews have lived in the region of North Africa that now constitutes the modern nation of Libya for more than 2,300 years, initially under Phoenician, Greek, and then Roman rule, some 400 years before the destruction of the Second Temple in Jerusalem and a full millennium before the rise of Islam in Arabia. The eastern (Cyrenaica) and western (Tripolitania) regions of Libya found themselves conquered by tribes from the Arabian Peninsula in the mid-seventh century CE during their invasion of North Africa and mostly ruled under various Muslim caliphates thereafter. Ottoman Turkish rule came to Tripoli in 1551 and somewhat later to Benghazi, sometimes with direct rule from Constantinople, but more commonly through local pashas. Italy invaded and conquered Libya from the Ottomans in 1911, and it remained an Italian colony until the defeat of the World War II Axis powers in North Africa in 1943, when Tripolitania and Cyrenaica fell under British administration. (A third region, Fezzan in the south, was under French administration.) The three administrative regions, with different tribal loyalties, united into an independent kingdom in 1951. King Idris was deposed in 1969 in an army coup led by Muammar Qadhafi. With major centers in the ports of Tripoli in the west and Benghazi in the east, Libya's Jewish Ottoman and post-Ottoman population at its peak was about 38,000, with 21,000 in Tripoli, 4,500 in Benghazi, and the remainder in smaller cities and villages. More than 90 percent of the Jewish community left between 1948 and 1951, leaving 2,500 in Tripoli and 400 in Benghazi, and Jewish life essentially came to an end in 1967, prior to the coup. Most of the Community went to Israel, where there are now an estimated 120,000 Jews from Libya

and their descendants, with some 3,000 in Rome and smaller numbers elsewhere. (See chapter 9, pp. 185–86.)

The texture of Jewish life in Libya, as described by the Libyan Jews themselves, was far from smooth. As the main minority, they were subject to *dhimmi* status, entailing the constant risk of murder, robbery, and desecration of synagogues.[1] It was not surprising that the Jews welcomed European intervention, first in the form of Italian colonization[2] and second through actions by the British Military Administration right after World War II. The Jews' high hopes for Europe were dashed initially by the Italian Fascist government, allied to Hitler and willing to see Libyan Jews die in Italian or German internment camps;[3] and then by the British, who stood by as Jews were murdered in 1945 and 1948. Though Libya's independence was negotiated by the United Nations, and its constitution officially embodied the Universal Declaration of Human Rights, over the 1950s

1. A digital map of the Jewish communities of Libya created by Eddie Ashkenazie et al. (still under construction) may be found at the Diarna website, www.diarna.org. The stories of the Jews' dire and dangerous plight and appeals to the Alliance Israélite Universelle from Libya are detailed in David Littman, "Jews under Muslim Rule in the Late Nineteenth Century," *Wiener Library Bulletin* 28 (1975): 35–36, 69–72.

2. Though the Jews might have expected France to intervene, following their appeals to the AIU, it was Italy that asserted its supposed rights to *la quarta sponda*, its fourth shore, as in Roman times. Libyan Jews embraced Italian culture and were until shortly before the Fascist period appreciated in return for their role as intermediaries. See Ministero delle Colonie, Mostra Coloniale di Genova, *Le Scuole Italiane in Tripoli* (Rome: Tipografia Nazionale G. Bertoro, 1914); Elia Artom, "L'Importanza dell'Elemento Ebraico nella Popolazione della Tripolitania," in *Atti del Secondo Congresso di Studi Coloniali* (Naples: Centro di Studi Coloniali, 1934), vol. 4, 116–27.

3. For Giado, an Italian internment camp, see Maurice Roumani, *The Jews of Libya: Coexistence, Persecution, Resettlement* (Brighton: Sussex University Press, 2008), 34–35; also David Meghnagi, unpublished paper, n.d., "Il Campo di Giado"; for Germany, see Yossi Sucary, *Benghazi—Bergen-Belsen*, trans. Yardenne Greenspan (San Bernadino: Createspace, 2016) (a fictional but accurate portrayal).

and 1960s indigenous Jews saw themselves become stateless hostages.[4] Finally in 1967, King Idris himself declared that he could no longer protect the Jews from rioting Muslims, and they were airlifted out to Italy in Libyan and Italian planes under the aegis of the American Jewish Joint Distribution Committee.

History is one thing, memory is another. Memory is what we remember. The events of our common cultural and emotional portrait—with a little taste of Proust's *madeleines*[5]—which serves as a bridge of collective group identity across the generations.

These memories encompass our unique *piyyutim* (hymns) for life-cycle events such as the Brit Milah, Bar Mitzvah, Simchat Torah, and Yom Kippur; of the memories of the beautiful beaches of Benghazi, such as the Giuliana Beach; of the Bar Gambrinus in Tripoli; the great football team Aurora, the Maccabi team, and the Ben Yehudah Club; the story of Alfonso Pagani, the "man in the box";[6] of Journo's *Il Ribelle*; of thousands of photos and documentaries such as the *Last Jews of Libya*; and of the stories of David Gerbi, such as his tale of the *qaffa* (the basket and the computer), as well as his exciting adventures about returning to Libya. These memories were once published in the magazine *Trabulsia Farsi* (Rome) and continue to appear in *Ada* in Israel and websites such as that of Vivienne Roumani-Denn (www.jewsof libya.com). It is a question of experiences, emotions, and symbols. It is a question of linguistic codes, as David Meghnagi writes, linguistic memories of a cosmopolitan commingling that is still in daily use. I refer for example to the typical dialogue that Meghnagi cites. When two Libyan Jewish women meet in New York, one says to the other,

---

4. See Leone Carpi, "La Condizione giuridica degli ebrei nel Regno Unito di Libia," *Rivista di Studi Politici Internazionali* 30, no. 1 (January–March 1963): 87–92.

5. For Proust, memory was suddenly reawakened and came flooding back when he tasted the humble coffee cakes, the *madeleines*, of his childhood.

6. Alfonso Pagani escaped from Libya by hiding in a crate and being transported by air to Malta. "L'Uomo della cassa" made international headlines. With thanks to Miriam Pagani for allowing us to read her late husband's unpublished manuscript.

"Eze surprise, 'amlcili, sono veramente frhana to meet you!" To cite a passage from the chapter by Meghnagi that appears in this volume:

> The apogee of this interlacing of worlds and cultures could be achieved speaking three or four languages at the same time, depending on whom one was talking to, passing from one language to another with the same person . . . according to the subject. . . . It was an oasis in which a Jew could feel Italian or Maltese, Greek or Arab, while continuing to be Jewish. It was a great interior treasure that not everyone realized they had. (See chapter 13, p. 269.)

We need to preserve our memories to avoid distortions and anonymity, before our people's discourse or way of speaking, especially among the young, disappears and they become submerged beneath newer, more universal memories of modern daily life. This reminds me of a true story from the Jewish Federation of New York in which the author asked the audience who remembered the name of the mother of Jesus, and almost everyone knew the answer. Then he asked who remembered the name of the mother of Moses. Only one person stood up and said with pride, "Yoshebel." Then the lecturer responded that he was close, but the correct name was "Yocheved." After the end of the lecture this person said to the speaker that the correct name was indeed Yoshebel, and cited as proof Cecil B. DeMille's *The Ten Commandments*. I do not think that any of us want to see our memories "corrected" like that. We want authentic memories.

My own family left Benghazi, crossed the ocean, and has been in America for fifty years already. As memories blend and spill into identity, especially in the twenty-first century, it is a question unavoidably of multiple identities. We need to clarify first of all the identity of Libyan Jews in general, in Italy, in Israel, and in America. The Community cannot be restricted to and does not completely fit the definition of "Arab Jews."

With regard to the Arab identity or "Arabness" of Middle Eastern Jews, we are reminded by the Israeli sociologist, Yehouda Shenhav, in his book, *The Arab Jews*, that this category is "neither natural nor necessarily consistent and coherent . . . given the long history of rupture between them . . . the label was edited out by historical circumstances, particularly the rise of Jewish and Arab nationalism."[7] Arabness may be at best a shared cultural code but it was not an identity, as another Israeli scholar, Amnon Raz-Krakotzkin, has pointed out. "It was a cultural-linguistic reality," as Raz-Krakotzkin says, quoted in Lital Levy's profound essay, "Historicizing the Concept of Arab Jews in the *Mashriq*,"[8] an important contribution to understanding the subject. Moreover, and most importantly, Jews could not be and were not admitted to Arab identity, whether in the *Mashriq* or *Maghrib*, because Arabs are or perceive themselves to be the main pillar of the Islamic *'umma* or Community of Believers, from which Jews and other infidels are automatically excluded and relegated to the inferior status of subordinate *dhimmi*. Ironically, almost parallel to the unprecedented effort of the Jewish intellectuals to join the Arab revival and nationalist movements, the "champions of Muslim reformism . . . Muhammed Abdu and Rashid Ridah and their later followers engaged in a form of 'dejudaization' of Muslim tradition . . . and offered a modern restatement of Islam's criticism of the Jews and Judaism."[9] Not surprisingly, the majority of Jews in the Middle East and North Africa sought the protection of European powers and the freedom of Western culture. Exacerbated by political enmity between Jewish and Arab nationalism, the definitive Arab rejection of Jews as Arabs is succinctly encapsulated in Albert Memmi's oft-quoted realization that "because we

---

7. Yehouda Shenhav, *The Arab Jews: A Postcolonial Reading of Nationalism, Religion, and Ethnicity* (Stanford: Stanford University Press, 2006), 9.

8. Lital Levy, "Historicizing the Concept of Arab Jews in the *Mashriq*," *Jewish Quarterly Review* 98, no. 4 (Fall 2008): 452–69.

9. Michel Abitbol, "Jews of Muslim Lands in the Modern Period: History and Historiography," 44–65, in Peter Y. Medding, ed., *Sephardic Jewry and Mizrahi Jews* (Oxford: Oxford University Press, 2007), 47. For a full discussion of this paradigmatic change in Muslim attitudes in the modern period, see Ronald Nettler and Suha Taji-Farouki, eds., *Muslim-Jewish Encounters, Intellectual Traditions and Modern Politics* (Amsterdam: Overseas Publishers Association and Harwood, 1998), esp. Ronald Nettler, chap. 1, "Early Islam, Modern Islam and Judaism: The *Isra'iliyyat* in Modern Islamic Thought," 1–13.

were born in these so-called Arab countries, we share their languages, their customs, and their cultures to an extent that is not negligible," but "the Arabs did not respect the Jewish Arabs . . . and it is far too late to become Jewish Arabs again."[10] The broader contexts of these developments in history, historiography, and culture are synthesized in Benbassa, Attias, and Abitbol (2006) and Harvey E. Goldberg (1996).[11] And so there can be no "next year in Tripoli."[12]

From another point of view, the Jews of Libya now resident in Italy encounter a convergence, an almost total one, with the Italian Jewish Community of Rome, but at the same time there is a historical divergence, because the Community's historical points of reference are not Luzzatto, Ginzberg, Modigliani, Cassuto, and Benamozegh (all important figures in Italian Jewish culture), but rather the Libyan figures of Mordekhai Ha-Kohen, Shimon Labi, and Avraham Khalfon. As time has passed, the convergences have become stronger than the divergences and an amalgamation, a melting pot, has taken place. Returning to the metaphor of midlife, though, one has to grow and recognize oneself in an independent identity before one can give one's best to the Community.

We, the Jews of Libya, as in almost all the Arab countries, closed up shop in Libya and were uprooted fifty years ago, but we left there the proverbial nail on the wall of Djoha, the hero of Middle Eastern jokes, fables, and proverbs. I recall the fable about Djoha when he was

10. Quoted by Shenhav, *Arab Jews*, 9. See Albert Memmi, *Juifs et Arabes* (Paris: Gallimard, 1974); English translation, *Jews and Arabs*, trans. Eleanor Levieux (Chicago: J. Philip O'Hara, 1975), esp. the chapter "What Is an Arab Jew?," 19–29; 20; and note on p. 29, quoted here.

11. See Esther Benbassa, Jean-Christophe Attias, and Michel Abitbol, *Juifs et musulmans: une histoire partagée, un dialogue à construire* (Paris: Découverte, 2006); and Harvey E. Goldberg, ed., *Sephardi and Middle Eastern Jewries: History and Culture in the Modern Era* (Bloomington: Indiana University Press, 1996), 1–55.

12. See Jacques Roumani, review, "Modern Middle Eastern Jewish Thought: Writings on Identity, Politics, and Culture, 1893–1958 by Moshe Behar and Zvi Ben-Dor Benite," in *Sephardic Horizons* 3, no. 2 (Summer 2013), www.sephardichorizons.org.

forced to rent out his house. He rented it all out except for one nail on the wall that he asked the tenant not to touch, and the new occupant said "all right."[13] Eventually Djoha's frequent visits to check on his nail annoyed the tenant so much that the latter moved out. Well, we also metaphorically revisit within ourselves this nail that the new occupants in Libya unknowingly guard, but no one can take it down from the wall.

In Libyan taste (where we mix many different spices to create a unique culinary sensation), we have tried to collect in one volume some essential aspects of the memory and identity of the Jewish Community. It is both for specialists and for all interested readers.

In June 2017, the Jews of Libya commemorated the jubilee of their complete exodus in 1967 from this North African land, an exodus that had begun with a mass migration to Israel in 1948–1949. Jews have resided in Libya since Phoenician times, seventeen centuries before their encounter with the Arab conquest in 644–646 AD. Their disappearance from Libya, like most other Jewish communities in North Africa and the Middle East, led to their fragmentation across the globe as well as reconstitution in two major centers, Israel and Italy. Distinctive Libyan Jewish traditions and a broad cultural heritage have survived and prospered in different places in Israel and in Rome, Italy, where Libyan Jews are recognized for their vibrant contribution to Italian Jewry. Nevertheless, with the passage of time, the Community is increasingly marking a transition, as memories fade among the younger generations and multiple identities begin to overshadow those inherited from past centuries.

The history of Jewish Libya has been well documented by some key authors,[14] complementing other books on Libyan Jewry written

---

13. See Dr. Gayed's blog, "Goha's Nail," January 1, 2011: http://dr-gayed.blog spot.com/search?updated-min=2011-01-01.

14. E.g., Renzo De Felice, *Ebrei in un paese arabo: Gli ebrei nella Libia contemporanea tra colonialism, nazionalismo arabo e sionismo* (Bologna: Il Mulino, 1978); English translation, *Jews in an Arab Land: Libya, 1835–1970*, trans. Judith Roumani

from the perspectives of anthropology, sociology, religion, and personal experiences.[15] In comparison to these well-known works from the point of view of a single author, this book offers instead an anthology where different authors highlight key and unique aspects of culture and society in Jewish Libya, including the diversity of cosmopolitan and local Jewish men and women within the community, their spatial and cultural environment under colonial influence, and traditional culinary specialties.

Addressed to the general as well as the scholarly reader, the anthology is intended to commemorate, celebrate, and preserve key elements of the Libyan Jewish heritage of popular interest and evoke a lively intergenerational exchange among the two hundred thousand Jews of Libyan origin worldwide, as well as with other Jews from North Africa. Similar books and anthologies have appeared on the Jews of the Maghreb (Morocco, Algeria, and Tunisia), such as the recent *Jewish Culture and Society in North Africa*,[16] where Libyan Jewry is typically absent. The present anthology, consisting of all original essays except the first two, will fill a gap in the genre and open comparisons with other vanished Jewish societies of the Maghreb and the Levant.

While the scope of the anthology covers all of Libyan Jewry, the voices of the community in Italy are highlighted since much of this

(Austin: University of Texas Press, 1985); Yaakov Haggiag-Lilluf, *The History of the Libyan Jews* [in Heb.] (Or Yehuda: World Organization of Libyan Jews, 2000); Maurice M. Roumani, *The Jews of Libya: Coexistence, Persecution, Resettlement* (Brighton: Sussex Academic Press, 2008).

15. E.g., Rachel Simon, *Change within Tradition among Jewish Women in Libya* (Seattle: University of Washington Press, 1992); Harvey Goldberg, *Jewish Life in Muslim Libya: Rivals and Relatives* (Chicago and London: University of Chicago Press, 1990); Abraham Khalfon, *Maʿaseh Tzaddikim*, edited with introduction, notes, and index by Asaf Raviv (Ashkelon: Peer HaQodesh, 2009); David Gerbi, *Costruttori di Pace: Storia di un ebreo profugo della Libia* (Rome: Edizioni Appunti di Viaggio, 2003); Arthur Journo, *Il ribelle* (Florence: Lettere, 2003).

16. *Jewish Culture and Society in North Africa*, ed. Emily Benichou Gottreich and Daniel J. Schroeter (Bloomington: Indiana University Press, 2011).

community's rich internal life after its exodus from Libya in 1967 is yet to be fully documented. As it has become well established in Rome, the Libyan community has turned to reflect on the meaning of its past and its sustainability in the future, given ongoing trends merging young Libyan Jews into mainstream Italian society.

Through a combination of text and image, this anthology is designed to provide the nonspecialist reader with a contextual understanding of Jewish Libya and a timely reference to this vibrant community. It should enrich the Jewish landscape of North Africa.

Our twelve contributors present very diverse approaches to various aspects of Libyan Jewish life and culture. It is important to remember that (as documented by archaeologists) our collective history reaches far back in time to ancient times. Shimon Applebaum, a British Israeli archaeologist who was stationed in Cyrenaica during the British Military Administration (1943–1951), writes about the Jewish Revolt against Rome in Cyrenaica in 115–117 CE (also known as the Revolt of the Diaspora) in his chapter "The Jewish Revolt against the Romans in Cyrenaica, 115–117 CE: Archaeological Evidence, Causes, and Course of the Revolt." Applebaum has studied the revolt, brutally put down, of this large and flourishing ancient Jewish Community, involving Egypt, Cyprus, and Mesopotamia as well as Eretz Yisrael. The menorah carved on a rock road in Cyrenaica, photographed a little earlier by an Italian archaeologist during the Fascist period, and actually a piece of graffiti, is one of the first examples of the use of the menorah as a political symbol. Survivors of the revolt may have fled south into the Sahara, eventually leading a defense against the Muslim invasion and helping create a Berber-Jewish syncretism as far west as southern Morocco.[17] Applebaum's chapter is reproduced from his *Jews and Greeks in Ancient Cyrene* (1979).[18]

17. For a historical novel on this subject, see Albert Memmi, *The Desert: or the Life and Adventures of Jubair Wali al-Mammi*, trans. Judith Roumani (Syracuse: Syracuse University Press, 2015).

18. Shimon Applebaum, *Jews and Greeks in Ancient Cyrene* (Leiden: Brill, 1979).

Maurice M. Roumani sheds light on the long centuries bridging Roman times and the colonial period ("Libyan Jews in the Islamic Arab and Ottoman Periods"). When Arabs invaded in the seventh century, they met organized resistance for a time from Jews and Berbers allied under La Kahena, the Jewish chieftain-queen. But it failed and the Muslim invaders swept on as far as Spain. Jewish communities survived, especially in the Jebel Nafusa Mountains near Tripoli, suffering persecution again under the Almohads and the Banu Hilal Bedouin invaders in later centuries. Such sufferings are recorded by poets and discussed later in our volume by Harvey E. Goldberg. From the sixteenth and seventeenth centuries under the Ottomans and the local dynasty of the Qaramanlis, Jews generally recovered and prospered, especially in the coastal towns, establishing trading links around and across the Mediterranean that would be invaluable in the Italian colonial period, as several of our other writers point out.

Hamos Guetta's evocative piece ("*Mafrum, Haraimi, Tebiha, Bsisa*, and Other Culinary Specialities: Tastes, Symbols, and Meaning") discussing traditions and food captures life in the old Jewish quarters of Tripoli, the *haras* where even in the mid-twentieth century life seemed to have changed little since Ottoman times. His child's-eye view shows us the world of women, largely excluded from the economic life of men, but lively with song and tradition and especially the lore and labor of cooking in their open courtyards. Rachel Simon, later in the book, confirms many of the insights here from a more academic point of view.

Harvey E. Goldberg, in a scholarly, anthropological study— "Tradition with Modernity: From Ottoman Times (1835–1911) to Italian Encounters (1900–)"—likewise fleshes out these remembered impressions. He records how, because books were rare, Jewish learning was largely oral; how the Beth Din of Tripoli had its own versions of Jewish law not accepted elsewhere but suitable for local conditions; and how local tradition could trump modernity (in a notorious case of traditional marriage that led to the firing of Libya's chief rabbi by the colonial authorities).

Sumikazu Yoda brings us a linguistic study of the particular Judeo-Arabic dialect of Tripoli ("Libyan Judeo-Arabic: The Arabic Dialect and the Judeo-Arabic of the Jews of Tripoli"). Interestingly, he recorded this dialect in Israel among Libyan Jews who had left Libya in the late 1940s and early 1950s. Somewhat isolated in Israel within their *ma'abarot, moshavim,* or villages, they have preserved Judeo-Arabic better than those more Italianized Jews who stayed on in Libya and moved to Italy in 1967. Later on in our volume, Samuele Zarrugh has more to say on the Jews of Benghazi and their Judeo-Arabic.

From the late 1940s and early 1950s, when Jews began to leave, and definitively by 1967, when the last of them left, the echoing voices in Judeo-Arabic and tantalizing scents of food being prepared before each Jewish holiday were fading away. Jews left behind an urban landscape of not only the humble homes surrounding open courtyards in the *hara,* homes soon occupied by Muslims, but also magnificent synagogues and public and commercial buildings designed by Jewish architects during the Italian period. Jack Arbib's visually rich essay ("The Vanishing Landscape: A Retrospective Glance at the Topos of Libyan Jews") documents much of this with "before" and "after" pictures, depicting a sad story of neglect, destruction, and desecration. He also indicates the shared spaces where Jews, Muslims, and even Christians had once interacted. These shared spaces were themselves largely created during colonial times.

Rachel Simon, in "Libyan Jewish Women as a Marginalized Vanguard in the Late Nineteenth and Early Twentieth Centuries," reveals how women in a traditional environment could also be modernizers or voices for continuity and change. She discusses areas in which women could potentially be active, pinpointing family life, work, education, and occasional participation in public life.

This paper and the following one complement each other. "Libyan Jewish Women in Italy and Israel Today," by Gheula Canarutto Nemni, is based on interviews with three representative groups of Libyan Jewish women today: conservative/traditional, middle of the road, and modernizing. Both essays highlight the enterprising nature of Libyan Jewish women, the real pillars of their families through the generations, loyal to tradition yet able to serve as a vanguard and seize opportunities to better the lot of their loved ones. Vivienne Roumani-Denn's excerpts from interviews of both women and men in the following chapter allow us to understand the family from the male point of view as well. One of her interviewees explains that, within his family, "Mother was the captain of the ship," validating the findings of Simon and Canarutto Nemni. Roumani-Denn's own mother's opinion about her daughter not being free to walk the streets for fear of being bothered by Muslim males (by the 1950s and 1960s Libyan Jewish women had dressed in European clothes for decades and were never actually veiled, only perhaps adding a small headscarf) also reflects comments by the respondents of Canarutto Nemni.

A cluster of articles on voices, both collective and individual, follows. In her "Life Interrupted: Interviews with Jews of Libyan Origin," Roumani-Denn draws on her archive of recorded interviews. Libyan Jews fill a wide and diverse spectrum of careers and activities along traditional and modern lines. Whether successful entrepreneurs, professionals, leading national and international figures, academics and artists, or rabbis, they are linked by a common Libyan Jewish experience that they may or may not view as part of their new identities. A streak of fearlessness, of risk taking, characterizes not only women but also Jewish men from Libya and is expressed in extraordinarily successful careers achieved against all odds. This is accompanied by and stems from a very high degree of confidence-inducing warmth and love within the family. The insights by Guetta, Canarutto Nemni, and Simon are confirmed and echoed through these interviews.

On an individual level, Jacques Roumani's interview of Samuele Zarrugh ("Growing Up Jewish in Benghazi: An Interview with Samuele Zarrugh") shows a person who comes from a very warm and supportive family and who thus, with the self-confidence this creates, has been ready to do extraordinary things. The family did not live in the Jewish area of Benghazi but somewhat outside it in a Muslim neighborhood. Samuele attended a Muslim high school and studied business economics at the University of Benghazi, an unusual course for a Jew in Libya. After the expulsion in 1967, he and his family did not gravitate to Rome like the majority but moved to Livorno, a much smaller Jewish Community. As a three-term president of the Jewish Community, he has become a factor in local affairs. Samuele's family bears out the paradigms of a close, loving Jewish family and also shows the closer relationships between Muslims and Jews in Benghazi than in Tripoli.

Our final section relates to the undeniable sufferings to which Libyan Jews have been subject. A chapter by Goldberg, "Violence and the Liturgical/Literary Tradition: Joining the Chorus while Retaining Your Voice," presents *piyyutim* composed to commemorate dangerous events from which the Jews of Libya escaped; thus these are hymns thanking God for their deliverance. Such compositions entered the liturgical tradition of Libyan Jews from the eighteenth century on, and in some cases they have remained part of it to this day. In other cases, only a faint memory remains of these rare *piyyutim*.

"Yossi Sucary's Novel *Benghazi—Bergen-Belsen* in the Context of North African Jewish Literature of the Holocaust," by Judith Roumani, introduces a new novel, written originally in Hebrew, which brings to life the Holocaust experience of several hundred Libyan Jews with British citizenship who were taken from Libya and interned in Bergen-Belsen. Other Jews, particularly from Cyrenaica, with French, Tunisian, or Libyan citizenship, suffered deportation and internment, either in Tunisia or in the desert of Tripolitania. Those with Italian citizenship were taken to Italy and placed in camps there. These unknown stories of the long reach of the Holocaust also deserve to be told.

"Libyan Jews between Memory and History," by David Meghnagi, the third coeditor of this volume, in his chapter based on personal memory, interrogates the relationship between memory and history, aspiring toward preservation of memory and continuity of identity. Identity is not only in the present, but depends for its maintenance on memory, and the memories of Libyan Jews lie in both strong and positive traditions and the trauma suffered in the land of their origins.

Thus, the combination of a proud and intense religious and traditional life, a strong family life, and historical trauma, the editors believe, form the memory and the identity of the Jews of Libya, and serve as a launchpad for their entry into the ceaselessly changing modern world as fully modern people.

Jacques Roumani, March 1944–December 2016, did not live to see the final version of this anthology on the Jews of Libya. The other two editors would like to give their profound thanks to the colleagues and friends of Jacques who have participated in its publication:
Liliana Di Nola-Baron and Mark Lazerson (especially), for invaluable help with translation into English. Annette Fromm, expert bibliographer. Andrew Septimus, right-hand son-in-law. Judith Roumani Saphra, more than a cousin; Elisa Septimus and David Roumani, for endless willingness to help on many levels.

Claudio Procaccia for his invitation to deliver a lecture in 2015 on which this introduction is based. Shimon Doron, director of the Museum of Libyan Jewry, Or Yehuda, Israel, for his interest, moral support, and photos and contacts provided, and Avi Pedahtzur for photograph permissions. Pedahtzur Benattiyah of the Or Shalom Cultural Center of Libyan Jewry, Bat Yam, Israel, for his interest and for photographs promptly provided from his collection; Eyal David and Nava Barazani for their interest and support; and the latter for a beautiful afternoon of Libyan Jewish art. Thanks also to Nahid Dayyanim Gerstein and Sharon Horowitz of the Library of Congress; Eleanor Yadin of the New York Public Library; and Arthur Kiron, for bibliographical help on a rare book from Livorno.

All the authors in this volume, for their contributions and belief in this project, and for their patience;

Friends of Jacques Roumani for their generous assistance in his memory to enable this publication: Anonymous (several); Klas and Paula Hersson Ringskog; Mark Lazerson; Debra and Marvin Feuer; Ariel Grun; Arnold and Lisa Rosenthal; Elana and Jesse Mendelson; Sarah, Isaac, and Claire Jonas; Joseph and Lexie Tuchman; Dana Septimus and Joe Feldman; Gail and Yash Shirazi; Nahid and Steve Gerstein; Shira Krimsky; Tali and Michael Gevaryahu; Lauren Packer; Hasson Family; Daniel Septimus; Barbara and John Robbins; Elan

Aiken and Eva Bein; David and Keren Itzkowitz; David Kramer; Chavie Berman; Yonatan Buckman; Eve Partouche; Jonathan Geller; Andrew Rubin; Deborah Halpern; Natan Fisher; Becky Silberman; Jackie Soleimani; Anat Penini; Lana Greenland; Rosamond Timberg; Joshua and Anna London; Katie and David Colburn; and Tobie Beckerman.

We gratefully acknowledge E. J. Brill, publishers, for generously allowing us to republish a chapter from Shimon Applebaum's book, *Jews and Greeks in Ancient Cyrene* (Leiden: Brill, 1979); and, with thanks also to Norman Stillman, and to Maurice Roumani himself, a portion of the entry on "Libya" by Maurice M. Roumani in Norman Stillman, ed., *Encyclopedia of Jews in Islamic Lands* (Leiden: Brill, 2010). Profound thanks to Ronald Bruce St. John, Aryeh and Elana Bourkoff, and Lucette Lagnado. We also acknowledge all those who have granted permission for us to reproduce photographs and those who offered help with marketing and promotion, and of course Deborah Manion and the experts at Syracuse University Press who have believed in this project and made it into a book.

♦ ♦ ♦

PART ONE

History

AS A BRITISH-TRAINED ARCHAEOLOGIST, Shimon Applebaum had
the good fortune to enter Cyrenaica as a sergeant with the Palestine
Brigade during the war around 1943. He was put in charge of antiquities for Cyrenaica for the British Military Administration, which, as
he says, was a responsibility far exceeding his rank. During a period
of eighteen months he identified the remains of large ancient Jewish
communities in Cyrene and other Roman-era towns and found evidence of their struggle against the Romans. Jewish settlement in Libya
may go back as far as the time of the First Temple. The Jews' revolt
against their masters lasted from 115 to 117 CE and was occasioned
by land appropriations, heavy taxation, loss of economic opportunities, and discrimination against Jews that favored Greek settlers. The
fury of the Jews' destruction of pagan images, temples, and official
buildings is remarkable. The Jewish rebels under Lukuas planned to
gather support in Alexandria and reach the Holy Land, but they were
routed in Egypt. Lukuas did indeed manage to break into Palestine
before being finally defeated. The Jewish rebels' surviving remnants
may have fled into the Sahara Desert and Judaized certain Berber
tribes as they migrated westward across the Sahara, in the process
becoming Berberized themselves. Applebaum in his preface acknowl-
edges input into his 1979 book from Pietro Romanelli, an Italian
archeologist of Fascist times, who had published in Italy in 1943 an
in-depth archaeological study *La Cirenaica romana*, obviously not

available to Applebaum when he was on the ground. Though it served Fascist colonial claims, Romanelli's work was serious and thorough, and contains the only photograph we have of the menorah carved on the Roman rock road, as a symbol of Jewish rebellion.

Maurice M. Roumani takes up the story of Jews in Libya during the Islamic Arab and Ottoman centuries, from the seventh century on. He notes the development of renewed small Jewish settlements from the third century on and also discusses Jewish merchants who came from Alexandria and the Jewish-led Berber resistance to the Arab invasion in the seventh century. Though Jews were persecuted during the Arab, Bedouin, and Almohad conquests of the seventh, eleventh, and twelfth centuries, they were not forced to convert and so managed to remain Jewish.

The four centuries of Ottoman rule from 1555 on, after brief Christian incursions, allowed the Jews in Libya to thrive and grow (within the limits of their inferior status under Islam), expanding their philanthropic institutions and serving as economic intermediaries among Libyans, Ottomans, and Europeans into the twentieth century.

These two essays on little-known aspects of Libyan Jewish history lead us into more recent times and topics, as the long Arab era and then the Ottoman period gave way in the early twentieth century to the briefer Italian colonial regime.

1

• • •

The Jewish Revolt against the Romans in Cyrenaica, 115–117 CE

Archaeological Evidence, Causes, and Course of the Revolt

SHIMON APPLEBAUM

An examination of the physiography of Cyrenaica and the factors which molded her settlement and economy, has shown that the seasonal cycle and the two forms of economy inherent in the conditions of the country have exercised a decisive influence on her history, causing a constant tension and a repeated oscillation between mixed farming and the raising of livestock, between settled agriculture and nomadic pastoralism. The concentration of the Jewish peasantry on the state lands, which were more sensitive than any other category to the results of the above alternation, as most of them were on the desert fringes, open to political vicissitudes and the arbitrary character of the rulers, caused the Jews to suffer to a greater degree than other elements from a reaction in favor of pastoralism and extensive agriculture at the end of Ptolemaic rule and at the beginning of Roman domination.

This chapter is a slightly shortened version of the "Summing Up" section of Shimon Applebaum, "The Jewish Revolt against the Romans in Cyrenaica, 115–117 CE: Causes and Course of the Revolt," in *Jews and Greeks in Ancient Cyrene* (Leiden: E. J. Brill, 1979), 328–44. With many thanks and full credit acknowledgment to Koninklijke BRILL NV, who granted us permission to reprint. Spelling, punctuation, and citation style have been adjusted for the present publication.

The process of the restoration of the intensive economy took place in a period of growing conflict between Rome and the Jewish people. Nero's decision concerning tenant rights on the state domain was directed to the advantage of the population which had not suffered in this way—namely, the private landowners, which meant the Greek citizens of Cyrene. The penetration of extremist influence during the Great Rebellion of 66–73 therefore found a fertile field of activity among the multitude of landless and impoverished Jews in the country.

An analysis of the events of 73 at Cyrene has proved important in that it has revealed the close connection between them and activist revolutionary trends that fostered the messianic movement in Judaea; the same events led to the annihilation of the Hellenizing class of Cyrenaican Jewry, and thereby prepared the way for the rising of 115, since it left no buffer element between the Jewish masses and activist influence. The points of contact between the acts of Jonathan the Weaver and the ideology of Hirbet Qumran, chiefly as it is expressed in the scroll of "The War of the Sons of Light with the Sons of Darkness," prove, with other features of the rebellion under Trajan, the Sicarian content of the movement; Eusebius' reports on the movement's activity in the Western Desert and in the Thebais point to concentrations of insurgents on the desert fringes and to their penetration into Egypt along the desert routes.

But if we are permitted to trace the roots of the revolt in Cyrene to a combination of the Sicarian activist current and economic, chiefly agrarian, conditions implicit in the country itself, does this explanation hold good for all the centers of the movement in Trajan's time? If this is not the case, we are faced with the alternative: either the agrarian situation in Cyrenaica possessed no real importance for the historical episode under discussion, or Cyrene stood at the head of the movement and played the leading role in igniting the conflagration. Historical data are in favor of collusion between the Jews of Cyrene and Egypt, more especially in the rural areas outside Alexandria, at least from the time of Lucuas' incursion into the Nile valley. The Alexandrine Jews are referred to explicitly as "the allies" of the Jews of Cyrenaica, although both the historical and the papyrological evidence suggest that the Jews of the city in 116 were not the attackers but the attacked; nor did the Roman authorities treat their remnants as rebels.[1] But this evidence should not mislead us in our assessment of events in Alexandria; the widespread damage shows beyond all doubt that the broad strata of Alexandrian Jewry were drawn in to the defensive war against the Roman power by their own violent reaction, and at a certain point of time the initiative passed into their hands (the capture of the Serapeium); we may be sure that the activist element was also present. The Romans, for their part, could permit themselves some clemency at the end of the struggle, or at least a show of compassion towards the miserable remnant.

It is equally erroneous to see in the struggle waged by the Jews of Alexandria with the Greeks of the city for equality of rights a factor in the war of 116. It was certainly not a struggle for Greek citizenship. The striving for such citizenship belonged logically to the Hellenizing group in Alexandrine Jewry, meaning the wealthy and the well-to-do among them, and was bound up with an attitude that harmonious co-existence with Greek neighbors must be sought by all possible means. The sharp antagonisms between the Jewish masses of Alexandria and their Greek neighbors originated elsewhere and their sources were more complex; the most prominent were the radiation of national influence from Eretz Yisrael, differences of religion and custom, relations with Rome as a ruling power, and above all, the ethnicintellectual compactness of the Jews themselves.

The aggressive Jewish movement in Egypt seems to have originated chiefly in the rural districts, hence it may be possible to perceive among its causes an agrarian economic factor. The situation of the Egyptian fellahin (peasants) had always been difficult, and had been in a state of crisis throughout the later period of Ptolemaic rule. Roman administration had not modified this situation in any fundamental

1. G. Alon, *History of the Jews* (1954) vol. 1, 248; see also A. Tcherikover, *The Jews in Egypt in the Hellenistic Roman Age in the Light of the Papyri* (1963), 163–66.

fashion. Milne has surveyed the economy of Egypt in the first century CE in a way that can be summarized as a condemnation of the regime.[2] He observed that the Romans transferred to themselves those lands previously granted to private proprietors, imposed the poll tax on the majority of the population (especially the peasants), and subjected the merchant class to an inexorable system of licensing. They confiscated the temple estates in return for an annual grant-in-aid, and thrust the greater number of administrative functions upon Egyptian citizens, who had to discharge them without remuneration. The system of currency introduced by Rome into Egypt was valid only within the province's frontiers, thus affecting adversely its export and import trade. Although the economic position improved temporarily at the beginning of the Roman occupation, thanks to improved conditions of security and order and the restoration of the irrigation system, most of Egypt's production—chiefly her grain—was exported to Rome for her own benefit without requital, while the export trade as a whole was mainly in Roman hands.[3] Milne concludes that "before the end of the first century, the pauperization of the middle classes must have been fairly complete . . . and, as there was no more to be squeezed out of them, the pressure was transferred to the actual cultivators of the soil."

Bell does not contradict Milne's assessment, and thinks that in the first century CE, after the initial period of prosperity, the members of the Egyptian middle class already faced a burden of taxation beyond their capacity to bear, and that economic difficulties were now perceptible.[4] Villages which had been evacuated and abandoned by the flight of their inhabitants are known as early as 55–60.[5] These

---

2. *Journal of Roman Studies* 17, 1927, p. 1 sqq.: "The ruin of Egypt by Roman mismanagement."

3. Also in Jewish hands, according to Milne, but I am doubtful whether the evidence is sufficient to confirm his opinion. It is that of Josephus, *C. Ap.* II, 64, which hardly favors Milne's statement.

4. *Cambridge Ancient History* 10, 1934, 314–15.

5. Thus also M. Rostovtzeff, *A Social and Economic History of the Roman Empire* (1937), p. 295, and especially pp. 298, 677, on the situation of the fellaheen.

data would therefore suggest that in Trajan's day the economic conditions of Egypt were such as to foster a rebellious mood among certain elements of the population. Milne explains the clash between Jews and Greeks in Alexandria partly in terms of the economic situation described. But these factors applied more especially to the rural areas, and if we cannot yet point to a real agrarian crisis, growing poverty is perceptible in the steadily increasing difficulty in finding candidates to fill honorary official positions in the provincial centers. The elements of the Egyptian situation, therefore, do not contradict the explanation given for Cyrene, and were equally likely to act as one insurrectionary factor among several.

In Judaea, on the other hand, the agrarian factors are prominent, and the evidence for them reaches us through the sayings of the talmudic scholar and the documents of Ben Kosba in a clearer form than in any other province except Egypt.

Cyprus constitutes a weak link in the approach which sees the agrarian factor as one of the factors in the Jewish rebellion. Here the Jewish outbreak assumed no less violent and murderous a form than in Cyrenaica, yet the proofs of an agrarian element are slender and almost nonexistent. All that can be said is, that the use of the island's agricultural produce by the Jews of Judaea in Second Temple times encourages a belief that a Jewish rural population existed in Cyprus, and the little that is known of the extent of the revolt and the distribution of Jewish archaeological finds suggests the presence of Jews throughout the island and that they were not confined to the cities.

We are therefore forced to conclude that the agrarian factor was common to two centers of the rising—Cyrene and Egypt (the movement in Judaea did not attain the dimensions of a war, being faced by an overwhelming Roman force)—but the degree of decisiveness of the factor cannot be proved in Egypt, while the position in Cyprus is obscure. The decisive universal factor was psychological—the messianic aspiration derived from the destruction of the Temple and the activist ideology, of which the Sicarian is an example, intensified to no small degree by the economic situation. It is to the peculiarity of the conditions of Cyrenaica, however, that we may ascribe specific features of the revolt. In Mesopotamia, on the other hand, the Jewish struggle originated as an organic part of the entire population's reaction to the Roman invasion, although doubtless the influence of events within the Roman Empire was also considerable.

Having examined the impulses at work in the rising, we must consider the nature of its manifestations. These can be divided into three topics: (a) the massacre of the gentiles; (b) the destruction of gentile temples and images; and (c) the destruction of the enemy's habitation centers. The visible traces of the second and third phenomena are most prominent in Cyrenaica but are also to be found in Alexandria and Salamis of Cyprus. Only one fact can be stated with certainty on the entire question: the two sides fought savagely and slew without mercy.

The aim of the destruction of pagan cults and images does not constitute a problem if the general objects of the movement are considered. The Maccabees[6] and the activists of 66–70[7] behaved in much the same fashion. The educated pagan was doubtless equal to doubting whether his cultic images were more than symbols of the deities he worshipped, but the written testimony must be interpreted to mean that the simple Greek and Roman saw in the image the god himself. Plato writes: "We behold the laws of the gods clearly and honor them, setting up images and statues in their honor, and although they are not alive when we worship them, we consider them to be the living gods themselves, who extend to us abundant good will and grace on that account."[8] In case we should think that Plato's words applied only to the fourth century BC but not to the second century CE, we have the words of Plutarch, priest of Delphi (120–146 CE): "As philosophers claim, those who do not learn to understand names correctly

6. I *1Maccabees*. 2, 45; 5, 63. For a Hellenistic statue at Beth Shean (Beisan) decapitated, probably by the Jews in the reign of John Hyrcanus (135–104 BC), see *The Ancient Historian and His Materials: Essays in Honour of C. E. Stevens* (ed. B. Levick), 1976, 66–67.

7. Josephus, *Vita*, 12 (65).

8. Plato, *Leg.* 11, 931A.

misuse things also like those Greeks who, not having studied, are
in the habit of calling bronze objects, paintings and things of stone,
not statues or offerings to the gods, but 'gods,' and even dare to say
that Lacheres clothed Athena, and that Dionysios trimmed the golden
curls of Apollo."[9]

Even after the middle of the second century CE, when the Jewish
scholars had begun to take a more lenient view of statues, distinguishing between those used for idolatrous worship and those designed
for mere ornament—since they no longer feared that Jews would be
led astray by images—they nevertheless persisted in their austere attitude to all images of the emperors and all actions associated with
their cult.[10] But in the earlier part of the second century they had not
yet reached leniency even in spheres outside the imperial cult, and,
clearly, the revolutionary activists even less so. Even subsequently, we
hear of R. Nahum ben Samai at the end of the second century, who
refused to look upon a coin because it bore the image of Caesar.[11] The
degree of courage and hostility vis-à-vis the alien power involved in
the smashing of the idols is made clear by the testimony of John of
Ephesus,[12] who relates that as late as the year 572 the statues of Trajan
were still standing in Persia, and the Persians feared to pass by them.
But we should not think that iconoclastic actions were confined to the
Jews. Occasionally imperial statues became the targets of other rebels
in times of revolt. Plutarch too, after the extract already quoted, pro-
ceeds to refer to "the statue of Zeus Capitolinus which was burnt and
destroyed in the civil war."[13] The *Res gestae Divi Augusti* tell us that
Mark Antony plundered numerous dedications, including statues,

9. *Moralia*, de Is. Et Os., 71. E. Bevan, *Holy Images*, 1940, pp. 20 seq. E. R.
Dodds, *The Greeks and the Irrational*, 1963, 292–94.

10. E. Urbach, "Rulings on Idolatry and the Archeological and Historical Reality," *Eretz Yisrael* 5, 1958, pp. 199 sqq.; see also H. A. Wolfson, *Philo*, 1948, I,
pp. 14 sqq.

11. Jer., *AZ* 7, 42c.

12. Johannes Ephesi, (Schönfelder), 251–53.

13. *Moralia*, De Is. Et Os., 71; cf. Tacitus, *History*, III, 71, 19–20.

from the temples of Asia, although this desecration did not reach the point of destroying the images themselves.[14]

The destruction of gentile settlements becomes increasingly clear as the excavation of the city of Cyrene progresses, and details amounting to a comprehensive picture of what occurred in the province have been assembled above. The work of destruction embraces most of the country, despite the defectiveness of our information on various settlements. The picture at Alexandria and Salamis is similar. It is hard not to see in this destruction, more especially in Cyrene and Cyprus, judging by the number of casualties which occurred there, the result of a premeditated plan. The systematic character of the demolition at Cyrene (e.g., the felling of the internal columns of the Temple of Zeus and of the peristasis of the Temple of Apollo) does not dispel the impression. Both this writer and Professor Fuks[15] have put forward a reason for this work of destruction: it was a corollary of the determination to abandon the lands of the Diaspora and to concentrate in Eretz Yisrael. But it was also directed against certain factors, and the question is, against which ones? The Greeks, the Romans, or all idolators indiscriminately? Many scholars rely on ancient sources and thus tend to see the Jewish effort as directed first and foremost against the Greeks.[16] Their view finds support in the texts of Eusebius, Orosius, and Syncellus.[17] There is no doubt, of course, that a great proportion of the victims of the events in Cyrenaica, Cyprus, and Alexandria were Greek-speakers, because they were the inhabitants of the urban centers

---

14. E. G. Hardy, *Monumentum. Ancyranum*, 1923, 108–9, ch. xxiv (IV, 49–51); cf. Dio LI, 17; Strabo, X III, 30 (595); XIV, 13 (637).

15. *JRS S I*, 1961, 104.

16. Cf. J. M. Jost, *Geschicht der Isr'aeliten*, III, 1822, 221–25; Tcherikover, *The Jews in Egypt*, 178, sees the movement as directed primarily against the Greeks. Fuks too sees its beginning in Alexandria and Cyprus as a clash of Jews and Greeks (*JRS* 5 I, p. 102); cf. Lepper, *Trajan's Parthian War*, 92. But Xiphilinus, *Eplt. Dio.* LXV II I, 68, says explicitly: "The Jews from the vicinity of Cyrene . . . exterminated the Romans and the Greeks."

17. *HE* IV, 2, 3; *Chron.* II, 164 (*PL* II, .554 (346–47); *vers. Arm.*, 219; VII, 12, 6; I, 657.

where the revolt raged most violently. But the revolt blazed up also in the Egyptian countryside, and in two places at least we hear of collisions between the Egyptian villagers and the Jewish insurgents.[18] In Alexandria the rising appears as a continuation of the constant clashes between Greeks and Jews which were a recurrent phenomenon during the first century CE, but this does not prove that only the Greeks were the objects of Jewish hostility. We do not hear, for instance, of the spread of the movement to Greek Asia Minor, where antiSemitism had manifested itself in the early days of the Empire,[19] and an anti-Jewish literature existed much like that in Egypt.[20] In Babylonia, as emerges from the revolt of Seleucia against Trajan, Jews and Greeks shared a common front against Rome. We must therefore conclude that only in the Hellenic-Roman cities was the Jewish onslaught directed against the Greeks, as they were the majority, and because the Jewish urban communities were concentrated in the Hellenized cities of the eastern Empire. But the leaders of the insurgents must have known perfectly well that they had no prospect of defeating the Greeks, or any other community, without colliding with the Roman power. The very scope of the rebellion shows that the movement made no distinction between Greek and Roman, hence its purpose was to destroy not only the pagan cults but also the Roman government. It is hard to think, however, that the insurgents hoped to overthrow the entire Roman Empire at one blow; their immediate objective seems to have been Eretz Yisrael. This is the meaning of the Cyrenaican Jewish advance upon Egypt, their struggle for the Delta junction at Memphis, Lukuas' break-in to Eretz Yisrael, and Lulianus' and Pappus' organization of Jewish infiltration from Cyprus to Syria and Judaea. It may indeed be supposed, on the evidence of the Apocalyptic literature, that the ingathering of the exiles to Eretz Yisrael was regarded as a

18. F. Tcherikover, A. Fuks, *Corpus Papyrorum Judaicarum*, nos. 438, 450.

19. Josephus, *Ant.*, XVI, 6, 4 (167–68); 6, 6 (171); XIV, IO, 8 (214); IO, 16 (234); IO, 21 (244).

20. The anti-Jewish writer Apollonius Molon, born at Alabanda in Caria, was active in Rhodes.

precondition of the messianic kingdom. This aim, inspired by expectation of the Messiah, is expressed in its clearest form in an Egyptian-Jewish source—in the writings of Philo Judaeus, who says: "And even if [the Jews] are slaves at the ends of the world under the enemies who have led them captive—at one signal and in one day all of them shall be freed, and their unanimous conversion to virtue will strike their masters with amazement . . . and when this unexpected liberation comes, they, who were originally scattered over Greece and the barbarian lands, over islands and continents, shall arise with one impulse, hastening from all quarters to the destination shown to them, with a divine insight beyond the power of human nature, invisible to others and visible only to them, as they pass from exile to their motherland . . . and as they go, the ruins shall become cities again and the ravaged land shall become fruitful."[21]

The reasons for the failure of the rebellion remain to be examined. The rebel forces were doubtless far inferior to the Roman in military qualities, training, and discipline. But their ability should not be underestimated: the evidence already summarized indicates that the Cyrenean insurgents probably underwent a period of physical and military training in the desert regions for a number of years, and the possibility should not be discounted that a number of Egyptian Jews received similar training. Nor should it be forgotten that no small part of the Jews of Egypt and Libya were cultivators whose forefathers had served for generations in the Ptolemaic armies and had earned their livelihood as military settlers under the same dynasties. The Libyan Jews' march across the desert from Cyrenaica to Egypt itself testifies to physical endurance and organized morale. The route had been traversed in ancient times by the armies of Egypt (Apries) and Persia—twice in the reign of Arkesilaos II—and also by the forces of Magas and Euergetes II. In that period the coastal plain was better settled than it is today; the winter rain collects in rock-basins, and ancient cisterns

21. Philo, *De poemis et praemiis*, XXVIII–XXIX (165–66).

1. Menorah carved on rock road in Cyrenaica by Jewish rebels, 115–117 CE. Source: Pietro Romanelli's *La Cirenaica Romana* (Rome: Airelli, 1943).

are to be found in considerable numbers along the coastal belt.[22] The season would also have facilitated the march, for Lucuas' men moved on Egypt in the rainy season of the early months of 116. In 1805 an American force 600-strong, under the command of Captain William Eaton, made the march from Alexandria to Bomba in eastern Cyrenaica, albeit with much privation, in thirty days.[23] The overthrowing of the inner columns of the Temple of Zeus and of the outer peristasis of the Temple of Apollo in the Sanctuary of Cyrene required technical

22. O. Bates, *The Eastern Libyans*, 1914, pp. 6 sqq.

23. Bates, p. 13; for a bibliography of the journey, *Dictionary of American Biography* 5, 1930, sv. Eaton, William, p. 613.

skill,[24] and implies a degree of organized effort exerted on a considerable scale. The general impression is, indeed, that the Jews of Libya acted as the spearhead of the entire movement. Unlike them or the Jews of the Egyptian countryside on the other hand, the Jews of Alexandria lacked a military tradition and probably had received no moral preparation for the struggle; they were the attacked, not the attackers, and their combat methods were probably those of men experienced in rioting and street-fighting.

In the light of the events we have portrayed, therefore, we may conclude that it was the Jews of Cyrene and the Egyptian countryside who acted in a coordinated fashion according to a prepared plan; the same is perhaps to be assumed with regard to the Jews of Cyprus, but we know nothing of their military conditions. It is still more difficult to determine whether some sort of coordination developed between the Jews of Cyrene and Egypt, on the one hand, and those of Cyprus on the other.

If we endeavor to formulate the strategic object of the Jews of Cyrene and Egypt, then, it was directed to achieving two aims. The first stage aimed at the liquidation of lesser resistance at the enemy's weakest point, Cyrene, and the establishment of contact with the strongest Jewish center outside Judaea, that is, Egypt, which was also a vital crossroads and the base of Rome's corn supply. The aim of the second stage was to annihilate with united forces the Roman garrison of Egypt, which had been weakened in 115–116 by the dispatch of a detachment of the Third Legion Cyrenaica to Mesopotamia and Judaea.[25]

24. The columns of the peristasis of the Temple of Zeus at Cyrene are now known to have been overthrown in the Christian period (see p. 352 in Applebaum's work), but the inner columns of the naos suffered in 115–117. For the Temple of Apollo, whose outer columns were overthrown in 115–117, see the chapter, "The War," 261–344, in Applebaum's work.

25. See A. Kasher, *Zion* 41, 1976, pp. 127 sqq., [Heb.], on the question of the dispatch of Roman forces from Egypt to the Parthian campaign (especially pp. 130–32). The evidence is not impressive, concerning chiefly the whole or part of III Cyrenaica and the Ala Augusta. It is difficult to estimate the Roman garrison's

The second stage of the Jewish plan was the most crucial, as its success depended on the insurgents' ability to capture Alexandria and to seize control of the sea in order to pass on swiftly to Eretz Yisrael. The Jewish victory in Cyrenaica may have given the Jews control of the adjacent sea, if Apollonia was taken, while, as we have noted, the revolt perhaps affected Jaffa, and Jews seem to have crossed from Cyprus to Syria and Judaea. But such control of the sea would have been far from complete, as witness the fact that most of the insurgents reached Egypt from Cyrenaica by land across the desert.

It may be supposed that the inhibiting factor was the Roman fleet—the classis Alexandrina, stationed at Alexandria.[26] The capture of the city would have enabled the Jews to close the seaways and cut off the corn supply, so starving the capital of the Empire. The fighting may indeed have affected this supply adversely for a period, since an inscription[27] commemorates *T. Flavius Macer, curator frumenti comparandi urbis factus a divi Traiano Augusto*, which may reflect a corn shortage in Egypt known to have existed in 99 but might equally have been the result of measures taken due to the war situation during the years 115–118. But the Jewish plan to capture the city of Alexandria, if it existed, was frustrated, and this was the vital failure of the rising.

The Jews of Alexandria did not seize the initiative when the moment was ripe, perhaps due to the opposition of their comfortable classes; doubtless they were also influenced by the proximity of the Roman garrison and by memory of past failures.

---

strength at the time of the rebellion; in 83 it included two legions, three alae of cavalry and eight cohorts of infantry, four of which were *equitatae*, (Lesquier, *L' armée romaine d' Egypte*, pp. 103 sqq.), totaling some 17,500 men. Under Hadrian, after the removal of the two former legions and their replacement by one legion only, the garrison consisted, according to Cheesman's estimate (*The Auxilia of the Roman Army*, 1914, pp. 163–64), of 2,500 cavalry, 750 mounted infantry, and 10,950 infantry.

26. Momsen, Hubner, et al., Corpus Inscriptionum Latinarum 2, 1970 etc.

27. H. Dessau, *Inscriptiones Latinae Selectae*, 1435; *Cambridge Ancient History* 11, 1936, p. 213, n. 2.

The failure in Alexandria produced two grave consequences: the Jewish advance upon Judaea was stopped, and the Roman forces in Syria were able to mount a counterattack by sea at a time chosen by themselves. The rebels' plan required the swift liquidation of the imperial forces in Egypt, in order to concentrate as large as possible a force in Eretz Yisrael for the decisive struggle with the principal Roman armies. This aim explains the consistent Jewish policy of annihilation carried out towards the Greeks and Romans equally, and the method of "scorched earth" followed in Cyrenaica and Egypt, the object of which was to leave no effective opposition in the rear. A sea-crossing would have ensured the success of this operation, but Alexandria remained untaken and the battle for the Delta crossroads near Memphis ended with defeat. Further, the resistance in the remaining districts of Egypt exceeded what was anticipated. Fighting continued along the entire Nile valley in the form of local engagements, and it would seem that the insurgents failed, due to the great distances over which the struggle was waged, to concentrate enough force at one point to bring the contest to a decision before the legions advanced to join the battle. Characteristic of this situation was the far-flung fighting between the two remote poles of Memphis and the Thebais, if the latter theatre may be regarded as the outcome of an attack by activists who had crossed from Cyrenaica by the oases of the western desert. This division and dispersion of the rebel forces must be counted among the factors of the Jewish failure.

The movement in Trajan's reign reveals, where inner class relationships are concerned, certain common features with processes in Judaea in the years 66–70. To judge by the premature outbreak in Alexandria in October 115, and by the passive attitude of the Jewish population of the city till it was attacked by the Greeks in 116, most of the wealthier class stood aside from the revolt, whereas in Cyrene, the elimination of the Hellenizing upper group in 73 had opened the way for the radicalization of the Jewish masses and their adherence to the revolutionary movement. While the Jewish upper class in Jerusalem and Judaea did revolt in 66, it did so because it was swept away by the more powerful current of the social revolution—which was intimately connected with the extremist and Zealot trends—and was destroyed as a result. At that time the wealthy of the Diaspora in Alexandria and Cyrene recoiled from rebellion; in Egypt they collaborated with Rome to bring the extremists to book. In the Diaspora revolt in Trajan's time, they stood aside, but were nevertheless overwhelmed and destroyed.

It may be doubted whether there ever arose in the early Roman Empire any movement which so imperiled Roman authority as did the Jewish Diaspora revolt in the reign of Trajan. None of Rome's subject peoples had risen in active rebellion on this scale, and none was located both within and without the imperial frontiers and distributed over several important provinces of the Empire itself. Nor do we know of any instance of so extensive a degree of cooperation between various communities which were both within the Empire and hostile to it. The aid given by the tribes of southern Britain to the peoples of northern Gaul in Julius Caesar's time preceded the principate,[28] and if the Dacian king Decebalus was in correspondence with the king of Parthia in order to strengthen his position against Rome,[29] he did not succeed in forming an effective military alliance.[30] Tacitus, writing not long before the Jewish rebellion, could express his satisfaction at the disunion and fratricidal strife of the Germans, and pray "that this mutual hatred persist and continue among the peoples if they cannot love us, since . . . fate can grant no greater boon than the quarrels of our enemies."[31] It remains but to add that the Parthian kingdom, for all its internal weaknesses, was the only power within reach of the Roman Empire capable of measuring up to her, and therefore constituted a constant threat to Rome. Scanty as is our knowledge of the relations the Jews of the Empire and Parthia during the period of

28. Caes, *BG*, 4, 2 o.

29. Pliny, *Ep*. X, 74.

30. Debevoise (*A Political History of Parthia*, 1938, p. 217) thinks that the mailed cavalrymen seen on Trajan's Column may be Parthians, in which case Pacorus aided Decebalus by actually sending military assistance.

31. Tacitus, *Germ.*, 33.

115–117 or immediately before, it is hard to refrain from supposing that the Jews saw in Parthia a potential ally, and that the Parthian rulers were ready to exploit Jewish hostility to Rome in the event of a military confrontation.

Jewish tradition saw the rebellion of Ben Kosba as a continuation of the Diaspora rising,[32] and even if this is incorrect, it is clear that the events of 115–117 influenced the outlook of Hadrian, who ascended the imperial throne a short time after the *tumultus* had passed its height, and had previously taken part in its suppression in Cyprus. From Trajan he doubtless derived his estimate of the Jewish people as an important factor and a grave problem bearing on the safety of the eastern frontier. This attitude was also affected by his sympathy for Hellenism, which inclined him to see the Jews of Eretz Yisrael as an element which marred the integrity of Hellenism in the east. The *tumultus*, the last great collision between Jews and Greeks in the Hellenistic and Roman periods, must have made a deep impression upon him, and may have decisively influenced his decision, fifteen years later, to transform Jerusalem into a citadel of Graeco-Roman civilization.

The revolt's failure led directly to the destruction of the three important Jewish centers of Cyrene, Egypt, and Cyprus. The archaeological evidence in Cyrenaica can be interpreted to indicate the renewal there of Jewish settlement as early as the third century, but the supposition needs further confirmation.[33] Jewish communities existed in Cyprus, according to inscriptions, by the fourth century, when the decree prohibiting Jewish entry appears to have been forgotten.

---

32. Yeivin, *Bar Kokhba* 2, pp. 42, 66; Rattner, *Seder 'Olam*, 30.

33. An epitaph from Ptolemais, the style of whose letters seems to belong to the third century, is Jewish (*Notizia Archeologica del Ministerio delle Colonie I*, 1915, p. 152, fig. 52). It is also possible that Jewish influence went to the making of the heresy of Sabellius, who lived at Ptolemais. (Cf. Bonaiuti, *Nuova Antologia*, II, 1950, p. 183.) In the fourth century Jewish ships were plying between Alexandria and Cyrene (Synes. *Epp.* 4). Cf. also Antiochi monachi, *De insomniis* (*PG*, 89, col. 1692). I am indebted for this reference to Drs. B. Jones and P. Llewelyn of the University College of North Wales, also to Professor Anthony Birley, who sent it to me.

2. Inscription from ancient Cyrene relating to Jewish Revolt. Courtesy of MOJL, Museum of Libyan Jews, Or Yehuda, Israel.

Papyrological material in Egypt conveys that "Jewish life in the country was completely paralyzed";[34] only in the third century do we hear again of evidence for the existence of a Jewish population consisting of more than scattered individuals.[35] The annihilation of these three large communities may well have intensified national feeling in Eretz Yisrael—one case at least is known of a Cyrenaican Jew who fought among Ben Kosba's warriors[36]—but had not these Diaspora centers met their end under Trajan, they might have furnished vital assistance to Judaea's war against Hadrian. Their ruin doomed the second revolt to failure before it had begun.

34. *CPJ* I, p. 94 (Prolegomena): "The general impression is that of a complete breakdown of Jewish life in Egypt."
35. Ibid.
36. Yadin, *Israel Exploration Journal* I, 1961, p. 46, no. 11 (Nahal Hever).

As a result of the rising (Pulmus Qitos), the scholars of Eretz Yisrael prohibited the teaching of Greek to the younger generation.[37] The prohibition, indeed, did not last, if it was ever rigorously applied—and some recent scholars have ascribed to it no more than qualified application—for the family of Rabban Gamliel "permitted the teaching of Greek to [its] sons because they were associated with the Roman government."[38] By the early third century, many epitaphs were being written in Greek in the great cemetery of Beth Shea'rim. But this did not mean that the Kulturkampf of Judaism and Hellenism was at an end; it merely died down, and revived in a different form in the struggle between Judaism and Christianity in the fourth century.

The failure of the rising also terminated the period of the active onslaught of Judaism as a missionary religion proselytizing among gentiles outside Eretz Yisrael. The collision, symbolized by the confrontation of the God of Israel and the god Serapis,[39] no longer takes political form, except perhaps when imperial statues are smashed at Tiberias in the following century.[40] On the other hand, it is not impossible that the defeat under Trajan caused the expansion of Jewish influence over the African continent. The report of the Judaization of Libyan tribes in the Aurez Mountains of Algeria lacks, apparently, reliable evidence, and it is not easy to prove that Jewish influence in western Africa originated in the flight of Jews from Cyrenaica westward before and after the revolt. Yet archaeology permits no doubt that reciprocal influences were at work between Libyan Jewry and Libyan-speakers in the first century CE. The conclusion to be drawn from Jonathan the Weaver's departure to the desert—which hints at the dispersal of extremist elements on the fringes of the Sahara and derives confirmation from the instructive analogies of Hirbet Qumran and the work

37. M. *Sota*, IX, 12; cf. S. Liebermann, *Hellenism in Jewish Palestine*, 1950, pp. 100–101.

38. *Tosefet Sotah*, XV, 5.

39. P. Oxy. 1242; cf. Musurillo, *The Acts of the Pagan Martyrs* (1954), pp. 162 sqq.

40. Jer., *AZ*, IV, 43.

of the Sanusi order in Cyrenaica in the present century—assists the credibility of an influence exerted by the insurgents upon the nomadic Libyan tribes and even of active cooperation between them. The result of such influence is likely to have been the spread of Judaism over north and central Africa after the rebellion's failure.[41]

The Jewish activist movement found its last expression in the rebellion of Ben Kosba. But where the Diaspora was concerned, R. Simeon bar Yohai's words on the massacre of the Jews of Egypt by Marcius Turbo sum up the situation: "In that hour the horn of Israel was torn out, and will not return to its place till the son of David comes."[42]

Bibliography

Bates, O. *The Eastern Libyans.* 1914.

Boeck, A., et al. *Inscriptiones Graecae.* 1873–.

Busolt, G. *Griechische Staatskunde.* Vols. 1 and 2. 1920, 1926.

Cagnat, R., and G. Lafaye. *Inscriptiones Graecae ad res Romanas pertinentes.* 1911–1927.

Dessau, H. *Inscriptiones Latinae Selectae.* Vols. 1–3. 1892–1916.

Diehl, E. *Inscriptiones Latinae Christianae Veteres.* Vols. 1–3. 1925–1931.

Dittenberger, W. *Orientis Graecae Inscriptiones Selectae.* 1903–1905.

Enciclopedia Italiana. 1929–1939.

Frank, Tenney, ed. *An Economic Survey of Ancient Rome.* Vols. 1–4. 1933–1940.

Geographical Journal. 1893–.

Giornale della società asiatica Italiana. 1887–.

Graffin, R., and F. Nau. *Patrologia Orientalis.*

Historia. 1950–.

Israel Exploration Journal. 1950–.

Jacoby, F. *Die Fragmente der griechischen Historiker.* 1926.

Jewish Quarterly Review. 1889–.

Journal of Egyptian Archaeology. 1914–.

---

41. J. Basnage, *Histoire des Juifs*, 1716, VII, p. 185; Marcier, *Histoire de l'Afrique Septentrionale*, 1888, I, p. 137; for a criticism of these views, Hirschberg, *Journal of African History*, 4, pp. 313 sqq.

42. Jer., *Sukkot*, 5, 55b.

Journal of Hellenic Studies. 1880–.

Journal of Jewish Studies. 1948/49–.

Journal of Roman Studies. 1910–

Journal of the Palestine Oriental Society. 1920/21–.

Klein, S. *Jüdische-palästinensisches Corpus Inscriptionum.* 1920.

La Parola del Passato. 1946–.

Migne, J. P. *Cursus Patrologiae, Series Graeca.* 1886.

Migne, J. P. *Cursus Patrologiae, Series Latina.* 1844.

Milne, J. P. *A History of Egypt under Roman Rule. 1924.*

Monumenta Germanica Historica (Auctorum antiquissimorum). 1877–.

Müller, C. *Fragmenta Historicorum Graecorum.* 1841–1870.

Norsa, M., and G. Vitelli. *Studi e testi: Il papiro greco Vaticano.* Vol. 2. 1931.

Notizie archeologici del Ministerio delle Colonie. Vol. 1, 1915; vol. 2, 1916; vol. 3, 1922; vol. 4, 1927.

Numismatic Chronicle. 1860–.

Palestine Exploration Quarterly. 1937–.

Papers of the British School at Rome. 1895–.

Pauly, A., G. Wissowa, and W. Kroll. *Realenzyklopädie der Classischen Altertumswissenschaft.* 1893–.

Preisigke, F. *Namenbuch enthaltend alle Menschennamen soweit sie in griechischen Urkunden Ägyptens sich vorfinden.* 1922.

Quaderni dell archeologia della Libia. 1950–.

Quarterly of the Department of Antiquities of Palestine. 1932–1949.

Rowe, A., D. Buttle, and J. Gray. *The Cyrenaican Expedition of the University of Manchester.* 1952. 1956.

Schürer, E. *Geschichte des jüdischen Volkes im Zeitalter Jesu Christi.* Vols. 1–3. 1909.

Tarn, W. W., and G. T. Griffith. *Hellenistic Civilization.* 1952.

Tcherikover, V. *Hellenistic Civilization and the Jews.* 1959.

2

◆ ◆ ◆

Libyan Jews in the Islamic Arab
and Ottoman Periods

MAURICE M. ROUMANI

The Islamic Middle Ages

Not much is known about the Jews of Libya at the time of the Arab conquest of North Africa in the seventh century, when the Arab governor of Egypt took Cyrenaica and Tripolitania from the Byzantines in 642. According to Jewish and Arab traditions, the Arabs encountered some resistance from the Jewish and Berber populations. There are legends about Jewish queens, such as La Kahena in Algeria, leading the Jews and Berbers against the invaders. The great Arab historian Ibn Khaldun (d. 1406) notes that some of the Berber tribes had accepted Judaism, among them the Nafusa, who lived in the mountainous regions of western Tripolitania. (The Jews of the Nafusa region are specifically mentioned in a responsum of Haninay Gaon in the tenth century.) In general, the Jewish communities were dispersed and their culture was primitive.

Documents from the Cairo Geniza indicate that there were Jewish communities in the principal towns of Libya from the ninth through

This chapter originally appeared as two sections ("Islamic Middle Ages" and "Under Ottoman Rule") in Maurice Roumani, "Libya," in *Encyclopedia of Jews in the Islamic World*, ed. Norman Stillman (Leiden: Koninklijke Brill NV, 2010), 250–52. It is reprinted here with many thanks and full credit acknowledgment to Koninklijke Brill NV, who granted us permission to reprint.

the twelfth centuries. Some of the Jewish merchants mentioned in the Geniza documents had family names like Itrabulsi and Lebdi, indicating origins in Tripoli and Lebda (ancient Leptis Magna). A certain Yusuf ibn Ya'qub al-Itrabulsi was a business agent of Joseph ibn 'Awkal, the Jewish merchant prince and intermediary of the Palestinian and Babylonian yeshivot in Fustat. Jewish merchants sailed with goods from Alexandria to Barqa in eastern Libya, thence to Tripoli, and from there to al-Mahdiyya on the Tunisian coast and onward to Sicily and al-Andalus. Jewish judges in Barqa corresponded with their colleagues in Egypt.

With the Banu Hilal and Banu Sulaym Bedouin invasions of the mid-eleventh century, the coastal towns of Cyrenaica and Tripolitania suffered greatly and the devastation of local agriculture led to famines. The Almohad conquest in the twelfth century and the ensuing persecution led many Libyan Jews to seek asylum in Egypt. Jews from Barqa appear in the Geniza records as recipients of welfare during the eleventh and twelfth centuries, and a Jewish refugee from the Jebel Nafusa region was hired as a teacher.

Since Tripolitania and Cyrenaica were at the far eastern periphery of their vast empire, the Almohads apparently did not impose conversion upon the conquered non-Muslim population as was their practice elsewhere. Nonetheless, Almohad rule in the twelfth and thirteenth centuries was very cruel, so much so that an anonymous poet wrote a rejoinder to Abraham ibn Ezra's famous lament *Aha Yarad* (O There Descended) cataloguing the communities destroyed by the Almohads. The unknown poet asks Ibn Ezra why he did not mention the suffering of Surman, Mesallata, and Misurata, all towns in Tripolitania. But the poet mentions onerous taxes and exile, not death or forced conversion. A Tripolitanian manuscript of Ibn Ezra's poem adds Sabrat (ancient Sabratha) and a place called Tura (perhaps somewhere in the Jebel Nafusa) as places for which the poet weeps. Tombstones with Hebrew inscriptions that appear to be from this period also indicate an open Jewish existence during the Almohad period when the region was administered by local governors.

There are few details about Libyan Jewry for the immediate post-Almohad centuries. Conditions seem to have worsened after 1510 with the Spanish occupation of Tripoli. The Spaniards remained until 1530, when the Knights of Malta took their place until 1551. The Spanish domination was very hard on Jews. Many families fled Tripoli and moved to Tajura and Gharian; some fled to Italy, mostly to Rome. Although some of these families later returned to Tripoli, they faced economic decay, continual insecurity because of frictions between Ottomans and Christians, discrimination and restrictions imposed by the Spaniards, and almost complete isolation between the Jewish community in Tripoli and the Jews of the interior.

Under Ottoman Rule

In 1551 the Ottomans entered the scene as the rulers of Libya. Their dominion continued until 1911. The Ottoman Empire ruled Tripoli through pashas and deys until 1711, and during this period the Jews, their number reinforced by the arrival of Spanish refugees and families from Livorno, flourished both economically and culturally. The major figure of this cultural renaissance was Rabbi Shimon Labi from Spain. He was passing through North Africa on his way to Palestine, but in 1549 he agreed to remain in Tripoli as the community's rabbi.

From 1711 until 1835 Libya was ruled by an independent hereditary monarchy, the Qaramanlis, whose power extended over Cyrenaica and Tripolitania. While this period was marked by civil wars between different local dynasties, invasions (like the attack of 'Ali Burghul on Tripoli in 1795, whose defeat was celebrated by a special local Purim), piracy activities that provoked military retaliation by foreign powers (like the one of the United States between 1801 and 1805), the Jewish community thrived because almost all of the commerce with Europe was in their hands. Under the relatively tolerant Qaramanlis, Libyan Jewry began to take on a cohesive identity separate from that of Tunisian Jewry.

With Libya as part of the Ottoman Empire, its Jews benefited from contacts with the many other Jewish communities of the Empire.

Toward the end of the Ottoman era, the local community could list sixty-nine rabbis, rabbinic judges, and representatives at the Sublime Porte. The Jews of Libya established a network of communal agencies whose beneficent activities ranged from helping the poor to religious education, synagogues, and yeshivot. But relations between Muslims and Jews were deteriorating: robberies, arson, and looting increased even though such acts were all violations of Ottoman policy. The Ottoman authorities tried to win the support of the local Jews by providing them with financial aid and appointing, in 1874, Eliahu Bekhor Hazan as *hakham bashi* (chief rabbi) of the Libyan Jewish community. Supported by Mordekhai Ha-Kohen, an influential adherent of the Haskalah (Jewish Enlightenment), Hazan modernized the Jewish educational curriculum by incorporating up-to-date European courses with the subjects traditionally studied. Ha-Kohen authored an important work on the history, customs, and culture of Libyan Jewry entitled *Higgid Mordekhay* (Mordecai Related).

* ◆ ◆

PART TWO

Folkways, Language, Habitat

OUR NEXT CLUSTER OF ARTICLES fleshes out more recent historical experiences.

Hamos Guetta, in a lyrical tone, describes the age-old relationship between food and traditional customs when he was growing up in mid-century Tripoli. Tradition still thrived and every Jewish holiday or life-cycle event had its own culinary tradition. Especially in the lives of women, in some cases very little had changed from Ottoman times, so that families still savored and participated in the special engaging folkways of Libyan Jewish life.

Harvey Goldberg records his conversations with Libyan Jews now in Israel as they discuss how they mediated tradition with modernity when in Libya. A dearth of Jewish books in Ottoman times had led to mainly oral education and to pragmatic legal decisions that were sometimes not in accordance with Jewish law but reflected local conditions. As Italian influence spread, there was tolerance toward such issues as sports on the Sabbath, but tradition could be called in to validate a clandestine "modern" marriage against the bride's parents' wishes. "Tradition with modernity" accurately describes the way Libyan Jews coped with the major historical changes affecting them in the colonial period.

Linguistic specialist Sumikazu Yoda contributes another aspect in reconstructing a threatened way of life: the particular form of Judeo-Arabic spoken by the Jews of Tripoli, preserved best by speakers who had emigrated to Israel in the late forties and early fifties. The reader may imagine how the sounds of Libyan Judeo-Arabic added to the scents and sights of food being cooked in the alleys and open-air kitchens of Tripoli's old Jewish quarters. It would only take an evocation of the built environment to reconstruct a lost way of life between these pages.

The lively sensorial picture fades, though, when we consider Jack Arbib's depiction of the "vanishing landscape" of Jewish Libya. Jewish homes taken over in 1967, wanton alteration and destruction of public buildings designed by Jewish architects, vandalism and desecration of once beautiful synagogues: these are the norm, as Arbib juxtaposes "then and now" photographs. From living Jewish habitats and public spaces shared with those of other religions, to the ruins and absences of today, is a sad transition.

3

• ◆ •

Mafrum, Haraimi, Tebiha, Bsisa, and Other Culinary Specialities

Tastes, Symbols, and Meaning

HAMOS GUETTA

The Bride

A bride, Sara, is standing in the sea and her skirt, or *sdad* (robe, covering), is pulled up and tied so as not to get wet; her hair is tied back with a brightly colored headscarf.[1] She is with a group of female friends, and amid laughter, loud discussions, and mutual instructions, they are washing the lamb's wool that will go into the mattress of the family about to be created.

Once the wool has been beaten and washed, the women are tired and hungry. Though their skirts were tied up around their knees, they got wet anyway. It's getting late; the wool is spread out, drying in the sunshine on the rocks, and hunger reminds them it's time for a lunch break. They are waiting for the groom to arrive; he has the honor and the pleasure of bringing large dishes of food for all of the bride's friends. When he comes, the women sit on the rocks near the wool in the sunshine and dip their hands into the couscous (the bread of all who live in

---

1. For more details and supplementary information for the topics in this chapter, please see the video on the author's website: http://www.italiaebraica.it/italiaebraica/video-gallery/viewvideo/514/racconti-di-hamos/purim--i-dolci-e-le-storie.html.

3. Women by the water, Tripoli, 1946. With thanks and acknowledgment to Hamos Guetta. Courtesy of Hamos Guetta Collection.

Libya) together with the sauce and meat. It's a rich meal that they are being served: there is meat, because the groom wants to make a good impression and not give rise to any criticism or complaints.

The almost-dry wool is carried on the women's backs, through the white alleys under small arches, while they hear the sound of brightly colored doors opening and closing: both friends and the curious know that Sara is going to get married. The wool is spread out in the future bride's house, a square house in the center of which is a hundred-square-meter patio open to the sky, where everything takes place and from which one can reach all of the rooms, including the one intended to be the residence of the new couple. It is the classic, three-part room (*mcielcia*) divided into three areas: in the center is a table and a chest of drawers with a mirror on top. In the drawers are the household books, all in Hebrew, books of prayer and wisdom. In the right-hand area there is a loft in which the parents sleep, underneath which is a cupboard; while on the left is another loft identical to the first, awaiting the children who will come.

The bathroom and kitchen are communal: in order to get to them you have to cross the open patio, even during rainy winter nights. The well of drinking water (*bir*) is on one side of the patio, while the one that collects rainwater (*majen*) is in the patio's center: its water is used only for washing.

The mother-in-law would check everything: she would open the drawers, inspect the daughter-in-law's linens, check whether her son was eating well (the kitchen was shared); and when she could, she would also check behavior in bed. Until the son, under pressure from his wife, rented another home somewhere else, the mother-in-law would be there, suspended between love and hatred, a companion for gossiping or a severe supervisor.

The Bath

Having a bath was a public event, out on the patio in a tin tub. Holding a glass in one hand, with the other my mamma was careful that I would not hit myself on the hard faucets of that tin tub. Someone would have filled the tub with water from the good well. In winter, some of the water would have been heated in the bottom half of the two-part couscous steamer over the *kanun* (a terra-cotta container full of charcoal embers). On Fridays, before sunset and the Sabbath arrived, we all had a bath, and that tin tub was the occasion for horseplay and games.

When the bath was over, a sugar candy was waiting for me, which I earned by making a nuisance of myself during the preparations for waxing, when the women would remove their superfluous hair. The melted sugar became long and elastic: this was the moment when I had to ask for the piece of candy, so before they prepared the sugar-wax a few pieces were set aside for me. Then my mother and her friends shut themselves up in the bedroom, and I together with all the other males were invited to take our distance. As long as I was very little, they would let me look; when I was bigger, I would imagine everything, guided by the screams caused by tearing out the hair.

Every home had a little white-haired old lady, who was not necessarily a close relative, but the elderly were never abandoned, and so with us there lived the "cousin of the grandma of my dad's cousin." That white hair, and the fact that I didn't really know who she was, intimidated me a little. You couldn't know everything. And you couldn't know who all the people who came into the house were. The hands that gave me the bath also changed: I knew it was my mother when she said, "Irrani Kabbara" (May the Lord sacrifice me in your stead).

The Rituals of Coffee and Tea

The goats were passing by our front door, and their loud bells gave notice to purchasers, who would come out with a container into which the shepherd would milk the nanny goat (an authentic local product). Jews, though, would serve goat's milk only to children or invalids. The precept in the Torah not to mix milk and meat was followed even though kitchens were small, and it would have been difficult to keep cheese or milk at home. It was a life full of rules, the life of the Jews of Libya. From that small kitchen, with its aluminum pots made from the carcasses of war planes, there emerged cooked meals for the whole family, and mother-in-law and daughter-in-law sat down together on a straw mat in the patio with the front door open. From there they could see the passersby and would often invite someone in for coffee or tea; many dishes were prepared sitting on that mat. On it many other household tasks were performed, such as crushing spices, cleaning grain, puffing up the wool inside the mattresses with toothed iron tools, weaving fabric, toasting coffee and other grains, refining, sieving, and grinding leaves for henna. Women got together sitting on the ground wearing the typical *barakan*, with their hair tied back, as if they were real workers, making quite a noise because of the brass mortar with which they would crush the spices. This mortar was a most precious object, whose cleaning and shining served as a visiting card for every home, and the women made it shine like gold.

4. Teatime. Courtesy of Hamos Guetta Collection.

Sitting on the straw mat, they talked about what time Shabbat was going to come in, work to be done before the festivals, purchases that had to be made, weddings, and henna. And when the news was bad, they would lower their voices, for example, when they talked about the time Rubena ran off with an Arab. This was a love that was absolutely forbidden, and the family reacted by observing a week of mourning.

"Your *auama* is miraculous," I would hear my mother's friends say. The *auama* was an oil lamp, with a wick formed by a jute fiber taken from a sack, covered with cotton and formed into a circle with a stitch and a circle of wrapping paper with a hole from which the wick, completely resting in the oil, emerged and floated on the water. And if it was not Shabbat—the day when the custom was to light the lamps to welcome the holy day—it was certainly an *auama* for praying for help, for protection, for healing, or merely for being successful with school homework. Friends who were not Jewish would often come by too and ask my mother to light an *auama*, and I remember lighting one myself when I had an important exam. Sometimes I would see one burning without any explanation, and the silent and sad atmosphere at home would discourage me from asking any questions.

The menfolk were often busy with activities relating to a small home factory or managing their business from home. Nonno Benia-mino would provide financing for the Arab farmers; the contracts were signed with a firm handshake, and trust was immense, so that even during the great crisis in 1930, Nonno did not have any problems providing food for the family.

I found this out a few years ago thanks to a discovery by my uncle: a manuscript by my Nonno, Hai Drikes z"l, which he made into a book and provided copies to all his children. In addition to the birth dates of his children, noted and described with exact religious references—such as, "Alfonso was born three days before Hanukkah, when hail fell that broke the roof of the green synagogue." What surprised me most in this book were the religious quotations, a song that later on we put to music, and some formulas with obscure meanings that even today I have not succeeded in understanding.

Nonno Hai, thanks to the women's help and labor, had at home a factory of scents: spices and perfume mixtures. My mother used to tell me that these mixtures and formulas were secret, so that when they were working the doors would be locked. I assume that my Nonno had written in the book some of these formulas. I have understood one of them, for a product that was used to turn away the evil eye and change moods. Because it's impossible to be a Libyan Jew without being a little superstitious.

Then there was a story told by mother, the heroine of the day: "When he turned the corner I took his wrist and with all my strength, anger, and fingernails, I wrenched the pistol from his hand." My mother used to sell coffee on the black market, obtained from the American military bases, whose language and customs she knew. A soldier in uniform had aimed his pistol and was threatening the man who would later be my father. The soldier had been trying to possess my mother. He was then disarmed by my father and handed over to the British command. The Libyan Jewish women had strong muscles toned by lifting heavy mortars and buckets of water, and they were familiar with tasks that today would be done by a machine. Tonina was one of the strong ones; she combined the sweetness of a slightly romantic and modern woman with the strength of a protective mother elephant. She had also grown up there in the patio open to the sky between a *kanun* and a mortar.

From coffee to tea, there were very precise rules for everything. Sitting on the matting, the women prepared the coffee on the *kanun*. Sitting on the matting, the women would roast the coffee inside a steel cylinder that they turned continually with a handle, resting on the burning coals, then mixed it with chickpeas that were also roasted so it would be lighter in taste and also on the pocket. Sitting on the matting in the open air, the women would have prepared some coffee for the master of the house.

Sometimes the coffee was given flavor with a leaf of wild geranium, other times with a distillation of orange flowers. Once I happened to go to the distiller of orange flower petals. I still remember: a man brought twenty jute sacks full and emptied the orange flowers in the patio; in the center were other mountains of flower petals like mine, and on one side was the distilling machine for the flowers. We waited in line to do the distilling and I became inebriated from the perfume of the flowers, the perfume of my childhood. As I waited my turn, I watched a sheep chewing slowly outside the door. The wait seemed endless until I got home finally with bottles full of the precious liquid. It wasn't necessary to go to the kitchen to make the coffee. The *kanun* could be put anywhere you liked, and so the coffee was prepared after it had just been ground right next to the mat. Scents were not lacking in the house of Nonno Hai, but the smell of fresh coffee, from the grain to the drink, was sublime and aroused the best of feelings.

Tea, in contrast, was purchased loose and ready for use and came in two kinds, basically: an intense green tea, strong and sweet, to have after an abundant meal; and black tea for welcoming guests. The ritual required that one drink three cups in succession, one of which would be flavored with nuts toasted in a pan.

We children would be given tea with a *roschetta* or *kak* (a small circular crisp biscuit), which we would break in two, trying to use it like a straw, but before the tea was soaked up the piece of biscuit would fall into the liquid and things got complicated. The allowance was one *kak* each; those left over were put up on a high shelf in the kitchen, and quite often Mamma would catch me standing on an upside-down tin bucket stealing another *kak*.

Purim

Drinks were accompanied by a piece of *kak*, sweet or salty, depending on the hour of the day. If a guest happened to visit around the festival of Purim, he was in luck: the sweets served were full of honey and rich with almonds, and servings were generous, because the custom was to send dishes of food from one family to another. Comparisons with Rachele's *debla* (fried manicotti) and Sara's *burika* (bourekas often stuffed with ground almonds) were to be expected, but the best ones were always those that were made at home.

A woman would be judged by the taste of her food above any other quality. That is how it was for the family and relatives. Each woman gave unstintingly of her own efforts and the help of her children or other members of the family. Turn the handle and pull out the dough, they taught me, even though I was a boy; when the festivals were looming, there was so much work to be done, and some help stretching out the dough for the *debla* was important. Already, at the age of four, they put me up on the stool to turn the *mafrum* (vegetables stuffed with meat) as they fried, just as many other children had to, and who, even today, in these real odors will imagine times that are no more. Besides the *debla*, the *makrota* (semolina cakes stuffed with dates), the *burikas* with almonds, and the amaretti (cookies made with almonds and ground apricot pits), in the dish that we used to send to all the neighbors and relatives for Purim we used to add some *kak* as well to make it bigger. The receivers of the gifts were not only Jews but also Christians, Arabs, Maltese, Americans, and more or less all the people who lived around our house with whom we were in good relations. I remember that my mother insisted I bring a dish of food to one lady, not only on Purim but every Shabbat; though she had been born Jewish, she had converted to Christianity and for that reason her family did not recognize her. According to my mother, the lady in question was nostalgic for her

5. Preparing matzah for Passover. Courtesy of Hamos Guetta Collection.

origins and she was sure that that plate of food gave her great comfort. Then there was the so-called rabbi's plate, filled with everything, so that the rabbi would not feel obliged to get up or to ask: couscous, *mafrum*, *tbiha* (stewed beef and beans), *tershi* (creamed pumpkin), and *mesaiiere* (mixed condiment of oil, pepper, and salt). There was quite an art in getting everything onto the same plate, and another challenge for a child like me to get to my destination without spilling anything.

It's not right for a man to cook, my mother used to say, but she didn't disdain male help when it came to folding the laundry. So men were good for folding large pieces of laundry and for shopping outside, in the open markets, where women did not dare set foot due to fear or jealousy from the men at home. So the father could contribute to Purim by buying colored torrone (pistachio, sesame, and honey candy) of pink, green, and yellow from Faju, the best Jewish pastry shop, whose recipes were secret and still remain so today, though the heirs have moved to Netanya in Israel.

Shabbat

From Thursday on, the spices were already being ground for Shabbat: the mixture of seven spices to flavor the vegetables stuffed with meat, cumin and *karuia* (caraway) to spice the fish, and ground almonds for the sweets. The vegetables were cleaned as well, and everything was prepared on the mat. On some Fridays in the summer I would go to my father's shop in Suk el Turk, where I would often see the Maltese fisherman arriving with a big fish (*cernia*) in his hands. He didn't want to be paid; this was his gesture of gratitude to my Nonno, who had made it possible for him to buy his boat. Then on Friday morning the cooking was completed on the *kanun*. The Shabbat menu was almost boring: *haraimi* (spicy fish in a red sauce), *mafrum,* couscous, always the same food and the same dishes, but what made the *haraimi* different was the degree of spiciness, the freshness of the spices, the quality of the fish, and the cooking. Every dish was followed by commentary, which would not always be delicate or kind toward the cook, but the plates would always be returned polished clean with the slipper of perfumed bread made at home and decorated with egg wash and sesame.

For the women, the couscous was not just a dish but a circle of life, a process that began on the mat where the grains were cleaned of impurities, run through the mill for grinding, and returned again to the mat. Then there was the lighting of the *kanun*, dampening the couscous in the *qasaa* (a large bowl), and then cooking it in the steamer. The imprecise fit between the lower and upper pots was corrected with bands made of dampened paper, since the steam should not escape from the sides but pass up through the couscous. And to flavor it they would put pumpkin and celery in the water. Though it was a neutral dish, the couscous had a unique perfume that, when mixed with the dishes for various occasions, would tell us the exact date and the day of the week.

This odor was precise, unique, and identifiable by every Jew in the *hara* (the Jewish quarter of Tripoli); it would last for many hours, as long as the cooking time for the couscous. Once an hour it was tipped into the *qasaa*, pulled apart by hand, fluffed up, and returned to the

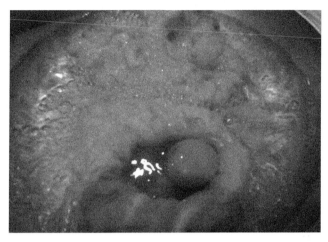

6. *Sfenza*. Courtesy of Hamos Guetta Collection.

cooking pot. As they waited, between one stage of cooking and the next, the women of the house would go off and hang the laundry on the terrace or go about other tasks. But one eye, and the utmost attention, were on the couscous, until it reached the table and its final judgment.

What could be different between one couscous and the next? My father would comment on it as if he were eating it for the first time. He hadn't been present when it had been worked on, opened by hand, when the individual grains had been separated with the *garble* (sieve). And so it was easy for him to say, "Last week it was softer."

The odors from the patio never stopped telling us which day and which hour it was, coffee, tea, grinding, spices, and distillations, so that on Shabbat morning we would wake up to the smell of the *dfina* (Sephardic cholent), the pot with the stuffed intestines, the *polpette* of *semola* (semolina dumplings), beans, meat, and potatoes. Since on Shabbat we could not light the fire, the big pot with the *dfina* was resting on the *kanun,* which had been lit just before sunset on Friday, before the holy day came in. Inside the *kanun* we would put a good supply of charcoal, with a nice large piece in the center that would burn all night and for a large portion of the following day. On the *kanun* was the pot, and on top of this a thick fabric cover, instead of a lid, as if it were buried in the material (*dfina* actually does mean "buried").

To have the fire still burning for Shabbat lunch was important, but it was also important for the coffee, which had to be drunk while still hot. The spiced coffee was prepared on Friday, and to keep it hot it was immersed in the *dfina* in a bottle of reinforced glass. On Shabbat morning, before we went to the synagogue, we drank that coffee, which had a special taste; when it was poured, it was important that we not drip on our good Shabbat clothes the drops of fat and oil that came out with the bottle from the *dfina*.

Pesach (Passover)

Three months before the festival of Pesach, we were already talking about it as if it were a threat. The women were beginning to divide the tasks and plan the work. The entire house, and everything that was in it, was turned upside down as if it was going to be rebuilt: they painted and cleaned so much that not a single speck of flour would survive that hysterical cleaning.

We had to empty the closets and wash all the clothes; anyone who didn't have a well in their house had to take them to the public fountain where, on a wooden plank, they were beaten for cleanliness and then hung out on the terrace, where it looked as if there was a competition for whiteness with the neighbors. The children would accompany their mothers and play hide-and-seek among the linens, then slide downstairs on the handrail. Children were entrusted with cleaning out the old threads of *meshnoa* (dried meat).

Inside, the house was emptied of objects, because walls and floors had to be perfectly washed with bucketfuls of water. Pots, dishes, and silverware had to be immersed in boiling water. In the days before Pesach, only essential things were kept inside the house, and the walls were repainted with whitewash. During the 1940s, this habit of cleaning for *Pasqua* (the word is used in Jewish custom, as well as being in common use in Italian), and the use of quicklime to repaint the houses once a year, stemmed the spread of epidemics.

In their brief encounters before Passover, the women had only one theme: "Where have you got to in your cleaning?" The most organized ones would close up the house a week before the holiday, barring the door even to their husbands. "It's all cleaned and sealed," they would say, "nothing and no one can come in, you never know whether their shoes have trodden in places that are impure or dirty with flour."

A month before Pesach, my father would bring home a little lamb. We small children would play with it and take care of it, giving it food and water, until a week before the holiday. Then we would encounter it again, served up to us during the entire holiday of Pesach, without our suffering any traumas of vegetarianism. The most important role was and still is given to the lamb's shank bone, which is an object mentioned in the Haggadah (Passover reading).

The matzah crackers for Passover were made in silence, because the flour was not supposed to touch the water, and if we talked some saliva might come out so that the crackers without yeast might become unkosher. Prior to the holiday, we children finally understood what was the purpose of the well in the center of the terrace or patio, a well without water whose sides were covered with a cylinder of iron. The adults brought wood to "light the well," which was in reality a cylindrical oven where the *ftere*, (matzah crackers), were baked. The rules were ironclad. The flour came from a special crop and had to be kneaded with one hand, in silence, standing in the shade—a task that was not easy, finding some shade in Tripoli—and then baked on vertical walls with the burning fire beneath. All of this could take no more than eighteen minutes, or the matzah would not be kosher. The smell on the day of baking the matzah was unique. Eight days of eating matzah, unleavened bread, change the body's metabolism and, after the first three days of enthusiasm for the holidays and detoxification from yeast, each of us was counting the days until we could eat again what was prohibited for the eight days.

The holiday would begin the day before, with roasted lamb, which was eaten outside the house, on the sidewalk, in order not to dirty the still very clean interior. We would handle the small bones with our fingers and we would still eat a little yeast bread before it was forbidden. For dinner we would eat the lamb stew with leeks and the next day stuffed lamb parts in all their forms, *asban* and *masran* (stuffed innards).

In the morning, while we were still drowsy, from the smell in the air we knew it was already Pesach. The stuffed lamb parts were made only at Pesach and had an intense smell. We could not wait for the prayers in the synagogue to be over in order to have lunch, to comment and to live the festival as a family, with our own sounds, and then sleep after lunch with full stomachs.

Our habit was to keep a little of the flour from which the *ftera* had been made to use on the morning of the eighth day to make *mimunas*. That was surely the day of scents: we had to make a sort of round bread roll for each member of the family, putting a boiled egg in the middle and adding spices like coriander and anise. The smell of yeast joined with that of the eggs fried with little cubes of *liia*, lamb fat, small rounds of *mergaz* (sausage), and paprika and garlic, a dish that would take until Pesach of the next year to digest, but which was a delight for the taste buds, and everyone would eat with pleasure the *mimuna* with the special frittata.

The Main Holidays

The most important holidays always had the same menu, with small creative variations applied by the mothers, but at Pesach the problem was how to eat the *haraimi* by dipping the bread in the sauce, something that was our habit, but which was difficult to replicate with the matzah.

Every holiday had its own scent: we would smell the wax of the little candle used to light the oil lamps on Hanukkah; the sweet biscuits of Shavuot that had been baked long and slow in the ovens; and the richest sesame bread from the public oven, enriched with the scent of prickly pear leaves that the bakers would use to humidify the ovens made of terra-cotta tiles. The ovens were generally built at street level and the pans of bread would be put on the sidewalk, while the baker did his work standing inside a cave-like space in front of the oven's

7. Biscuits for Shavuot baked by Erminia Tammam.
Photo by Judith Roumani.

mouth. There were hundreds of pans, each one belonging to a family
that could recognize it due to special signs on the bread. My family's
bread had two cuts along the side and a small hole in the middle, but
that was not the only thing that distinguished it. "Obviously" these
were the most beautiful loaves of all, because every mother was convinced that her own bread was the best; if their husbands would taste
the bread at the home of a friend and find it good, they would tell
their wives in order to stimulate them to do better.

My mother wasn't tired enough when Emilia, Aunt Malu, came
by, and Emilia convinced her to put herself forward as a volunteer to
clean the synagogue. So, when the house had been cleaned, she ran to
the synagogue with rags and buckets. The holy place made that work
almost a relief for the spirit; during a break she would drink some coffee brought from home in a thermos and eat a piece of *bocca di dama*
(sponge cake) left over from the *seudot* (ritual meals) of the day before.
Women took advantage of the synagogue being empty to say their
own prayers and to tie their scarves onto the *Sifrei Torah* (handwritten
Torah scrolls) inside the *Aron Hakodesh* (Holy Ark in the direction of
which one prays). During the cleaning they would also repair the cur-
tains of the *Aron Hakodesh*, and if it was a big repair the work would
be done at home on the mat.

The *tallitim* (rectangular prayer shawls with fringes on the corners
and shorter ones on the sides) would also come home for washing and

mending and then the terrace was festooned, as for a holiday, and the neighbors would be full of gratitude and admiration. The next day, she was not allowed to approach the *Sefer Torah*, and so she would ask a man, "Could you please get the blue scarf with white and yellow stripes for me from the *Aron Hakodesh*?" A real trophy to bring home: later on, in a propitiatory rite, the knot would be undone over the head of the person in the house most in need of help, as a sign of blessing and to take away the evil eye.

A large part of the responsibility for any dirt on the *tallitim* was due to the *askarot*, the commemorations, real festivals, occasions for men and women to be at the synagogue together. The family concerned would make a point of bringing to the synagogue the best dishes—biscuits (*kak*), almonds, *mafrum*, eggs, chickpeas, and abundant drinks—and nobody at all would think of the one commemorated. Whatever was left over would be taken to the Garfa, the home for the elderly. Women would take responsibility to care for an old person and would take socks back to mend on the mat, returning to the home with something useful and staying a little to give some help.

A husband's antics pretending to eat would not go unobserved by his wife, who had labored so much over that dish. "Why don't you eat your *tebiha*? Is it not good?" At first he will deny that he's not eating, then he'll admit that he has tasted something at the synagogue for Sion's *askara*. It's known that Sion's wife is famous for her *mafrum*; and the issue makes the wife annoyed, so she doesn't insist that the husband eat, but keeps her bad humor until bedtime.

On Shabbat we could not light a fire, or pay the Arab baker to warm the rice, so we would send the pan to the baker together with a piece of bread on the side to compensate him; the baker would put these together until he had a full bag and then sell it. We could not always have access to the *kanun*, because charcoal was pricey, and in times of poverty it was not unusual to see a woman go to a neighbor to ask her for an already burning piece of charcoal. Thus she would exchange a piece that had gone out for a burning piece, even if the neighbor would look as if she didn't want to accept the piece that had gone out; then after a little back-and-forth, the charcoal that had gone

8. Children bringing lambs for Passover. Courtesy of
Hamos Guetta Collection.

out was put in the place of the burning piece that had been given to
the borrower.

Israel

On the State of Israel's independence day, one was forbidden to celebrate in Libya. My mother didn't care, though, and she would unfail-
ingly cook the holiday foods even on Yom Haazmaut. In the morning,
we would go to school as usual, and if Independence Day fell on a
Saturday or Sunday, we would go to the synagogue to pray for Yom
Haazmaut. My mother's recommendation was not to wear holiday
clothes so as not to draw attention to ourselves as we went to the
synagogue, where we avoided saying the prayers in a loud voice. Libya
considered Israel an enemy country, and multiple laws prevented us
from having normal relations with our relatives who had emigrated to
Eretz Israel, people we had not set eyes on or heard from for twenty
years. It was such a serious thing to have relations with Israel that
the family of my friend Franco Meghnagi had not even told him that
he had two brothers in Israel: he discovered it only in 1967, the year
when all the Jews left Libya for good. The word "Israel" was taboo, it
was obliterated from atlases, and it was unknown in school books. The

only possibility that was allowed was to study Torah in the afternoon. We craftily transformed the Talmud Torah School into a study center for the Hebrew language, the language of the new State of Israel erased by the Libyan government, together with the Jews' civil rights.

Winter in Tripoli

Winter in Tripoli was rarely harsh, but we still caught colds that my mother fought by having us drink a mixture of wine, olive oil, and honey or sugar in the morning, a real bombshell that often had miraculous effects. If after that we ended up in bed with a cough and the flu, a poultice of kerosene on the chest would be necessary. The fumes and the heat were unbearable for us children, but we got well fast. If we had an earache, Mamma's remedy was a wad filled with black pepper and sprinkled with *arak* (an alcoholic drink with anise), which was placed in the earhole. The effect was some heat that healed our otitis.

In the morning, when we would wake up for school, the winter breakfast was *sahleb*, a porridge made from millet flour flavored with cinnamon and sugar. In Italy millet is given to birds, but *sahleb* is a wonderful dish that my children have always had and continue to eat.

Coming out of the Roma Italian School at 1:30 p.m., having lunch and arriving in time for Talmud Torah at 2:30, was a real challenge. My mother would manage it because she was one of the first women in Tripoli to have a driver's license; she would carry us and so many friends, filling up her romantic, rounded Morris with twelve children.

When the smell of pencils and erasers was erased by that of boiled chickpeas, it was clear to everyone that it was a day of celebration. Probably someone had had a baby boy and the custom was to give a coin to all the boys in the Talmud Torah, together with chickpeas boiled with salt and celery and the Belgian chocolate that all we youngsters loved, Choco Prince. We studied less, the giving out of the chickpeas extended our recess time, and the snack was upgraded. If the birth was in the family of a relative or friend, two days of fun were guaranteed, with the celebration of the Zohar on the evening of the seventh day after the birth during which mothers, aunts, and relatives extended themselves to feed all the guests. The next day, the day of the *milah* or circumcision, which allows the baby to join the Jewish people, was the crucial one. The air was full of the smell of sweets, the sound of blessings, the *besamim* (perfumes), and the warmth of the crowd that pressed around the *mohel* (the rabbi who was there to cut the foreskin) to see him at work and right afterward to comment on the *milah*—whether it was well done, whether the rabbi had been good or not, whether he had been more decisive or less so as he cut, whether the baby had cried a little or a lot. If he only cried a little, the credit went not to the mohel but to the gauze soaked in wine that they had given the baby to suck on. From the same bottle, the rabbi would drink a little of the wine, and pour the rest over the little member to disinfect it. The story goes that not all the *milot* were perfect, and some problems had come up over the years. But the ceremony always finished in the same way: the baby drunk and sleeping, the relatives around the tables rich with salted almonds and *lagbi* (chlorophyll of palm) when it was the season, a white drink that was slightly alcoholic, sweet but not too sweet, and that had to be drunk during the twenty-four hours after harvesting because it went off immediately, so that after three days it was dangerous and could cause colic.

In the Tripoli of my childhood, as well, there was plenty of street food. There was no need for a special occasion for tasty snacks. The streets were full of the carts of street vendors of prickly pears (we made accounts at the end by counting the rinds); we could also taste grilled corn on the cob or a *sfenza*, a fried doughnut made only of flour, or more simply a sandwich of tuna and so much *fel fel* (hot peppers). One day, next to an apartment building under construction, sitting on the ground having a break were some Arab workers, and my father sat down with them and invited me to dip into olive oil, as they were doing. Poor, hungry workers would ask the vendor who was frying to have the *sfenza* absorb as much oil as possible, turning it with the *saffud*, a pointed iron tool with which he managed and turned his fritters. Rich people, on the other hand, would have him add an egg, which as it fried would attach itself to the ring in the center of the dough.

Yom Kippur

The time when food played a fundamental role was before and after Yom Kippur, the twenty-six-hour fast. Before sunset, a meal that was halfway between lunch and dinner and rich with many kinds of food, was eaten to prepare us for the kilometers we would have to walk to get to the old green synagogue (the Hadra Synagogue) in the *hara* where my grandfather went to pray, then we would walk back home to sleep. The following morning, still fasting, we went back to the synagogue but the walk, which had been so pleasurable the evening before on a full stomach, now seemed endless, especially since we had to pass by the Arab bread ovens with their unmistakable smells. Finally we arrived at the synagogue where the prayers were being recited, while the children amused themselves with games. Then there were the final, very long hours when the mind was fixed on food, on what we would have liked to be eating, on our favorite dishes that came into the mind. When the prayers finished with "El Nora Alila" and the shofar, we went home—fortunately not to our own home, which was very far, but to the home of an aunt who lived near the synagogue. To get there we didn't need an address, it was enough to close our eyes and follow the scent of coffee with *zahar* (orange flower water), *bulu* (sweet rolls), and the *safra* (semolina cake). We could have got confused only because the other houses had prepared the same things to break the fast. Finally, we went home for dinner and what we had been imagining eating all afternoon, though it became impossible after the first few mouthfuls of *nukides* (Tripolitanian gnocchi made of flour and eggs), because after twenty-six hours of having no food in the stomach we could not put anything else in it. The plans made with friends to go out after dinner became only dreams as the *nukides* went down into the stomach. Between the family chatting and the pillows that were attacked, night came on and we went to sleep, because the next day was a regular day and everyone had to go to work.

Regular days would not last very long, though, because right after Yom Kippur came Sukkot, the festival of booths, the most enjoyable one for children, whose responsibility it was to build and decorate the booth. For eight days we would eat in the booth, and the most observant would also sleep there, even if it rained, under a roof that was anything but waterproof. Besides hanging oil lamps inside, there was the custom to decorate the ceiling by hanging symbolic fruit like pomegranates and dates. As for all important occasions, the food was special: the only difference was that the smells of the food spread through the entire house because the dishes were brought from the kitchen, up the stairs, and onto the terrace where the booth stood, leaving a wake of aromas. Eating dinner and looking at the moon and the stars through the gaps between the palm fronds that covered the booth was particularly exciting for us children.

Henna Party

A husband had to be found for Sina, who was already over twenty. Even if she hadn't been invited to the next henna party, someone would make sure that she would be. The henna was the celebration that took place a few days before an actual wedding. Followed by a long procession with colored candles and singing accompanied by the *darbuka* (the local drum), the future bride, dressed in red and adorned with a belt and large pieces of jewelry, walked with her face covered across the entire *hara* until she reached the house where the celebration was to take place. The guests were already there. The men, who were free to move around, circulated among the tables and musicians, in their best clothes, while the young women like Sina sat on chairs lined up in a row where they were on show for the eyes of possible suitors. Sina, as everyone did, borrowed the *sdad* from Rina, the necklace and bracelets from Aunt Halu, and the *hzam* (a wide metal belt) from her mother. If someone noticed her and wanted to ask her to be his wife, he would send an emissary with some money in his hand. The young men circulated around the girls and made the money jingle in their pockets.

The ambassador received the money from the young man (the more money, the more convincing the proposal would be), and he had to put it in the girl's hand and then tell her the name of the young man who sent it. The girl had to decide right away whether to accept the money or not. Just a few seconds to decide whether you should accept the courting of someone who perhaps you had not been expecting. Often the money was returned, but if it was accepted the news would spread beyond the party in a few minutes.

The next day, the suitor would send the girl some well-appreciated sweets: *bocca di dama* (sponge cake) rich in almonds, as well as a replica of the rare sweets of Purim. Then, in the presence of her mother, the young man would meet the girl for the first time. Other meetings would not be allowed until the parents had made an agreement about the dowry, the house, and the work: a business deal between the parents often ended up interrupting the dreams of love. The interruptions because of business issues were often followed by elopements and stories, marvelous stories, of secret love affairs.

Halu was not well off, but she was very beautiful; Alfonso, from a wealthy family, had asked her to be his wife, and the negotiations had been difficult. In the end, the future mother-in-law agreed that Halu's family could give her as a wife with her six gold bracelets, and that they should provide the henna party. But there was no money for the party and so, following Tonina's advice, Halu had three bracelets made in brass and sold three of her gold bracelets. With the profit she paid for the party; when the mother-in-law discovered the stratagem, Halu and Alfonso were already married.

Bsisa

Life in Tripoli was overflowing with propitiatory rites, prayers with a specific purpose, and dishes eaten for good luck. The *bsisa* was one of the latter: a mixture of grain, coriander, anise, almonds and sesame ground together that formed a sort of cereal to which were added dates, whole almonds, and small candies. The mothers would toast and grind everything next to the mat of straw, and in the evening, when the father arrived and everyone was there, he would read a short blessing for the home and family. Still today, *bsisa* is prepared in a bowl in which a piece of gold jewelry and the keys to the home or the workplace are added for good luck; the mother soaks everything with olive oil and everyone eats a portion. It is generally eaten on the new year of Nissan, but also when one begins something new and important, such as for a birth, a marriage, or building a house. Sometimes a little is put aside in a container that is hidden somewhere to bring luck, but the risk is always that when Passover comes a little *bsisa* will be forgotten somewhere. This shouldn't happen because yeast is not allowed: if then it is discovered after Pesach, it is damaging for us because, despite all the cleaning, the house had not been kosher on Pesach.

These are the tastes, smells, scents, and meanings of the foods of our childhood, sensations that give access to a world now disappeared.

4

• ◆ •

Tradition with Modernity

From Ottoman Times (1835–1911)
to Italian Encounters (1900–)

HARVEY E. GOLDBERG

When describing the religious life of a Jewish community, it is customary to speak of rabbinic leaders, important books, or religious ideas and movements. These topics are certainly relevant when discussing the Jews who lived in Libya. This essay, however, will also consider "ordinary Jews," who were taught from an early age to be loyal to their families' and communities' traditions but who also had to meet the challenges of an evolving world for which classic Judaic texts did not always provide clear and detailed guidelines. My perspective is that of a partial outsider. I did not grow up within a Jewish community in Libya, but I have encountered people from that land over the course of forty-five years. These encounters led me to delve into their past, which has meant a constant search for books and documents and also engagement with many people who shared with me their stories and points of view.

The following incident, from my first extensive contact with Jews from Libya in Moshav Shalva, which is located south of Kiryat Gat in southern Israel, may illustrate the impetus for this search. I attended synagogue prayers one Sabbath morning, and because I was a guest of the village I was "called up" to recite the blessings over the reading of the Torah. I knew the blessings by heart and had carried out such a *mitzvah* (religious deed) on numerous occasions in Ashkenazi synagogues, but still I was a bit nervous. This is because of a slight difference in the Ashkenazi and Sephardi versions of the second blessing, and also because the decorum of going up to and coming down from the *bimah* (platform) where the Torah is read varies slightly in each community. Nevertheless, my performance of the *mitzvah* passed smoothly and I was congratulated warmly upon resuming my place among the congregants. I reflected upon the power of this ritual. I had come from a middle-class family in New York City, and these congregants had come from a mountainous region south of Tripoli (Jebel Nafusa). I had received a general education, learning broadly about the European/Christian world, and their formal education consisted of a few years in a synagogue school. My approach to Jewish life had been filtered through several generations of savants linking Jewish tradition and modern European scholarship, and their upbringing knew nothing of these interpretations. But in the space of a few minutes, when I ascended to the Torah, uttered two blessings, and then descended from the *bimah*, our worlds intersected with a sense of communion, both between us as people and with "the tradition" that we shared. Since then, I have sought to elaborate upon this experience, which combined an attachment to a revered text and a growing familiarity with a community.

Libraries and Life

In European eyes, the regions of Libya often were a source of trouble: a lair of corsairs challenging Mediterranean shipping, or the territory across which Erwin Rommel advanced toward Egypt during World War II. Libya's marginality in relation to larger population centers is a geographical fact, and it is referenced by a person who renewed Jewish life in the region in the sixteenth century: Rabbi Shimon Labi. One source briefly mentions Rabbi Labi as passing through the area while headed toward the Land of Israel but then deciding to remain in Tripoli because Jews there did not even know how to recite the blessings properly. Little is known about Labi's life or his concrete activities in Tripoli, but he is recognized throughout the Sephardi world, and beyond, as author of the popular *piyyut* "Bar Yohai."

There is scant information regarding Libyan Jewry in the following centuries. Some religious figures, such as the *payyetan* R. Moshe
ibn Jenah of the seventeenth century or R. Mas'ud Hai Reqah, who
was educated in Izmir and moved to Tripoli in the mid-eighteenth
century, left written legacies. Reqah authored a commentary on Maimonides' *Mishneh Torah*, became the head of the *bet din* in Tripoli,
and taught a generation of Torah scholars. It is only from the late
eighteenth century that we have some sort of continuous historical
picture of Jewish life in the city. Mordekhai Ha-Kohen, born in 1856,
later speculated that perhaps earlier rabbis had left no historical writings because "the captivity and plunder that befell them caused the
loss of their chronicles and cherished objects."

Ha-Kohen's own book, at first unpublished, seems to have come
together around the turn of the twentieth century.[1] He utilized manuscripts of a chronicle compiled by Rabbi Avraham Khalfon (b. 1741–
d. 1819). Rabbi Asaf Raviv has done an extensive search of manuscripts
put together by Khalfon.[2] Raviv, while lauding Khalfon's extensive
knowledge and understanding of Torah, points out how much of his
effort was devoted to collecting and copying manuscripts that reached
him; at one time he refers to Khalfon's approach as "encyclopedic."

1. Mordekhai Ha-Kohen, *Higgid Mordekhay: Histoire de la Libye et de ses Juifs,
lieux d'habitation et coutumes*, ed. Harvey E. Goldberg (Jerusalem: Ben-Zvi Institute) [in Heb.].

2. A. Khalfon, *Ma'aseh Tzaddikim*, edited with introduction, notes, and index
by Asaf Raviv (Ashkelon: Peer HaQodesh, 2009). I only came across this by chance.
We know that there are (were) manuscripts of Avraham Khalfon that were never published. Some disappeared, others reached Israel, and others appeared elsewhere. This
manuscript existed in the Ben-Zvi Library (brought from Tunis by Robert Attal),
and Raviv—who serves as a rabbi in one of the moshavim in the Negev—took it
upon himself to publish it, with an extended introduction that provides more information on Khalfon and his work than appears anywhere else. Raviv did an excellent
job. Publication of the book was supported—apparently—by a family in the moshav
(I believe many of the residents are from Gerba), and the publication honors Khalfon's memory. The publisher is a small press in Ashkelon that is active in publishing
liturgical and other sacred books that are in use in synagogues and among families.

9. In the *hara* of Tripoli. Courtesy of Hamos Guetta Collection.

Raviv's thorough exploration underlines the reality that Tripoli, and the towns in its hinterland, suffered from a dearth of printed books.

This situation also is evident in the spoken language (Judeo-Arabic) of the Jews of the region. When once interviewing a man from Tripoli, trying to determine the location of his residence in the Jewish Quarter, he answered that his home was not far from a certain yeshiva. He then inquired if I knew what a yeshiva was. Upon asking him for his explanation, he replied, "it is like a library"—*sifriya*—a place housing many books. This linguistic usage was confirmed by several other people and strongly suggests the paucity of printed books in the region.

A similar impression arises from the word *siddur*, as this Hebrew term (that means "prayer book" in many Jewish communities) became part of the spoken Judeo-Arabic in Libya to mean "printed book." I surmise that this reflects a situation where, for a long time, the only printed books with which Jews had frequent contact were prayer books. These, for the most part, were printed in Livorno and typically were given to boys on the celebratory occasion that we now call "Bar Mitzvah" (in Libya the occasion was frequently referred to as *tfillin*—putting on of phylacteries). In various ways, Jewish life reflected traditions circulating within the life of the community, and handed down over generations, rather than constant attention to the details enshrined in texts.

Mordekhai Ha-Kohen, in his discussion of the *bet din* in Tripoli, calls attention to the gap between tradition as embodied in life and tradition as inscribed in books. He depicts a division of intellectual labor. The learned of the community were split into those who were scholars of the Talmud, the theoretical source of rabbinic law, and the rabbinic judges who were responsible for practical decisions in the context of the court. The former would refrain from studying the literature of the *posqim*, or the codes, that contained concrete judgments made with regard to specific cases that had come up over the course of the centuries. Moreover, in addition to the knowledge of halakhic writings that developed over time in different Jewish centers, there also existed a more local tradition. It consisted of a set of norms and practices that was viewed as binding and hallowed by years of observance, despite the fact that they may not have been firmly anchored in the general literature. Members of the *bet din* frequently made their decisions in terms of these local traditions.

An ancient practice, enforced in Tripoli through the end of the nineteenth century, provided that payment be made to the judges in the *bet din* by the winning litigant. This practice, in fact, was explicitly prohibited in the *Shulḥan 'Arukh*, a compendium of religious laws authored in the sixteenth century. While the *Shulḥan 'Arukh* became the standard code in much of the Jewish world, including Tripoli, in this matter local custom held its own. In the late nineteenth century, however, pressure grew to change the practice so that rabbinic judges would receive a salary from community funds. Actual reform in the matter was undertaken only after the Italians took over the city of Tripoli.[3]

---

3. Ha-Kohen, *Higgid*, 255ff. R. De Felice, *Jews in an Arab Land: Libya, 1835–1870*, trans. J. Roumani (Austin: University of Texas Press, 1985), 37; Khalfon, *Lanu u-Levanenu* (For Us and Our Children after Us) (Netanya: privately published, 1986), 166–68, contains some memoirs concerning aspects of the court related to this practice.

Mordecai Ha-Kohen was critical of the fact that the judges in Tripoli persisted in following local customs rather than consulting earlier decisions found in the literature of the *posqim*, but it is possible to view the same situation in another light. The community itself, as embodied in daily life in the context of family and synagogue, continued to be the locus of loyalty and a guide to behavior. As new situations arose, local religious habits shaped the life of Jews more than the formal rabbinic rulings. This traditional, nonideological, religious orientation tolerated and adjusted to new patterns of behavior emerging in the twentieth century without undermining a basic sense of continuity and identity. This internal dynamic enabled changes to be absorbed without ripping Jewish society apart.

For those who grew up with the notion that Jews are subdivided into religious categories, it requires a bit of mental stretching to grasp this orientation. When talking to Jews from Libya, I have not infrequently heard the statement that "we all were religious." At the same time, I have had other discussions that often were surprising, suggesting that this blanket statement is far too simple. On one occasion, forty years ago, I was chatting casually with one of the leaders of Moshav Porat in Israel. The conversation moved to topics in Jewish history, and he referred to the period in Jewish history when Christianity began to spread. "The Jews were foolish," he ventured, because they insisted on people being circumcised. Many people would have become Jewish if not for this insistence, he reasoned. It was obvious that my interlocutor did not harbor ideas about dropping *brit milah* from Jewish practice. He maintained a religious way of life as did the other members of the moshav. But the ease with which he was willing to play mentally with an option that was quite at odds with central Jewish norms struck me as quite distinct from what I was accustomed to hearing when in interaction with Orthodox Jews. It alerted me to listen carefully to perspectives on religion when they were expressed by other Jews from Libya whom I met.

Several examples were provided by the late Ya'akov Guweta from Benghazi, who was the principal of a Jewish school there before immigrating to Israel. Guweta's education led him to read books on Jewish history that reached the city, either written in, or translated into, Hebrew. At one point, he mentioned to me how he was influenced by the writings of the great nineteenth-century historian, Heinrich Graetz. He recalled that he became convinced upon reading Graetz that the Zohar had been written in Spain in the thirteenth century by Moshe de Leon and that it was not produced by the *Tanna* Rabbi Shimon Bar Yohai according to widely accepted tradition. This broadening of historical horizons, however, did not dislodge Guweta's Jewish commitments. His continuing attachment and loyalty to them was made clear in another conversation in which he related his bewilderment with the complex situation upon arriving as a new immigrant in Israel.

Guweta depicted how he was confounded and embarrassed when people asked him whether he was religious (*dati*) or nonreligious (*lo dati*). "Neither category made sense to me," he claimed. Guweta was not comfortable answering *dati*, a term he perceived to mean that one was extremely pious, strictly following every detail of the commandments; but neither could he readily answer *lo dati*, "as if I ate non-kosher food and separated myself from the life of the synagogue."[4]

This dilemma was undoubtedly experienced by many newcomers whose sense of bewilderment has been left unrecorded.

Everyday Accommodations

Shifting from the realm of ideas and attitudes to that of practice, descriptions of various spheres of life in Libya indicate that many Jews there felt that they could adopt contemporary styles of behavior while remaining attached to Jewish tradition. Some features of European comportment became routine but were not seen as turning one's back on Jewish norms. In Tripoli there were numerous families who, in the summer, spent much time at the seashore including on Shabbat (the Sabbath). They could prepare in advance so as not to have

---

4. H. E. Goldberg, ed., *Sephardi and Middle Eastern Jewries: History and Culture in the Modern Era* (Bloomington: Indiana University Press and New York: Jewish Theological Seminary of America, 1996), 44.

to cook on Shabbat, and they did not feel that relaxing at the beach and swimming in the sea constituted a violation of central Shabbat norms. While there were rabbis elsewhere in the Jewish world who found reasons to prohibit swimming on Shabbat, and others considered it contrary to the spirit of that hallowed day, a widespread attitude among Jews in Tripoli was that it was an acceptable practice that did not undermine the basic rules or sense of belonging to the community. The details or logic of rabbinic rulings were not crucial in maintaining this attitude.

On one occasion I did encounter a reference to a text in discussing everyday life, but the atmosphere of the remark seemed to reinforce my overall understanding. As Italian life became entrenched after Libya was colonized, economically mobile Jews took on aspects of Italian lifestyles, including the way they dressed and general mores of public appearance. The family of an engineer, Moshe Haddad, had moved outside of the Old City and built a synagogue there. Haddad, in his house in Netanya in Israel, painted pictures of life in Tripoli including a portrait of his family's synagogue that showed a mixture of men in European hats and those wearing a red fez. Another person from a similar background, who was active in the Maccabee sports and social club, explained that young men typically abandoned traditional head coverings, something that occasionally evoked critical comments from representatives of tradition. A standard retort on the part of his youthful contemporaries was the claim that, according to the *Shulḥan 'Arukh*, the wearing of a head covering at all times is a sign of special piety (*ḥasidut*) and not an essential religious duty. For most of his friends, he added, the question of wearing a head covering all day was not even an issue. Several people explained to me that they would keep a skullcap (*kipah*) in their pocket, in case there was a need for it during the day, and comfortably put it on their heads or kept it in their pockets according to the situation. They were proud of being conscientious about this, rather than being embarrassed by what might be considered religious laxity or inconsistency.

Modern pastimes also quickly became part of communal life and were not perceived as inimical to tradition. In an interview with

Rabbi Bekhor Sabban, who was one of the licensees in the *bet din* that assisted petitioners in presenting their cases before the judges, he testified that everyone knew of his enthusiasm for sports and his wholehearted support of a Jewish soccer team. His description gave no indication of tension between this passion and his rabbinic status or duties. Apparently many young people played soccer on Shabbat. In *Jews in an Arab Land* by historian Renzo De Felice, the author indicates that Rabbi Castelbolognesi, who reached Tripoli from Italy in 1934, began to oppose football on Shabbat though it had not been seen as a problem before. While in traditional terms there are activities that fit the spirit of Shabbat better than sports, this may be another instance of the community relying on its own religious instincts more than on rabbinic rulings. In fact Mordekhai Ha-Kohen, based on the accounts of elders describing the early part of the nineteenth century, records a practice of teams engaging in competitive physical combat in the Jewish quarter every Shabbat afternoon.[5]

One should assume that in any group there will be diversity and not everyone will adopt the same median path. In the latter part of the nineteenth century, there were those who opposed the proposed innovation of Rabbi Eliahu Bekhor Hazan to teach Italian as part of the education of young Jewish boys.[6] In the early decades of the twentieth century, elementary Italian education became widespread, even while there were still people who sensed that this presented them with a cultural world that was new and challenging. This may be illustrated by a discussion I had with Moshe Ji'an who came from the coastal town of Misurata. Ji'an's schooling exposed him to an Italian curriculum along with his traditional studies in a Misurata synagogue. After World War II, he studied further with other young men at the Neveh Shalom Yeshiva in Tripoli, and he was among the groups that immigrated to Israel early, in late 1948. Ji'an kept many papers and notes from his school years, ranging from the maps of Italy that he

5. Ha-Kohen, *Higgid*, 118–19.
6. Ibid., 236ff.

drew in the government school to the exercises of his Hebrew studies. Before leaving Tripoli, he gathered these papers together in a binder. Then, he sketched a title page to this collection and decorated it like the opening page of a volume of the Talmud. He humorously designated this collection *Masekhet Eruvin*, the name of the tractate of the Talmud dealing with "mixtures of diverse substances." This telling expression illustrates that, for Ji'an, bringing together Italian education and religious socialization required some effort.

Reactions to Change

There were other local responses to the growing presence of European influence in the town that attempted to ward it off. A group of pious individuals led by a rabbi, associated with a synagogue known as Dar Burta, constituted themselves as a "society of reproof." They acted, in the words of one of the former members, as a "secret police," reporting infringements of Jewish law by individuals in the community to their rabbi. For example, they might catch someone going quietly into his shop, before the Sabbath ended on Saturday evening, to fetch an item. Such a man would be handed a written "summons," demanding that he appear, contritely, at the Dar Burta synagogue. The only sanctions behind such a summons were a circle of public opinion and the individual's religious conscience.

In my experience, not all Jews in Tripoli knew of the existence of the Dar Burta group. Perhaps awareness of it was limited to those who lived in the Old City? One person from the New City reported that when riding a bicycle on Shabbat he would be careful to avoid the Old City because he might be roughed up there. But it would not be correct to envision these different parts of the city as entirely separate worlds. Some of those who had moved to the New City would attend synagogue in the Old City on festivals, maintaining a tie to where their family had prayed in the past.[7] The very same individuals could be viewed at times as modernizers and at times as traditionalists.

---

7. See the description of Yom Kippur in the previous chapter by Hamos Guetta.

That "modern" orientations coexisted with traditional patterns is clearly illustrated in a case that became well known in Libya and beyond: the dismissal of Rabbi Gustavo Castelbolognesi by Governor Italo Balbo, and his recall to Italy approximately a year and a half after he was appointed. The tense background to this case is discussed extensively by Renzo De Felice, but it reached a peak in an incident where modern sentiments and ideals clashed with tradition in a complex fashion. It entails a matter of private *qiddushin* (betrothals) that were carried out within a circle of Jews in Tripoli whom Balbo assumed to be "progressive."[8]

The Italian government's policy was to try to bring to Libya rabbis from Italy who, in addition to their rabbinic training, were familiar with contemporary European life and culture and would help encourage Jews in Libya to move in that direction. This, in fact, was similar to the approach of the Ottoman government when appointing a *hakham bashi* (chief rabbi) in the nineteenth century, as was illustrated with regard to Rabbi Eliahu Bekhor Hazan. Rabbi Castelbolognesi reached Tripoli late in 1934, a short time before Balbo was appointed governor early in 1935. Contrary to Balbo's expectations, Castelbolognesi became a strong advocate of preserving tradition. He argued against rules requiring Jewish children to attend school on Shabbat, something that had become widespread in Italy. In Balbo's eyes, by contrast, observing the Sabbath was nothing more than stubbornly holding on to old customs.

Tensions like these alerted Balbo to any sign of Castelbolognesi defending tradition against what Balbo saw as advancement toward Italian civilization. This is the context for his vigorous reaction in the case of private *qiddushin*. A forty-year-old man had been trying to court a young woman aged fifteen who studied in high school. Both the man and the family of the girl were from circles enmeshed in Italian culture and norms. Yet the future husband took a step in his courtship that reached deep into Jewish tradition. He drove with

8. De Felice, *Jews*, 143ff.

the woman to a spot where two friends were waiting, uttered the standard formula of *hare at mekudeshet li* (Behold, you are thereby consecrated to me), and then presented her with a ring that she did not reject. Having taken place in front of two adult male witnesses, this was enough to establish a relationship of *qiddushin* between the two, a condition that only could be changed by a formal divorce as stipulated in Jewish law. The man involved was quite modern according to the conventional understanding of that notion in Libya of those days, and he sought to marry a woman of similar background. Yet the means he employed epitomized a reliance on tradition.

The parents of the woman (whom they probably viewed as a "girl") objected vigorously. They approached the colonial government, speaking in terms of modern values and laws. They argued: how could the Italian regime tolerate such a regressive move? This argument resonated strongly with Balbo's perspective. He urged Castelbolognesi to pressure the local *bet din* to annul the *qiddushin*. Such a step is formally possible within rabbinic law (known as *hafqa'at qiddushin*), but it is an option that rabbis, over the centuries, have taken only reluctantly. The local *bet din*, for their part, upheld the validity of the *qiddushin*, even though they had been carried out privately (in front of only two witnesses), without any rabbinic involvement. Rabbi Castelbolognesi, continuing down the path he had carved out since arriving in Tripoli, refused to push the local rabbis away from adhering to tradition.

This incident challenges a simple view of "modern versus traditional." An Italianized Jew relied upon ancient tradition to carry out a modern act, marrying a woman solely based on his relationship with her and without involving her family. A modern rabbi, who had received a general education, turned out to be a staunch supporter of local rabbinic authority in Libya. To Balbo, however, the picture was clear and simple. Castelbolognesi was standing in the way of progress and he had to leave his position and return to Italy (this took place in mid-1935). In a long report sent to Mussolini, Balbo described the evolution of events in detail. He describes Castelbolognesi as having become "mesmerized" by the local Jewish community and their ways.[9] There is probably some truth to this depiction, but it deserves to be placed in a wider context.

I once chatted about Rabbi Castelbolognesi with Clara Levi, who was born in Padua and moved to Libya after racial laws were passed in Italy in 1938. Castelbolognesi had served as the chief rabbi of Padua from 1924 to 1933. In Tripoli, Levi had taught in a Jewish school and claimed to understand the rabbi's point of view. She said that he had a definite preference for the more traditional members of the community but did not express this simply in terms of religious norms. To him, as he explained after returning from Libya, some of those who were more Italianized in their outward appearance and mien were putting on airs vis-à-vis their fellow Jews and had yet to fully internalize a European way of life. The rabbi, according to Levi, was attracted to those who were Jewish through-and-through without any pretenses.

A Historical Perspective

We do not have direct access to Castelbolognesi's views, but I think his attitudes have to be placed in a historic context. He arrived in Tripoli more than a hundred years after the invasion of Algiers by France, an event that set in motion far-reaching changes in the lives of the Jews there and throughout the region. Castelbolognesi was well aware of the dramatic shifts that had affected European Jewry with regards to their traditional comportment, religious ideologies, and identities. Jewish leaders in Europe in the nineteenth century at first sought to export these patterns to their coreligionists in North Africa. By the mid-twentieth century, many dislocations and schisms within Jewish society were evident to the new rabbi arriving in Tripoli.

Communities in Libya still largely followed well-trodden paths of Jewish life, but pressures to change were evident. In an interview with Rabbi Khamus Agiv from Tripoli, who served as the rabbi of the city of Or Yehuda in Israel, he explained how in his generation few young

9. Ibid., 157–59.

people in Tripoli had any interest in continuing their traditional Jewish studies. It appeared that soon there would be few rabbis or other ritual specialists, and he personally was approached by the leadership of the community to continue his studies. They promised to support him if he took this direction rather than to train for some more common occupation. Developments like these provided a challenge to Castelbolognesi to work for the social and educational advancement of Jews in Libya while also seeking to preserve tradition or, in a more subtle fashion, aiming to guide Jewish practice as it changed gradually. Admittedly, this is historical speculation after the fact, while it is almost certain that Balbo had no way of gaining insight to such a nuanced approach.

In addition to the growing presence of Italy and of European life in general, influences from other directions were significant. The broad Muslim majority in Libya held on to its traditions as constituting the framework of everyday life and as a way of resisting European encroachment. From this angle, life in Libya was conducive to the continuation of time-honored practices. Even with the differences between Islam and Judaism, and the possibilities of tension, daily and seasonal routines entailed mutual religious respect. Jews were sensitive to the fact that Muslims fasted on Ramadan, while many Muslims were cognizant of Jewish practices and even took them into consideration. It was a common practice for some Jewish men in Tripoli, after Sabbath morning prayers in the synagogue, to stop by cafes owned by Muslims and to be served tea or coffee. It was understood that the Jews would come back later in the week and pay for what they had drunk. Rabbi Avraham Hai Addadi, in the nineteenth century, had criticized the practice but it was not abandoned. In fact, it continued to be part of Jewish-Muslim interaction in the years after independence, even with the many changes in relations between the communities.[10]

10. Eyal David, "The Daily Life of Upper-Middle Class Jews in the City of Tripoli in Libya (1951–1967)," M.A. thesis, Hebrew University of Jerusalem, 2014, 44 [in Heb.].

From the late 1930s on, Jewish life in Libya underwent a series of difficult and challenging events: from the appearance of the racial laws, through the bombings and forced transfers of World War II, to the anti-Jewish riots of 1945 and 1948 and the eventual migration of the vast majority of the population to Israel beginning in the spring of 1949. While daily life and communal structures were severely disrupted, the overall orientation of the community continued to be based on a taken-for-granted attachment to tradition. In Israel, as indicated, newcomers from North Africa were confronted with a whole new range of options with regard to the maintenance of Jewish life. Many continued with an ingrained combination of loyalty to established patterns along with incremental accommodation to new practicalities. In the next section I offer two anecdotes concerning ritual life in Israel that illustrate the special character of this orientation.

Continuity in Israel

An approach to religion that stresses tradition stands in contrast to two possible trends. One contrast is in relation to those who abandoned tradition and chose a secular outlook and lifestyle as their ideal. A different but significant contrast involves "orthodoxy," which idealizes the written word and the pronouncements of rabbis and often pushes toward seeking the more severe and restrictive option in the realm of religious behavior. Jews from Libya in Israel often have followed a path that is distinct from either of these trends, as I will show through accounts of two prayer situations that I came across, one in a home setting and the second in a synagogue.

In the 1980s, the father of a friend living in Netanya died, and I visited his home during the week of mourning—*shiv'ah*. The older visitors, born in Libya, had known the deceased from abroad. Men and women sat in the living room and the time for *minhah*—afternoon prayer—approached. Barely noticeably, the men rose, turned toward Jerusalem, and someone began to lead the *minhah* prayer. The women continued to sit in the living room, ceased their chatting, but otherwise nothing changed. In parallel Orthodox settings that I have experienced, either the women would leave the room or the men would move to a separate area for prayer. The situation I observed, where women remained in the room while prayer was conducted by men, seemed totally normal to the Libyan participants. While the behavior of the two genders was different—men recited the formal prayers while women did not—there was no hint that anyone felt this required their separation one from another.

The second occasion, also in Netanya, further suggests that the norms of gender separation that were prevalent in Libya were not as demanding as those prevalent in today's Orthodox practices. It took place during the Sabbath morning prayer in a Libyan synagogue, just before the public reading from the Torah. An old practice, both in Ashkenazi and Sephardi realms, has been to "auction off" honors connected to reading the Torah, especially the privilege of reciting the blessings (*brakhot*) linked to the public reading. The custom of auctioning this privilege has disappeared in many contemporary communities, but it is maintained in others, including some synagogues in Israel where it still constitutes a mechanism for funding synagogue upkeep. That particular morning, a woman participated in the bidding from the women's section behind the men, separated by a thin curtain. Having purchased the privilege of the right to this mitzvah, she designated a male member of her family to "go up" and bless the Torah. The event seemed quite routine to the other participants. Subsequently, I have heard that parallel scenes took place in Ashkenazi synagogues on the Lower East Side of New York City early in the twentieth century. Also, the medieval documents from the Cairo Geniza depict a woman purchasing the honor of reading from the Scroll of Esther, for her brother, during the Purim holiday.[11] Perhaps the taken-for-granted partial participation of women that I observed

---

11. S. D. Goitein, *A Mediterranean Society: The Jewish Communities of the Arab World as Portrayed in the Documents of the Cairo Geniza*, vol. 3, *The Family* (Berkeley: University of California Press, 1978), 24.

that Shabbat morning in Netanya is more in tune with Jewish practice over the centuries than the strict rules presented today as being the only options within Jewish tradition.

Both in Libya and in Israel, there was an attitude toward tradition that encouraged a preservation of familiar religious routines in a non-ideological fashion. The extremes of religious reaction that emerged in Europe in the modern period did not characterize the Jews in and from Libya. They did not promote a rabbinate based on new ideologies, and most were not attracted to a self-conscious orthodoxy seeking to defend itself against the encroachments of modernization. The community itself, as embodied in daily life in the context of family and synagogue, survived as a locus of loyalty and a guide to behavior for many.

5

⋅ ⋅ ⋅

Libyan Judeo-Arabic

*The Arabic Dialect and the
Judeo-Arabic of the Jews of Tripoli*

SUMIKAZU YODA

About Arabic in General

The Arabization of North Africa

It is presumed that the Arabization of North Africa took place in two stages. Before the Muslim conquerors arrived in Byzantine Cyrenaica and Tripolitania in the middle of the seventh century, the majority of the indigenous inhabitants of these areas, as in other areas of North Africa, had been speaking Berber dialects, some Latin dialects, or maybe dialects reminiscent of Punic. When the area was occupied by the Muslim conquerors, the indigenous people adopted Arabic, the language of their new rulers, as their own language and most of them converted to Islam, although some Jews maintained their faith. At first, immediately after the Muslim conquests, it seems that Arabic was used exclusively in some coastal towns, while in the vast inland area the Berber language was predominant. This situation is still found, for example, in Morocco, where about half of the population speak Berber dialects. In the eleventh century, a series of invasions by Bedouin tribes from the Arabian Peninsula passed over the Maghribi countries (e.g., the invasion of Banu Hilal). They preferred to settle in the hinterland and contributed to widening the Arabic-speaking area outside the towns.

Classical Arabic

As is well known, the term "Arabic" denotes Classical Arabic and variations such as standard Arabic, al-Fusha, literary Arabic, and so on. In this essay, I exclusively refer to "Classical Arabic" (henceforth CA), which is used mainly on official occasions, and "spoken dialects." The grammar of CA was established in the tenth century, and since then Arab intellectuals have preserved it as it was and have not allowed any grammatical changes. Meanwhile, the vocabulary developed as time went on; for Muslims it is a very important affair to write correct CA, the language in which the Quran is written. It became a language taught in school, so there are no native speakers of CA.

Spoken Dialects

In contrast, spoken dialects are used as the daily language, exclusively for speaking, although the situation nowadays shows some change, and occasions to write in spoken Arabic are increasing. Since spoken dialects are used in a vast area from Iraq in the east to Mauritania in the west (actually there are also small Arabic-speaking communities in Central Asian countries such as Uzbekistan, Iran, and Afghanistan), there are many varieties according to the following factors.

Geography. The first factor is a geographical one. Broadly speaking, the Arabic dialects are divided into two main geographical groups: Eastern dialects versus Western dialects (the latter are usually called "Maghribi dialects," to which the dialect of Libya belongs). The decisive criterion distinguishing these two groups is found in verb conjugation. The prefix for the first-person singular of the imperfect is represented by ʾa- in the Eastern dialects, whilst it is known by n- in the Western dialects. For example, "I write" is expressed as ʾaktub in the Jerusalem dialect (one of the Eastern dialects) and nəkčəb in the Arabic dialect of the Jews of Tripoli (henceforth TJ).

Traditional Lifestyle. The second factor is a social one: Bedouin dialects versus sedentary dialects. The sedentary dialects have developed in old towns conquered by the Arab army during the seventh and eighth centuries (Tripoli, Sfax, Sousa, Kairawan, Tunis, Constantine,

TABLE I: **Conjugation of the verb "to write" (imperfect)**

	Tripoli Jewish		Jerusalem	
	sg.	pl.	sg.	pl.
3.m.	yəkčəb	ykəčbu	yiktib	yikitbu
3.f.	čəkčəb		tiktib	
2.m.	čəkčəb	čkəčbu	tiktib	tikitbu
2.f.	čkəčbi		tikitbi	
I.	nəkčəb	nkəčbu	ʾaktib	niktib

Annaba, Algiers, Tlemcen, Fez, Rabat, Tanger, etc.) where the mother tongue of the indigenous people (including Jews) was not Arabic. The Bedouin dialects are those developed by the Bedouins who came with the stream of the invasion of Banu Hilal. It is worth noting that the terms "Bedouin dialect" and "sedentary dialect" are based on the historical background against which both dialects have developed, and they do not necessarily reflect the actual lifestyle of the speakers. For example, the Arabic dialect of the Muslims of Baghdad belongs to the Bedouin dialect, although the speakers are sedentary people, not Bedouin. The criterion to classify these two groups is merely based on the pronunciation of *qāf* of the CA; in the sedentary dialects, the CA *qāl* is reflected as *qʾ* or *k* (voiceless sounds), but in the Bedouin dialects as *ɡ* (voiced sound). In this respect, TJ belongs to the sedentary dialect, whilst the Arabic dialect of the Muslims of Tripoli (henceforth TM) belongs to the Bedouin dialect.

TABLE 2: **The distribution of the reflection of CA *q***

	CA	Sedentary dialects	Bedouin dialects
he said	qāla	qāl (TJ)	ɡāl (TM)
		ʾāl (Jerusalem)	ɡāl (Baghdād)

Religion. The third criterion is religion. In many Arabophone cities, the dialect of Jews shows some differences from that of Muslims, since Jews often lived in a distinct Jewish quarter of the town, separated, but not completely, from the Muslim quarter. Therefore it

סימן 75

המלה מלעיל, אבל היהודים מבטאים המלה מלרע, למשל: מִדָּה (שלחן), המשלמים
מבטאים מִדָּה והיהודים מבטאים מִידָּה, ובשמות העצם הכל מבטאים מלעיל, למשל
רָבְקָה, שָרָה, יְהוּדָה, חֲנֻיָּה עקרבא וכיוצא [קט:ב].

או ת׳, בין רפיה בין דגשה, בלתי שם הפרש מבטאים אותה קרובה למבטא ת׳
רפויה לאשכנזים, והמשלמים תועבי נודאאם, אשר לפי המסורת עיקרם פלשתים אך
כעת נתערבו בהם ערבים, הם מבטאים אות חיו כמבטא את׳ רפויה לאשכנזים.

המשולמים	היהודים	עברית	המשולמים	היהודים	עברית

הגיד מרדכי

סימן 75

[הגיד מרדכי והמעברות שבהם יהודי טריפולי]

תנועת היהודים בתקופת הזאת, כמו מה שתורה אותם החכם רבי שמעון לביא, ראשון
הוא לכל דבר שבקדושה וכמעשו הוא נְרם (עיין בס׳ 20 הערה 24), הוא תקן להם
סדר התפללה על הרוב כמנהג הספרדים, כי הוא מגרש קשטיליא, כמ׳ בהערה 24,
אך כמה מהנגים נשתנו ברוב הימים, תקן מגרש לעורי תלמוד תורה ומהנורים נעשה
תישים.

השפה המדברת׳ היא ערבית מהוללה ברברית, איסלקית. היהודים משנים קצת
מהמשלמים באיזה מלות[61] כי המשלמים גם מבטאם משנה, מבטאם [קט:א]

(61) בהיות גם דבר זה מפתח לחוקרים למצוא איזה ידיעות, ראיתי לסדר לפניך איזה
מלת המשוו׳[ם] בין היהודים[61] המשולמים.

המשולמים	היהודים	עברית	המשולמים	היהודים	עברית

10. "Differences between Tripolitanian Arabic and Tripolitanian Judeo-
Arabic, as recorded by Mordekhai Ha-Kohen," in *Higgid Mordekhay:
Histoire de la Libye et de ses Juifs, lieux d'habitation et coutumes*, ed. Harvey
E. Goldberg (Jerusalem: Ben-Zvi Institute, 1978), 232–33 (this table is not
found in the English translation). By permission of Harvey E. Goldberg.

is likely that Jewish dialects escaped certain linguistic developments
that Muslim dialects underwent; that is, Jewish dialects may preserve
more archaic elements that Muslim dialects have lost. On the contrary, Jewish dialects, being comparatively free from the influence of
literary Arabic, introduced linguistic innovations unknown in Muslim
dialects. From such innovative phenomena as well as the conservative
retention of older features, we can learn many important materials for
researching the history of Arabic dialects. In addition, Jewish dialects
contain a number of loan words from Hebrew and Aramaic that are
unknown to Muslims.

The difference between the Jewish and Muslim dialects varies from place to place. For example, in Tripoli, the difference is so great that the language type of Jewish and Muslim dialects is different: the Muslim dialect is a kind of Bedouin dialect,[1] and the Jewish dialect is a sedentary dialect. Meanwhile, in Jerusalem, the difference is slight and restricted to the vocabulary, and no special difference is felt in the phonology and morphology. In Tripoli this division has resulted from a demographic shift that took place after the invasion of Banu Hilal in the eleventh century. After the first Arabization, the inhabitants of Tripoli (both Jews and Muslims) began to speak a sedentary dialect. But at the second Arabization from the eleventh century onward, the Muslims were so strongly influenced by the Bedouin dialects of the invaders that their dialect acquired the most conspicuous characteristics of the Bedouin dialects, that is, the pronunciation of *g* for CA *q*, whilst the Jews escaped this phenomenon and their dialect remained a sedentary dialect. In addition, the immigration of Jews from other cities, including refugees from Spain after the Reconquista, should have some influence on the Jewish dialects of Libya.

The Arabic Dialect of the Jews of Libya

In Libya, the Jewish communities are found in cities or towns scattered along the Mediterranean coast from Benghazi to Zwara and in some villages of the mountainous area in southern Tripolitania. Although the linguistic details of these dialects are not clear because of the lack of investigation, for the time being we can call the dialects spoken by Jews in the actual Libyan territory "Libyan Jewish dialects."

Note that all Libyan Jewish dialects, from Benghazi to Zwara, are sedentary dialects; on the other hand, all dialects spoken by Muslims of Libya are Bedouin dialects.

---

1. TM is not a "pure" Bedouin dialect but it should be defined as a "Bedouinized sedentary dialect." TM has the most conspicuous characteristics of Bedouin dialect, i.e., the reflection of OA *qāf* as g, but it has some other characteristics of the sedentary dialects.

The Libyan Jewish dialects can be subclassified into three dialectal groups:

(1) Western coastal dialect, including Tripoli.

(2) Eastern coastal dialect, the center of which is Benghazi.

As for the coastal dialects, we can discern a slight difference in vocabulary between the eastern (Misurata-Zwara) and western parts (towns around Benghazi), thus it may be possible to divide further the coastal dialects into Eastern coastal and Western coastal dialects.

(3) Southern dialect (dialects of some villages in southern Tripolitania, such as Nalut, Yifren, and Gharyan).

The mountain dialects are different from the coastal dialects in many points, which will be shown in the following discussion by comparing them with Tripoli Jewish dialect.

Note that this classification is based on the experience of sporadic hearing during my fieldwork, not on scientific grounds. In order to clarify the situation, we should make further detailed research.

The Characteristics of the Arabic Dialect of the Jews of Tripoli (TJ)

The Reflection of the CA ḥ in TJ. In some positions, CA ḥ seems to be absent (i.e., inaudible), but in some other positions it can be audible as voiced ḥ (i.e., IPA h[ɦ], which is difficult to distinguish from a vowel). In the case of *āda ~ ḥāda*, the initial ḥ may or may not be audible, but it seems that the speaker is conscious of the existence of ḥ. And in the case of CA *daḥan* ("to anoint") reflected in TJ *dḥən*, it is apparently audible as *dən* without any trace of CA ḥ, but with attentive audition, a kind of friction between *d* and *ə* can be felt as a voiced glottal fricative ḥ.

TABLE 3: **The realization of CA ḥ in TJ**

TJ	CA
āda ~ ḥāda "this (m.)"	*ḥāḍā*
fāhəm "understanding"	*fāḥim*
dḥən "he anointed"	*daḥan*
kṛā "he hated"	*kariḥ*

On the other hand, for the case of *kṛā*, it is safe to say that the etymological *h* has completely disappeared, since this verb conjugates as
a third radical weak verb (compare *ṛmā*, "to throw"). If *kṛā* contains
the etymological *h*, its conjugation should be *kṛā* (3.m.sg.), **kəṛḥəč*
(3.f.sg.), **kṛəḥč* (2.m.sg. & 1.sg.) [kʀʸa:ʧ], and so on; compare *kčəb*,
"he wrote" (3.m.sg.), *kačbəč* (3.f.sg.), and *kčəbči* (2.m.sg. & 1.sg.).

TABLE 4: **The conjugation of TJ verb *kṛā* (< CA *karih-*) and *ṛmā***
(< CA *ramā*)

	kṛā < CA *karih-*		*ṛmā* < CA *ramā*	
	sg.	pl.	sg.	pl.
3.m.	*kṛā*	*kṛāw*	*ṛmā*	*ṛmāw*
3.f.	*kṛāč*		*ṛmāt*	
2.m.	*kṛīč*	*kṛīču*	*ṛmīč*	*ṛmīču*
2.f.	*kṛīči*		*ṛmīči*	
1.	*kṛīč*	*kṛīna*	*ṛmīč*	*ṛmīna*

The Pronunciation of r. In TJ, *r* is pronounced as uvular trill (IPA
[ʀ]) or uvular fricative (IPA [ʁ]), like the French *r*. In the Maghrib, no
Arabic dialect has been discovered where this uvular [ʀ] is standard
pronunciation for *r* other than TJ; but some people pronounce the
uvular trill or uvular fricative *r* as a personal linguistic habit.[2]

The Affrication of CA t and t̠ to č. CA *t* (ت) and *t̠* (ث) is, except for
some cases, reflected as *č* (IPA [ʧ]).

CA	TJ
t̠amāniyah	*čmənya*, "eight"
katabat	*kačbəč*, "she wrote"

2. The Arabic dialect of the Jews of Baghdad has both the uvular [ʀ] and trill [r],
each of which functions differently; uvular [ʀ] is exclusively for original Arabic words
and trill [r] is for words of Hebrew, Persian, and Turkish origin, and words recently
borrowed from OA or the Muslim dialect. In TJ there is no such usage and even *r* in
Italian words is pronounced with the uvular [ʀ].

But this affrication does not take place when Classical *t* or *ṯ* stands before *l, n, s, š, ṣ*.

CA	TJ
ṯalāṯah	tlāča, "three"
tusakkir	tsəkkər, "you shut"

The Stress as Distinctive Feature. The stress rule of TJ is as follows: the stress falls on *əCC* or *v̄C* nearest the end of the word, except for the following cases.

(1) All verbs of the 3.m.sg. perfect have ultimate stress: *ṭəbbáḥ* "he called," *fəršák* "he relaxed."

(2) Dissyllabic feminine nouns functioning as adjectives in the following patterns bear the stress on the ultimate syllable.

(a) CəCCá: *bīḍá* "white," *ḥəmṛá* "red," *ḥəyyá* "living," *məṛṛá* "bitter"

(c) CCūCá: *čfūḥá* "tasty" (f.), *ḥlūwá* "sweet" (f.)

(3) Some Hebrew words: *ətčūrá* "Torah," *ẓḍāqá* "charity"

(4) Some isolated cases: *ābādə́n* "never," *mīdá* "low table"

In most Arabic dialects the stress position is morphologically decided, so the stress does not usually function to distinguish meanings. But in TJ, because of the abovementioned exceptions, the stress now serves the distinctive feature.

TABLE 5: **Distinction by stress**

səkkár "he shut"	sə́kkər "shut!"
nəkčáb "it (m.) was written"	ná̃kčəb "I write"
ǧəllá "he boiled"	ǧə́lla "fruit"
məṛṛá "bitter (f.)"	mə́ṛṛa "time"
kəḥlá "black (f.)"	ká̃ḥla "a kind of fish"

The Use of Two Verbal Forms for "to take" and "to eat". In the Maghribi dialects, two different forms are attested for the verbs "to eat" and "to take" in the perfect: *klā* "to eat," *xdā* "to take," and *kāl* "to eat," *xād* "to take." As far as I have observed, the distribution of *klā-xdā* and *kāl-xād* of these verbs among the Maghribi dialects is complementary, that is, a given dialect possesses only one of the *klā-xdā* series (in most Maghribi dialects) or the *kāl-xād* series (Fez-Jewish, Maltese, Hassānîya [Mauritania], Bou Saâda [western Algeria]), whilst in Tripoli-Jewish dialect both *klā-xdā* and *kāl-xād* series coexist. However, even in Tripoli-Jewish dialect the use of *kāl-xād* series is restricted to the third-person of the perfect; in other persons, the *klā-xdā* series is used.

TABLE 6: **The conjugation of the verbs "to eat" and "to take"**

	to eat		to take	
	sg.	pl.	sg.	pl.
3.m.	*kāl ~ klā*	*kālu ~ klāw*	*xād ~ xdā*	*xādu ~ xdāw*
3.f.	*kālǝč ~ klāč*		*xādǝč ~ xdāt*	
2.m.	*klīč*	*klīču*	*xdīč*	*Xdīču*
2.f.	*klīči*		*xdīči*	
1.	*klīč*	*klīna*	*xdīč*	*Xdīna*

The Verb ṛā "to See". In TJ, the verb indicating "to see" is expressed by *ṛā* (< CA *raʕā*) with a complete conjugation; meanwhile, in most other Maghribi dialects, *šāf* is used and *ṛā* is used as a demonstrative pronoun: *ṛā-ni žīt-ik* "Here I came to you!" (Tunis-Muslim), or even if it is used as a verb, the conjugation is not completed; for example, in Tunis-Muslim dialect, *ṛā* is used only in the perfect.

TABLE 7: **The conjugation of the verb ṛā "to see"**

	perfect		imperfect	
	sg.	pl.	sg.	pl.
3.m.	*ṛā*	*ṛāw*	*yāṛa*	*yāṛāw*
3.f.	*ṛāč*		*čāṛa*	
2.m.	*ṛīč*	*ṛīču*	*čāṛa*	*čāṛāw*
2.f.	*ṛīči*		*čāṛāy*	
1.	*ṛīč*	*ṛīna*	*nāṛa*	*nāṛāw*

Foreign Elements in the Tripoli Jewish Dialect. Hebrew and Aramaic Words: Generally, the Arabic dialects of the Jews contain a number of words (mainly concerning Judaism) borrowed from Hebrew and Aramaic. Most of these words were adapted to the Arabic morphological system, but the stress tends to remain on the original position; the word on the pattern *CCāCa* bears the stress on the penultimate syllable, although Hebrew צדקה is reflexed in TJ as *ẓdāqá* "charity" with the stress on the ultimate syllable. And some Hebrew or Aramaic nouns have been so deeply assimilated to the Arabic morphological system that they take the so-called internal plural form; for example, Hebrew סדור is reflexed as *ṣaḍḍūṛ* and it means now "prayer book", and its plural is *ẓḍāḍəṛ* (not *ṣaḍḍūrīm) as *faṛṛūž* "rooster" and *fṛāžəž* "roosters".

In the following passage, some Hebrew and Aramaic origin words are cited.[3]

ᶜīnārᵊᶜ "evil eye" (< עין הרע), *bḍəq* "to check" (< בדק), *brāxā́* "blessing" (< ברכה), *būrīm* "Purim" (< פורים), *čānāx* "the Bible" (< תנ''ך), *čfəllīm* "Bar Mitzvah" (< תפילים) (*yəlbəs čfəllīm* "he is having his Bar Mitzvah"), *čfənnáq* "to be spoiled" (< התפנק), *čkəwwán* "to intend" (< התכוון), *ətčūrā́* "Bible" (< התורה), *dāwīd* "King David" (< דוד), *drəš* "to preach" (< דרש), *ḥāčān* "bridegroom" (pl. *ḥčənnīm*) (< חתן), *ḥnəkkā́* "Hanukkah" (< חנוכה), *ḥīlūlā́* "feast for saint's memorial day" (< הילולה), *īṛəs* "Eretz Israel" (< ארץ), *kābūḍ* "respect (< כבוד), *kāšīṛ* "kosher (food)" (pl. *kšīrīm*) (< כשר), *lḥālīq* "ḥaroset" (< Middle Arabic הליק < Aram. הילק ~ חילק), *məzzāl* "fortune" (pl. məzzālūč) (< מזל), *mīlā́* "circumcision" (pl. *mīlūč*) (< מילה), *mūīl* "circumciser" (< מוהל), *mūši* "the prophet Moses" (< משה), *məṣwā́* "commandment" (< מצווה), *rəbbi* "rabbi" (< רבי), *səkkā́* "Sukkot" (pl. *səkkūč*) (< סוכה), *səkkānā́* "danger" (< סכנה), *sīfər čūrā́* "the Torah" (< ספר תורה, pl. *sīfrē čūrā́* < ספרי תורה), *ṣaḍḍūṛ* "prayer book" (pl. *ṣḍāḍəṛ ~ ẓḍāḍəṛ*) (< סידור), *slīḥūč* "penitential prayers" (always in pl.) (< סליחות), *snā* "to hate" (< שנא), *šəbbāč* "Sabbath" (pl. *šbābəč*), (< שבת), *ṭāhūṛ* "kosher

3. Sumikazu Yoda, *A Description of the Arabic Dialect of the Jews of Tripoli (Libya): Grammar, Texts and Glossary* (Wiesbaden: Otto Harrassowitz, 2005), 361.

(food)" (pl. *ṭāūrīm*) (< טהור), *ṭṛīf* "nonkosher (food)" (< טרף), *xnab* "to steal" (< גנב), *yūsīf* "the prophet Joseph" (< יוסף), *ẓḍāqá̄* "charity" (< צדקה).

Italian Words. In Libya, because of the colonization by Italy from 1911, Italian became a language of administration and many Jews learned it. A number of Italian words expressing modern concepts were borrowed and took root in the Jewish dialects. Nevertheless, the shortness of the colonial period failed to provide sufficient time for these Italian words to be arabicized. Some of them, however, were adapted to the Arabic morphological system, for example, a verb *ḅāḷḷa* "to dance" (< It. *ballare*), which conjugates the Arabic way; *ḅāḷḷa* "he danced," *ḅāḷḷāč* "she danced," *ḅāḷḷīč* "I danced," *yḅāḷḷa* "he dances," *nḅāḷḷāw* "we dance," and so on; and some nouns *bānīnū* "sandwich" (< It. *panino*), *mərkānči* "rich" (< It. *mercant*), *bəšḳḷīṭṭa* "bicycle" (< It. *bicicletta*), *ḅāgāḷya* "luggage" (< It. *bagaglio*), *ḅāḷḷūn* "aeroplane" (< It. *pallone*), *ḅəṛṭəḷḷa ~ ḅəṛṭīḷḷa* "European hat" (< It. *berrettella*), *ḅūḷṣu* "wrist" (< It. *polso*), *fāmīlya* "family" (< It. *famiglia*), *fəṛmāčīya* "pharmacy" (< It. *farmacia*), *frūṭṭa* "fruit" (< It. *frutta*), *mūbīlya* "furniture" (< It. *mobilia*), *rīgālu* "gift" (< It. *regalo*).

A Special Language (Argot) of Peddlers

At least at the beginning of the twentieth century, there was a kind of special (secret) language of peddlers of Tripolitania.[4] This language was called *lašon ha-qodeš əṭ-ṭəwwāfa* (the peddlers' holy tongue) or simply *lašon ha-qodeš* (the holy tongue); the Muslims used to call it *ᶜabrāni* or *ᶜabrīya*, and it was used "in case of need." It seems that this *lašon* does not indicate a language but some special words incomprehensible to outsiders. The *lašon* consists of mainly Hebrew

---

4. Harvey Goldberg, "Al Leshonam ve-Tarbutam shel Yehudey Tripolitaniya," *Leshonenu* 38 (1974): 137–47, 138–40; and H. Goldberg, "Language and Culture of the Jews of Tripolitania: A Preliminary View," *Mediterranean Language Review* 1 (1983): 85–102, 90–91.

and Aramaic words such as *aton* "donkey" (Heb. אתון), *rexoš* "merchandise" (Heb. רכוש), *zōzim* "money" (Aram. זוזים), *mizbana* "sell" (Aram. מזבנא), and so on. And Mordekhai Ha-Kohen gives an example of a verb conjugation, which fits the Arabic verb conjugation (with some modifications by Yoda):

qāta "to bring" < Aram. *qā - ˀata* (קא אתא).

TABLE 8: **The conjugation of the verb *qāta* "to bring"**

	perfect		*imperfect*	
	sg.	pl.	sg.	pl.
3.m.	qāta	qātāw	yqāti	yqātīw
3.f.	-		-	
2.	-	qātītu*	tqāti	tqātīw
1.	-	qātīna	nqāti	nqātīw

According to the verb conjugation of the Arabic dialect of the Jews of Tripoli, the conjugation suffix should be *-ču; qātīču* (see below).

Compare with the same type of the conjugation of an Arabic verb; *nāda* "to call."

TABLE 9: **The conjugation of the verb *nāda* "to call"**

	perfect		*imperfect*	
	sg.	pl.	sg.	pl.
3.m.	nāda	nādāw	ynādi	ynādīw
3.f.	nādāč		tnādi	
2.m.	nādīč	nādīču	tnādi	tnādīw
2.f.	nādīči		tnādi	
1.	nādīč	nādīna	nnādi	nnādīw

Comparison with TM

Here I am going to show the most representative difference between Tripoli Jewish and Tripoli Muslim dialects.

TABLE 10: **Difference between Jewish dialect and Muslim dialect of Tripoli**

	Jewish dialect	*Muslim dialect*
CA *q*	*q*	*G*
CA *r*	uvular fricative: IPA [ʀ]	apical trill: IPA [r]
CA *t, ṯ*	*č (t)*	*T*
he said	*qāl*	*Gāl*
he did	*ᶜməl*	*dār*
he entered	*dxəl*	*xašš*
he saw	*ṛā*	*šāf*
he went back	*wəlla*	*ržaᶜ*
I hit him	*ḍṛəbč-u*	*ḍṛəbt-a*
they buy	*yəšrīw*	*yešru*
silver	*fəžra*	*fuḍḍa*

Already at the end of the nineteenth century, Mordekhai Ha-Kohen registered the differences between TJ and TM words in his work called *Higgid Mordekhay,* which describes the Jews of Tripolitania.[5]

Texts of TJ

*Life in Tripoli in the 1950s (Extract from a Narrative
of a Man Born in Tripoli in the late 1940s)*

(1) *āná, rkəbt-l-[H]āṛets[H],[6] fīya ᶜəšrīn ᶜām, wṣəlt l-hnāya mᶜa ṃṃālī-ya.[7]
(2) ᶜəšrīn ᶜām žīt hnāya. (3) kənč qbəl fi iṭālya, ṭəsᶜa šhūr, kənč ǧādi, āná
mᶜa ṃṃālī-ya, w-bəᶜdīn žīt ... l-hnāya l- ... l- [H]āṛets[H], [H]israēl[H]. (4)
[H]axšāv[H], a ... āná žīč mᶜa xəmsa xwāč, xəmsa xwāč, rəbᶜa wlād w-bənč*

5. Mordekhai Ha-Kohen, *Higgid Mordekhay: Histoire de la Libye et de ses Juifs, lieux d'habitation et coutumes,* ed. Harvey E. Goldberg (Jerusalem: Ben-Zvi Institute, 1978) [in Heb.] (the table is not found in the English translation).

6. Modern Hebrew words are put between superscript Hs.

7. Ha-Kohen, *Higgid Mordekhay,* 232–33.

... *zūz bnāč, rəbˤa wlād w-zūz bnāč, bəˤdīn xū-ya kān ǧādi fəll-iṭālya*[8], *bəˤdīn žā b-rūḥ-u. (5) žā b-rūḥ-u ḥūwa, w-žā mˤa-na bəˤdīn ža f-əl-ḥūš li ˤṭāw-ən-na ḥnāya ... fi* ^H*israēl*^H. *(6) ḥnān kənna fi iṭālya, bəˤdīn, qbəl ma-žnīa l-iṭālya kənna fi ṭrābləs. (7) kənna fi ṭrābləs, āná kənč fī-ha tsaˤṭāš-əl ˤām, w-kānu ˤənd-i xwāč-i w-bəˤdīn, kənt nəxdəm āná b-ruḥ-i. (8) nəxdəm b-rūḥ-i, kənt nə ... xdəmt nəqqāš fi ṣfāyṛ ən-nḥas w-fi ḥdīd, ḥdīd dhəb, ḥatča ḥdīd dhəb w-xlāxəl ... w-xlāxəl. (9) w-kənt nəxdəm ˤla rūḥ-i, kān ˤənd-i zūz zǧāṛ fī-ham tlaṭṭāš-əl ˤām. (10) xlāxəl lli ləbsū-ham fi ražlī-ham. (11) w-f-čəmma ḥatča la-ḥzāmāč, ḥzāmāt li ḥaṭṭu-ham f-lə-bṭən. (12) ḥzām, kīf lə-dhəb ṭrūf ṭrūf, mxəlltīn kbāṛ k-ḥāyda. (13)* ^H*axšāv*^H *āná kənč, waqtli kənč zǧīr, kəll-na āná ma ˤənd-i ṣḥāb b-zāyd, kānu ysəmmīw mūši w-dāvīd ... bzāyd ṣḥāb. (14) kənna nmšīw s-skūla, nmšīw s-skūla ˤli ražlī-na,* ^H*beyt sefer*^H *(15) xāṭəṛ kənna nqūlu skūla, ma-kānt-š ˤən-na kəlma* ^H*bidyūk*^H *f-əṭ-ṭrābəlsi, ṭrābəlsīya. (16) mūš qətl-ək, ˤa xāṭəṛ fi ṭrābləs yədwīw b-əl-ˤəṛbi mxəlltạ b-əṭṭalyān w-mxəlltạ b-əl-ˤəṛbi. (17) kənna nmšīw s-skūla ˤla ražlīna, ˤla ražlī-na, m-əl-ḥāṛa l-kbīra, ḥāṛa z-zǧīra w-l-ḥāṛa l-wəṣṭya*[9], *kənna sāknīn ǧādi, w-kənna nəmšīw ḥatča la-skūla fi ... səbˤa kilomətr bˤīda.*

Translation

(1) I embarked for Israel, [when] I was twenty years old, and I arrived here with my parents. (2) I came here at the age of twenty. (3) I was beforehand in Italy, for nine months, I was there, with my parents, and thereafter I came here, Israel. (4) Now ... I came with my five brothers, five brothers, four brothers and a sister ... two girls ... four boys and two girls, then my [elder] brother was there in Italy and later he came by himself. (5) He came by himself and he came

---

8. The insertion of the definite article before *italya* should be considered a slip of the tongue by the speaker.

9. The names of the Jewish quarters are *ḥāṛa l-kbīra, ḥāṛa z-zǧīra,* and *ḥāṛa l-wəṣṭya,* where the preceding noun *ḥāṛa* is without a definite article, but when preceded by a preposition or a conjunction, it takes the article *m-əl-ḥāṛa l-kbīra* "from the Great Quarter," *w-l-ḥāṛa l-wəṣṭya* "and the Middle Quarter." See Yoda, *Description of the Arabic Dialect,* 291.

with us later to the house which was given to us here in Israel. (6) We were in Italy and then, before we came to Italy, we were in Tripoli. (7) We were in Tripoli, and I was nineteen years old, I had my brothers, then I was working by myself. (8) I was working by myself, I worked as a smith for brass trays, bracelets, even bracelets and anklets. (9) I was working independently, I had two boys of thirteen years old. (10) Anklets which were worn on the ankle. (11) And there were belts as well, belts which were put on the belly. (12) In the belt some gold pieces are embedded like this. (13) Now when I was young, I had many friends, called Moshe, David . . . many friends. (14) We used to go to school *"beyt sefer"* on foot, (15) because we called it *"skūla,"* we didn't have an exact word in Tripolitanian (Arabic), (16) I didn't tell you that in Tripoli they speak in Arabic mixed with Italian and mixed with Arabic [*sic*]. (17) We used to go to school by foot from the Great Jewish quarter, the Small Jewish quarter and the Middle Jewish quarter; we were living there and we used to go to school . . . seven kilometers away.

Literary Idiom of the Jews of Tripoli (Literary Judeo-Tripolitanian)

The Jews in the Arabic-speaking area began to write Arabic in Hebrew script at least from the tenth century. This kind of Arabic is called "Judeo-Arabic," where Hebrew and Aramaic phrases from religious sources can be easily inserted. Many great Jewish works were written in this kind of Arabic, such as *The Guide for the Perplexed* by Maimonides or *The Book of Kuzari* by Yehuda Halevi. It seems that in that period some Jewish authors had a good knowledge of CA and supposedly they could write correct CA. However, they did not believe there was any prestige in the Quran, and so they were less restricted in the normative consciousness of grammar, thus the rate of grammatical deviation was somewhat higher than in Muslim documents.

In the Middle Ages, Judeo-Arabic was used for correspondence within a Jewish community and also with other Jewish communities, and seen in this light, this language functioned something like koine for Jewish communities. Therefore it was used for *responsa* among Jewish communities of the Middle East and the North Africa.

From the end of the Middle Ages onward, Judeo-Arabic began to contain more elements of the spoken dialect of each region than ever before. At least from the beginning of the twentieth century, Judeo-Arabic ceased to be a communication tool common for all Arabic-speaking Jews, but it became rather a communication tool within restricted regions; for example, a Judeo-Arabic text published in Tripoli is mainly written in a linguistic style where TJ contains some CA elements, so it is comprehensible for the Jews of Libya (and probably southern Tunisia). It is interesting enough that many Judeo-Arabic documents published in Tripoli contain some elements from the Tunisian dialect (e.g., instead of Tripolitanian *rā* "to see," Tunisian *šāf* is used). In addition, the proportion of the dialectal elements and CA elements varies considerably, probably according to the educational level of the intended readers; documents written for the ordinary people contain fewer CA elements.

Modern Judeo-Arabic seems to have been used in the beginning for religious matters, and this situation continued until the end of the mass immigration to the State of Israel after its foundation. During the Italian colonial period, it was used for the purpose of educating Jewish people about public health and so forth, and also in the twentieth century a number of newspapers were published in this language.

In Judeo-Arabic some letters may be added by a dot above or below, which can distinguish different sounds:

כ = *k*, כֿ = *x* (like German *ch* in *Bach*).

ג may have a dot above or below גֹ, גֿ or a slash ג'; one indicates *ǧ* (as French *r* in *Paris*) and another *ž* (as French *j* in *journal*) but the sound depends on the texts. In *Deghel Sion* (a monthly Zionist newspaper), גֿ = *ž*; גרידתנא *žrīdatna "our newspaper" (CA جريدتنا) and גֹ = *ǧ*; גרפת *ǧarfaċ "room (of)" (CA غرفة). On the other hand, in Erev Pesah (גֿ = *ž*; יכֿרגֿ *yaxraž "he goes out" (CA يخرج) and ג' = *ǧ*; תג'רבל *ǧǧarbal "she sifts through" (CA تغربل).

פֿ = *f*, צֿ = *ḍ* (as Arabic ض).

Besides the ligature אל = ﻻ is frequently used.

There is no fixed orthography, therefore one and the same word may be spelled in many ways; נתאעך, נתעך, מתעך "yours" (in TJ *nčā͑ək*). According to the style, the proportion of the (Pseudo-) Classical element varies. For example, there are two ways in which verbs may be negated:

לם (cf. CA لم):[10] סאבך לם דכלת פّי גמעيّת ציון "I did not enter (participate in) the Zionist organization"

מה . . . -ש (a verb is put between two elements, which is the normal negation of verbs in the modern spoken Arabic): מא קדרתש נפהמהא "I could not understand it."

Letters in the Judeo-Arabic of Tripoli. The following two letters written in the Judeo-Arabic of Tripoli in the early nineteenth century are cited from S. de Sacy (1810), with the original translation in French.[11]

בעّת יום כב חשוון תקם פה מרסיליא יעّא
א סניור מרדכי נגّאר יצّו מן חוّם מסלם עליך באّש אחّדّשו סנת אד אכّטין באש
נערפّך אّדי אגّמעא לבّרא כתבתלך בّריّא ועלמתך במא כאן ודלחין
נזידך אד אّחרפّין באש נחרצّך תמשי לענד סניور יעקב ותסלם עליה מן גّהّתי
יאסר ועّלא מאّדאמא ותקّולו נאניך סלّאמת אד אّכّיר צّלה תעّאّא יכّמל
עליך וקّולו איّדא יעّמל עلّייא גّמיל יקّדרשי יאכّودלי אסّראח באש נרווח לתّونّس
מעّא אّמّרכّב אّדي מאّשי פّיהّא עצّמאّן וקّولו באّיך ינّסّאني אّחّסّבّא דיّאّי מّעّא
דיّאّי ראّני עّאّמّל עّلّא אّלّה ועّليّך וכّדّاّך תّسّلّمّלّي עّلّא מّوّسּיّו עّلّא לّيّאّתّאّד ועّلّא מّאّדّאّם

This text contains Hebrew expressions in the form of *roš tevot*; בע'ת = בעזרת האל, יע'א = יעזרה אל, יצ'ו = ישמרהו צורו, חו'ם = חתום מטה, בא'ש = אחרי חרישת שלומך וטובתך, אחّדّשו = באّלף שלומות, besides some foreign words from European languages, סניور = signor (It.), מאّדّام, מאّדّאמא = madame (Fr.), מוّסּיّو = monsieur (Fr.).

---

10. CA لم is combined with a jussive verb, but in the Tripolitanian Judeo-Arabic, it may be combined with perfect verbs and indicates the negation of the past. Because of this different usage, this particle may be called a "pseudo-Classical element."

11. Silvestre de Sacy, *Grammaire arabe à l'usage des élèves de l'école spéciale des langues orientales vivants: avec figures* (Paris: De Bure, 1810), xv and Planche V (fig. 11), xvi (fig. 12).

11. Extract from personal letter in Judeo-Arabic of Tripoli. Courtesy of Sumikazu Yoda.

Translation: [Avec le secours de Dieu. Le 22 de Marcheschvan 560 [1800], à Marseille; que Dieu l'assiste! A M. Mardochée Najjar (que Dieu le garde!), de la part du soussigné, qui lui offre mille salutations. Après m'être informé du bon état de votre santé, je vous écris ces deux lignes pour vous instruire que la semaine dernière je vous ai écrit une lettre et donné avis de ce qui étoit arrivé. Aujourd'hui, je vous ajoute ces deux mots pour vous engager à aller chez M. Jacob. Saluez-le bien de ma part, ainsi que Madame, et dites à M. Jacob: Nous vous félicip tons de cet heureux événement, et nous prions Dieu de vous combler de plus en plus de bien. Dites-lui que, s'il veut me rendre service, il pourroit m'obtenir un congé pour que j'aille à Tunis par le même bâtiment par lequel doit partir Othman. Rappelez-lui, prenez garde qu'il ne m'oublie, que mon compte et le sien ne sont qu'un. Je n'ai de resource qu'en Dieu et en lui. Vous saluerez aussi de ma part M. Lieuu taud et Madame.]

תעלם יא מוחבנא אלדי קבלת אלבאלא מתעך נומרו כמסא ובעתהא
וכונת נרדר נביע כדאך לבאלא לוכרא אלדי באקיא בעד לחאגא
בזאיד לוכאן מא טלבוליש תלת שהור וגלא פדפע חאגא אלדי מא
חביתש נעמל מן גיר אורדני מתעך ויוצלך פי וצט האדי חסאב
למגבור טלע חק לבאלא רבע מייא וכמסין ריﭏ אבו דור ראני
זוזתהום פי חסאבך ומעא גיר האדי יאתיך אירימיסא דיאלהא

12. Extract from commercial letter in Judeo-Arabic of Tripoli. Courtesy of Sumikazu Yoda.

ותקדר תטמאן אׄדיבעאנאהא ביע טייב פי זמאן אׄדיחנאן פיה

ונקול נשאׄה אׄדי יכון כאטרך טאיב מן גׄיהתנא וכדׄאׄך תכון

מן ליום וקודאם ודלחין מא עדנא באש נטולו עליך אן בלכיר ואסלאם

Translation: [Sachez, mon cher ami, que j'ai reçu la balle, no. 5, et que je l'ai vendue. J'aurois pu vendre de même l'autre balle qui reste encore, et même à quelque chose de plus, si l'on ne m'avoit pas demandé trois mois de délai pour payer, chose que je n'ai pas voulu faire sans votre ordre. Vous recevrez, ci-inclus, le compte du produit: la valeur de la balle monte à 450 piastres fortes que j'ai passées à votre compte. La remise vous en parviendra par une autre occasion. Vous pouvez être assure que nous l'avons bien vendue pour le temps où nous sommes. Nous osons nous flatter que, s'il plait à Dieu, vous serez content de nous: vous le serez pareillement dorénavant. Nous n'avons, pour le présent, rien de plus à vous écrire, sinon de vous souhaiter toute sorte de bien. Adieu.]

Newspaper Degel Sion. Degel Sion was the first Jewish newspaper published in Tripoli. The first number was published in 1920.

אלחאלא אלחאצׄרה

פׄי אׄעדד אׄאוול מתע גׄרידתנא ביינא בלסאן

פׄציח אן גׄרידתנא האדׄי מקצודהא לתדׄאפׄע עלא

13. Masthead of *Deghel Sion* newspaper. Courtesy of Sumikazu Yoda.

חקוק קומנא ותגדידהו במואפקת לחרכה לצ'יונייא
וליס כאַרג' מנהא. חיתנא אחנאנ תאבעינ טריקתנא האדי
טאביעי וואג'ב עלינא לנדאכֿלו פֿי אומור יהוד
טראבלס ותאסיסאתהא איהודייה.

Translation: [The actual situation
In the first number of our newspaper, we explained in plain language that the aim of this our newspaper is to defend the rights of our nation and to renew it [*sic.*] according to the Zionist movement and not otherwise. Since we follow this our way, it is natural that we have to be involved also in the Jewish matter of Tripoli and the Jewish foundations.]

Conclusion

With the advent of the Muslim conquerors, the Jews of North Africa (including the area that is now Libya) adopted Arabic as their language and inherited it until their mass immigration to Israel and Italy. Even if the Jews have coexisted with Muslims, the Jews, having lived in physically restricted Jewish quarters, developed their special Arabic dialect distinct from that of Muslims. Especially in Tripoli, the Arabic dialect of Muslims suffered strongly the influence of the Bedouin dialects, whilst that of Jews has kept more original (or archaic) linguistic characteristics. In this respect, the investigation of the Jewish dialects may contribute to Arabic dialectology.

The Arabic dialect of the Jews of Tripoli has many characteristics that are not attested to in other Arabic dialects: the absence of *h*, the uvular trill *r*, the realization of CA *t* and *ṭ* as *č*, the distinctive stress, the special verbs "to eat" and "to take," and the use of the verb *ṛā* "to see."

As in other Jewish languages, the Arabic dialect of the Jews of Tripoli contains many Hebrew and Aramaic words, which have been morphologically arabicized. *Higgid Mordekhay* reports that at the beginning of the twentieth century, there was a kind of special language of peddlers of Tripolitania, which is called *lašon ha-qodeš əṭ-ṭawwāfa* or *lašon ha-qodeš*. This language consisted of mainly Hebrew and Aramaic words and was used in order not to be understood by outsiders.

The tradition of Judeo-Arabic (written Arabic in Hebrew script) is attested in Tripoli. Especially in the eighteenth through twentieth centuries, it was used for commercial or personal correspondence between Jews. In addition, at the beginning of the twentieth century, many booklets were published in the Tripolitanian Judeo-Arabic. These kinds of documents should be more deeply investigated, since some of them provide information on various aspects of the daily life of Jews of Tripoli at that period.

Although the Libyan Jews who emigrated from Libya exceeded 30,000 persons, the actual number of the speakers of this precious Arabic dialect is considerably decreasing. It is, therefore, an urgent task to investigate it in more detail, which may contribute to preserving a part of the cultural legacies of Libyan Jewry.

Bibliography

Fischer, Wolfdietrich, and Otto Jastrow. *Handbuch der arabischen Dialekte.* Wiesbaden: Otto Harrassowitz, 1980.

Goldberg, Harvey. "Al Leshonam ve-Tarbutam shel Yehudey Tripolitaniya." *Leshonenu* 38 (1974): 137–47.

———. "Language and Culture of the Jews of Tripolitania: A Preliminary View." *Mediterranean Language Review* 1 (1983): 85–102.

Ha-Kohen, Mordekhai. *Higgid Mordekhay: Histoire de la Libye et de ses Juifs, lieux d'habitation et coutumes.* [In Hebrew.] Edited by Harvey E. Goldberg. Jerusalem: Ben-Zvi Institute, 1978.

Marçais, William. "Comment l'Afrique du Nord a été arabisée." *Annales de l'Institut d'études orientales d'Alger* 4 (1938): 1–22; 14.

Sacy, Silvestre de. *Grammaire arabe à l'usage des élèves de l'école spéciale des langues orientales vivants: avec figures.* Paris: De Bure, 1810.

Simon, Rachel. "Deghel Sion." In *Encyclopedia of Jews in the Modern World*, Norman Stillman. Boston: Brill, 2010.

Yoda, Sumikazu. *A Description of the Arabic Dialect of the Jews of Tripoli (Libya): Grammar, Texts and Glossary.* Wiesbaden: Otto Harrassowitz, 2005.

6

✦ ✦ ✦

The Vanishing Landscape

A Retrospective Glance at the Topos of Libyan Jews

JACK ARBIB

The almost complete obliteration of Jewish toponomy in Libya, and ongoing civil war damage including destruction of relevant parts of the country's archaeological and architectural heritage, makes any attempt to faithfully catalogue landmarks connected to the long, uninterrupted Jewish presence in Libya (a continuous period of over 2,300 years) extremely complicated. Moreover, the process is affected by the unavailability of primary sources.

Over the ages, the Jewish component of the general population in Libya never developed a specific architectural vernacular (with possible exceptions of the structures of synagogues); rather, they followed and interacted with the flux of the dominant styles of the epochs. The more accessible testimonials are the Jewish quarters (the Hara Kbira and Hara Sghira in the Medina of Tripoli). These structures, which were built above a Roman encampment, date to the total reconstruction of the quarter under Spanish rule, with a subsequent (re)settlement of Jews in the area.

Our survey covers both rural and urban settlements. Concerning the latter, the focus is on the two main cities of Tripoli and Benghazi, while the Jewish presence in other smaller centers such as Misurata, Jefren, Homs, Zliten, and Tigrinna had traits of a mixed rural/urban fabric. The scope of this survey is limited by the availability of documentation, and by no means do the landmarks recalled here render a comprehensive overview of the variegated and complex Libyan Jewish heritage. Thus the partiality of this list is due not to deliberate choice but to objective limitations. In addition, this narrative will not indicate precise historical periods, and references to pre-Aliyah and post-Aliyah eras (in the period 1948 to 1952 the majority of the community and the totality of the *hara* population immigrated to Israel) are freely intermingled. While we will refer to the Jewish-specific topos, or *maqom*, we will not disregard the "contact zones," public spaces and institutions where the different communities interacted.

Cave Dwellings

Examples of the earliest Jewish homes in Libya are the troglodyte cave dwellings at Garian in the Jebel Nafusa range, continuously inhabited by Jewish families, who abandoned these dwellings when they immigrated to Israel in the late 1940s. On these we have some images from Italian sources from the time of the occupation and a remarkable series of pictures taken in 1947 by the journalist Amos Gordon, who had earlier visited Libya as a war correspondent embedded in the British Army. He was able to document the everyday life of the Jewish cave dwellers. After the Jews of Garian abandoned their houses and immigrated to Israel en masse, these caves were appropriated by Libyans who built new houses above them and annexed the caves as extravagantly decorated living rooms.

Metropolitan Areas

Tripoli

Under Ottoman rule, and before the conquest by the Italians in 1911, the Jewish presence in Tripoli was concentrated in the Jewish quarters of the Medina. The Medina has maintained, to this day, a pentagonal border that follows the polygonal geometry of the walls and fortifications built by the Spaniards in the sixteenth century. The orthogonal grid of the streets recalls the classic Roman layout, based on *cardo*

14. Garian (old postcard). With grateful thanks to MOJL, Museum of Libyan Jews, Or Yehuda, Israel.

16. Garian view. Courtesy of OSA, Or Shalom Archives, Bat Yam, Israel.

17. Garian. Photo by A. Gordon. Courtesy of MOJL, Museum of Libyan Jews, Or Yehuda, Israel.

15. Garian view. Source: *La Rinascita della Tripolitania: Memorie e Studi sui Quattro Anni di Governo del Conte Volpi Misurata*, ed. Giuseppe Volpi (Milan: Mondadori, 1926).

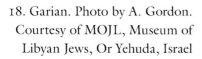

18. Garian. Photo by A. Gordon. Courtesy of MOJL, Museum of Libyan Jews, Or Yehuda, Israel

and *decuman*.[1] Two intersections are focal points of the urban layout, namely the intersection between the *cardo* and the northern *decuman* marked by the Arch of Marcus Aurelius (erected in 163 CE to honor the emperor, this tetrapylon structure was restored and cleaned up by an Italian excavation in 1933) and the Arba'a Arsat (four Roman columns) intersection between the *cardo* and the southern *decuman*, with each corner marked by a house originally belonging to a prominent family (Qaramanli, Gurgi, and Mahsen). These two intersections were frequented by all communities and were contact points between the various communities.

The Jewish quarters (Hara el Kebira and Hara el Sghira) were delimited (clockwise on the map below) by Bab el Jedid, then by the western wall, the northern wall, the Arch of Marcus Aurelius, and Arba'a Arsat. In this area all the homes, synagogues, yeshivas, and schools of the community were concentrated. Regarding business and trades, most Jewish activities were outside the compound, with shops, warehouses, offices, and workshops in business areas located further south, such as in Suk el Turk, Suk el Najjara, and Suk el Mushir.

---

1. Terms from Roman times defining the main artery (*cardo*) and the east to west street it perpendicularly crosses (*decuman*).

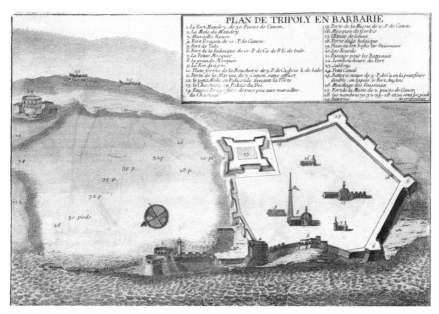

PLAN DE TRIPOLY EN BARBARIE

19. 1705 map of Tripoli. Courtesy of OSA, Or Shalom Archives, Bat Yam, Israel.

20. View of the *hara*, Tripoli. Courtesy of MOJL, Museum of Libyan Jews, Or Yehuda, Israel.

21. View of the *hara*, Tripoli. Courtesy of MOJL, Museum of Libyan Jews, Or Yehuda, Israel.

22. View of the *hara*, Tripoli. Courtesy
of MOJL, Museum of Libyan Jews,
Or Yehuda, Israel.

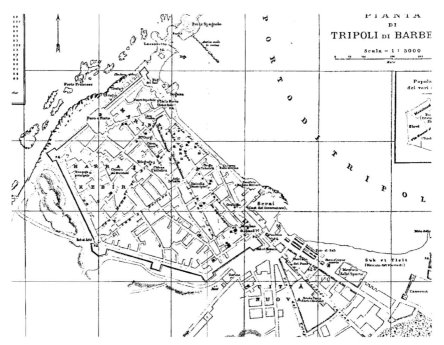

23. Map of Old City of Tripoli ca. 1920. Courtesy of OSA, Or Shalom
Archives, Bat Yam, Israel and Jack Arbib.

Synagogues

Until 1948–1950, at least thirty-three synagogues were active in the
hara. Some of them had important libraries with manuscripts and rare
books, locally printed or coming from world centers of Hebrew literature, such as Livorno, Venice, Leipzig, and Amsterdam. A partial list
includes Slat l'Kbira, Dar Bishi, Dar Al Ketra, Dar Suyed, Dar Bibi,
Al' Tlata, Al Fukia, Al Kabalia, Al Zatlawi, Dar Gerbi, Al Malti, Dar
Serussi, Al Frenk, Dar Abta, and Dar Curiel.

Slat l'Kbira (the Great Synagogue) was the largest synagogue in
Tripoli. This was the venue of many important events, the most mem-
orable being the visit of the Palestinian Jewish soldiers of the British
Eighth Army when they liberated Tripoli in 1943.

Sometime after the expulsion of the last Jews of Tripoli in 1967,
the building was turned into a mosque, with the addition of a minaret.

24. Great Synagogue, Tripoli (before 1967). Courtesy of OSA, Or Shalom
Archives, Bat Yam, Israel.

25. Great Synagogue, Tripoli. Courtesy of OSA, Or Shalom Archives, Bat Yam, Israel.

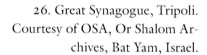

26. Great Synagogue, Tripoli. Courtesy of OSA, Or Shalom Archives, Bat Yam, Israel.

Dar Bishi was originally built in 1770 and became much dilapidated over the years. The Italian government wanted a "decorous" Italianate synagogue in Tripoli as an expression of progress and modernity under the new rulers. The new synagogue was designed by a young Jewish architect, Umberto Di Segni, who was born in Tripoli to an Italian family and later became one of the most important architects in the Fascist colonization of Libya. The building was redesigned

27. Great Synagogue, Tripoli. Courtesy of OSA, Or Shalom Archives, Bat Yam, Israel.

28. Great Synagogue, Tripoli, present state. Courtesy of OSA, Or Shalom Archives, Bat Yam, Israel.

in accordance with the European style very popular in synagogues built at that time. Dar Bishi was inaugurated in 1923 and was conveniently used by the government as a showcase of emancipation of the community and tolerance from the regime, hosting visits by Mussolini, royal family members, and dignitaries. The structure is still standing today, in sore condition after a botched attempt by the Libyans to rebuild the dome in a mosque style in the 1970s.

29. Great Synagogue,
Tripoli, present state.
Courtesy of OSA, Or
Shalom Archives, Bat
Yam, Israel.

30. Dar Bishi Synagogue. Courtesy of private collection. For Dar Bishi, see
also the admirable Diarna website, www.diarna.org.

31. Dar Bishi Synagogue. Old post-card. Courtesy of OSA, Or Shalom Archives, Bat Yam, Israel.

32. Dar Bishi Synagogue, present state. Courtesy of OSA, Or Shalom Archives, Bat Yam, Israel.

33. Dar Bishi Synagogue, present state. Courtesy of OSA, Or Shalom Archives, Bat Yam, Israel.

The Dar Bibi synagogue was founded in 1901 by Mordechai Angelo Bibi Arbib. It was located adjacent to the family home and had an *ishibet* (yeshiva) and a rich library (eight hundred books). The building was donated to the *kehillah* by Bibi's son Jacob when the family moved to a new house in the Italian neighborhood, and it hosted the synagogue, a library, a yeshiva, and a *gherfa* (old people's hospice). It was looted after 1967 and nowadays only rubble remains. Some memorial plaques (including the 1901 dedication inscription) and other religious objects have been removed and are now exhibited in the so-called museum in the Dar Al Serussi.

34. Dar Bibi Synagogue, present state. With thanks to Sergio Bian-concini, photographer.

35. Plaque from Dar Bibi. With grateful thanks to David Gerbi, photographer.

36. Plaque from Dar Bibi. With grateful thanks to David Gerbi, photographer.

37. Great Synagogue, Benghazi. Courtesy of OSA, Or Shalom Archives,
Bat Yam, Israel.

The Al' Tlata synagogue was said to have been established by followers of Shabbetai Zvi and was also said to have a *Ner tamid* (lamp)
dedicated to his memory. A follower of Shabbetai Zvi, Avraham
Miguel Cardozo, arrived in 1648 from Spain, and served as the personal physician to the bey of Tripoli. In 1673 he completed his book,
Boker Avraham, which he sent to Zvi for his approval.

The Slat l'Kbira (the Great Synagogue) in Benghazi. See illustration 37 for an interior view of the old synagogue.

Just as they did for Tripoli, the Italians wanted a modern synagogue
for Benghazi. This synagogue was built and inaugurated in the month
of Sivan 5689 (June/July 1920). It now operates as a Coptic church.

A replica of the Slat Boushayeff—Zliten synagogue exists in the
Zeitan moshav in Israel, where most of the Zliten community relo-
cated. It is now the site of an important annual festivity, attended by
Jews of Libyan origin from different places.

38. Great Synagogue, Benghazi. Courtesy of OSA, Or Shalom Archives, Bat Yam, Israel.

39. Great Synagogue, Benghazi. Courtesy of OSA, Or Shalom Archives, Bat Yam, Israel.

40. Boushayef Synagogue, Zliten. Courtesy of MOJL, Museum of Libyan Jews, Or Yehuda, Israel.

41. Boushayef Synagogue, Zliten. Courtesy of MOJL, Museum of Libyan Jews, Or Yehuda, Israel.

42. Derna. Courtesy of OSA, Or Shalom Archives, Bat Yam, Israel.

43. Derna. Courtesy of OSA, Or Shalom Archives, Bat Yam, Israel.

44. Derna. Courtesy of OSA, Or Shalom Archives, Bat Yam, Israel.

45. Derna. Courtesy of OSA, Or Shalom Archives, Bat Yam, Israel.

46. Homs Synagogue. Courtesy of OSA, Or Shalom Archives, Bat Yam, Israel.

47. Tigrinna Synagogue. Courtesy of OSA, Or Shalom Archives, Bat Yam, Israel.

48. Tigrinna Synagogue. Courtesy of OSA, Or Shalom Archives, Bat Yam, Israel.

49. Misurata Synagogue. Courtesy of MOJL, Museum of Libyan Jews, Or Yehuda, Israel.

Yeshivas

In a 1926 directory, the Italian Administration for Tripolitania lists six yeshivas in Tripoli:
- Ishibet Dar Bibi, Hara el Kebira Street No. 141
  Founded in 1901—800 books—Librarian Saul Tesciuba
- Ishibet Dar Sued, Hara el Kebira Street No. 90
  Founded 1863—1,667 books—Librarian Beniamino Barda
- Ishibet Dar Burta, Shara Mushi Burta
  2,100 books—Librarian Mushi Haddad
- Ishibet Dar Koha, Homet Garian Street—Librarian Isaac Meghnagi
- Ishibet Slat l'Kbira, Shara Slat l'Kbira—Librarian Nissim Haggiag
- Ishibet Sciueha, Shara Slanat
  Founded 1800—200 books—Librarian Rabbi Rahmin Aghib[2]

Dwellings

With the intention of improving health conditions in the Hara, the Italians initiated an interesting project for the construction of a cooperative housing project for indigenous Jews (*Israeliti indigeni*). The design, by Umberto Di Segni, was presented at the Triennale

2. The numbers of books in these yeshivas are quite impressive, and the reader may compare these details with the findings of Harvey E. Goldberg in his previous chapter with regard to Ottoman times.

50. Umberto Di Segni housing project. Source: Jack Arbib et al., *L'Ombra e la Luce: Note su Umberto di Segni, Architetto* (Nola: Il Laboratoio, 2010), 39.

Exhibition in Milan in 1933 but never executed, possibly because of objection from the very same people for whom it was intended.

Illustration 51 is a floor plan of the project, which included running water and toilets for the apartments and communal services.

Until the beginning of the twentieth century, the area had an organic urban fabric with cohabitation and integration of specific landmarks such as synagogues and yeshivas (*ishibot*) for Jews and mosques and *madraseh* for Muslims, while *suqs*, *funduqs*, *hammamat*, and *kushot* (public baking ovens) were shared by all communities.

The dwelling styles did not differentiate between communities but were based on the economic status of the owner. The more affluent merchants and landowners of all communities built mansions based on a central court around which all rooms and upper balconies opened up. With the ongoing decay and demolitions in the quarter and the appropriation of the buildings, tracing of the original identities is an

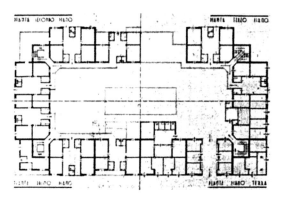

51. Umberto Di Segni housing project. Courtesy of private collection.

awkward task. Some of these buildings are listed in the *Guide for the Historical Landmarks of the Old City of Tripoli* published in 2010.

The Hush Al-Harem mansion, located in the Arba'a Arsat intersection, built by Yusuf Pasha at the end of the eighteenth century to host his harem, became later, around 1835, the seat of the Consulate of Tuscany. Around 1911 the mansion was bought by the Nahums, a rich family of silk merchants. It was restored in 1994 to serve as a Center for Popular Culture, with a collection of popular objects and costumes.

Hush Bashagha, located in the Suq Al Harrara, was home to a Jewish family and then bought by a Protestant missionary physician by the name of Mr. Reed, who ran a medical clinic for the locals.

Hush Rabbi Nissim was built under Qaramanli rule and was known as Rabbi Nissim's (or Nahum's) house.

Hush Angelo, built by Angelo Mordehai Arbib, grandfather of Bibi Arbib, housed a synagogue (Dar Bibi) built in 1901, a yeshiva, and a library. Bibi's son Jacob then donated the structure to the community to become an old people's home (*gherfa*) when the family moved to a newly built house in the Italian modern city outside the walls. The whole building was razed during the systematic destruction of Jewish buildings in the *hara* under Qaddafi's rule, as shown in illustrations 34–36 (p. 118). A marble plaque celebrating the inauguration of the temple in 1901, originally placed in the synagogue, is now exhibited in the Dar Al Serussi "museum."

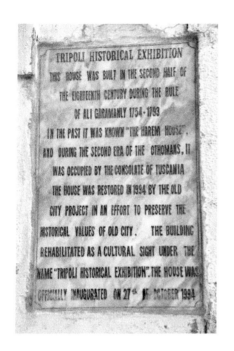

52. Nahum Mansion. Source: *Guide of Historical Landmarks of Old City* (Tripoli: n.p., 2010).

53. Nahum Mansion. Source: *Guide of Historical Landmarks of Old City* (Tripoli: n.p., 2010).

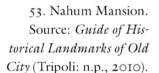

Dar Al Serussi, one of the most important buildings in the Medina, was built in the second half of the eighteenth century, during the Ottoman period, and housed a synagogue and a Jewish school. Under Qaddafi's rule it was restored to serve as a documentation center known as the Ahmad Al Nayeb House for Historical Information. Two rooms of the house contain a so-called Jewish Museum exhibiting items and ritual objects from destroyed Jewish homes and synagogues.

54. Nahum Mansion. Source:
*Guide of Historical Landmarks of
Old City* (Tripoli: n.p., 2010).

55. Nahum Mansion. Source: *Guide
of Historical Landmarks of Old City*
(Tripoli: n.p., 2010).

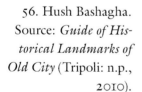

56. Hush Bashagha.
Source: *Guide of His-
torical Landmarks of
Old City* (Tripoli: n.p.,
2010).

57. Dar Al Serussi. Source: *Guide of Historical Landmarks of Old City* (Tripoli: n.p., 2010).

58. Dar Al Serussi. Courtesy of MOJL, Museum of Libyan Jews, Or Yehuda, Israel.

59. Dar Al Serussi. Courtesy of David Gerbi, photographer.

60. Dar Al Serussi.
Courtesy of David
Gerbi, photographer.

Banco di Roma

Both Turkish and Libyan sources indicate the establishment of this
bank as an instrument by the Italian government to collect intelligence inside the Turkish Empire and facilitate the conquest of Libya.

In order to operate in Libya, the Banco di Roma had to take over,
in 1907, an existing banking operation and building of the Eugenio
Arbib Corporation. Below is the first seat of the Banco di Roma in the
Medina, now restored as a branch of the Umma Bank.

After the conquest in 1911, the bank moved to larger premises
in the Merkez Square. This building too was restored around 2004.

Finally, under Fascism, in 1934 the bank moved to a new pres-
tigious building outside the Old Town on the newly built Piazza
Italia. The building is still standing and is now the seat of the Umma
Bank.

Banco di Napoli

This bank's story has also a Jewish angle. In the rush to open a branch
in Tripoli, the management was searching for suitable premises and
finally decided on this building, at the Arba'a Arsat intersection,
owned by the Labi family and previously occupied by the Othman
Bank. The rental started in 1913 and lasted until the bank moved to
new headquarters on the main avenue of the new city, where it operated until 1969.

61. Banco di Roma. Source: *Guide of Historical Landmarks of Old City* (Tripoli: n.p., 2010).

62. Banco di Roma. Source: *Guide of Historical Landmarks of Old City* (Tripoli: n.p., 2010).

63. Banco di Roma. Courtesy of private collection.

64. Banco di Roma. Courtesy
of private collection.

65. Banco di Roma.
Courtesy of Eric Salerno,
photographer.

66. Banco di Roma. Courtesy
of OSA, Or Shalom Archives,
Bat Yam, Israel.

67. Banco di Napoli. Source: *Guide of Historical Landmarks of Old City* (Tripoli: n.p., 2010).

Schools

Funduq B'Aishu, originally a three-story building, located in the zone of Bab El Bahr, damaged by the bombings in World War II, was used as a Jewish school until 1943, and now is a storehouse for fishermen's equipment.

Funduq Abudalghusa, located in Al-Halka Street, is a two-story compound that was occupied by Jewish shops of different trades, such as goldsmiths, silverware traders, and perfume and silk merchants.

Other schools:

Talmud Torah

Scuola Principe di Piemonte

Scuola Pietro Verri

Scuola Roma

Residential

Two Palazzi Nahum on the Corso (Halfalla Nahum).

Palazzo "Nafha," on the Corso. The popular wit coined an acronym based on the initials of the families living there (Nemni, Arbib, Fadlun, and Hassan). *Nafha* in the Libyan Judeo-Arabic dialect means pompousness.

Palazzo Haddad on the second principal avenue, the Corso Sicilia, was nicknamed "the Coliseum" because of its shape. Most of the tenants were Jewish families.

Casa Arbib—Corso corner Zenghet Hassuna Pasha.

68. Palazzo Nahum. Courtesy of Sergio Bianconcini, photographer.

69. Palazzo "Nafha." Courtesy of Sergio Bianconcini, photographer.

70. Palazzo Haddad. Courtesy of Sergio Bianconcini, photographer.

71. Casa Arbib. Courtesy of Sergio Bianconcini, photographer.

72. Casa Arbib. Courtesy of Sergio Bianconcini, photographer.

This house on the corner of the Corso and Hassuna Pasha Street was built in the 1920s by Jacob Arbib, Bibi's son, when the family moved from the *hara* to the new city planned by the Italians. It had two large apartments on the first floor for the family. The upper floor was later added after the family was forced to abandon the house in 1967. On the ground floor under the arcade stood the Gambrinus, a popular café with billiards.

The picture below is a view of the side of the house giving onto Hassuna Pasha Street. In the background is a four-story building where in Italian times the popular UPIM department store operated. Further up on the street there is the impressive mansion of Hassuna Pasha, mayor of Tripoli at the time of the Italian conquest, and home of the Qaramanlis.

Villas

Villa Zard, in the suburb of Giorgimpopoli:

This villa on the beach was designed in 1935 for the Zard family by one of the most important architects of the time, the Milanese

73. Villa Zard. Courtesy of private collection.

74. Villa Zard. Courtesy of private collection.

75. Villa Zard. Courtesy of private collection.

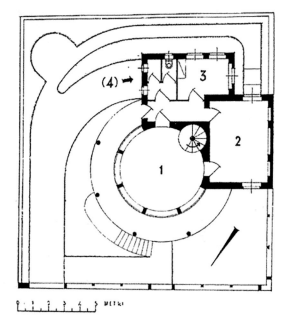

Giovanni Pellegrini, who counted many friends and clients in the Jewish community.

Villa Bambola, Feshlum:

    The Villa Bambola was a country house on an agricultural estate in the village of Feshlum, on the outskirts of Tripoli. It was built in the Turkish period and belonged to the Arbib family as a weekend retreat.

76. Villa Bambola. Courtesy of private collection.

Villa Zachino Habib, Città Giardino:

This was a spacious modernist villa, located in the Garden City quarter, and was bought in the aftermath of World War II by Zachino Habib, then president of the Jewish Community, from a top Italian apparatchik who had understandable reasons to move back to the motherland.

Contact Zones

The Monumento ai caduti, a memorial ossuary built by the Italians for soldiers fallen in the conquest of Libya, was located on an esplanade on the border of the *hara* facing the sea. The building was designed by Armando Brasini, and the erection was supervised by the young Jewish architect Umberto Di Segni, who also added a monumental escalade to the sea. Because of its adjacency to the Jewish quarter, the large open space in front of the monument became a convenient location for events of the community. It was used for school festivals, youth movement gatherings, a festive demonstration on the day of the declaration of Israel's independence, and also as a staging area for embarkation of

77. Monument, signed by Umberto Di Segni. Courtesy of private collection.

78. Monument. Courtesy of MOJL, Museum of Libyan Jews, Or Yehuda, Israel.

olim[3] on the ships docking in the nearby port. The building was dismantled by the Libyans in the 1960s and replaced by an ugly water tower.

Illustration 77 shows the perspective signed by Di Segni with the stairs he designed for access to the esplanade. Illustration 78 is a picture of Italian officials visiting the site after completion.

3. Emigrants to the Holy Land.

79. Monument. Courtesy of
MOJL, Museum of Libyan Jews,
Or Yehuda, Israel.

80. Monument. Courtesy of
MOJL, Museum of Libyan Jews,
Or Yehuda, Israel.

Above, from left to right, the monument with the pupils of the
nearby Pietro Verri Jewish school; the same location, with groups of
olim from the various communities preparing to board the ships; and
lastly (ill. 81) the water tower replacing the destroyed monument.

The Marcus Aurelius Arch was and still is a prominent landmark.
The Italians restored it in the spirit of glorification of the Roman Empire and of a native son turned emperor. Being at the crossing of the
two main arteries of the Medina, it has always been a reference point
for all inhabitants in all periods as a convenient place for meetings and
for a cup of tea in one of the stalls surrounding it.

To avoid any temptation of topolatry, it might be appropriate to
quote some lines from Yehuda Amichai's poem "Tourists": "You see
that arch from the Roman period? It's not important: but next to it

81. Monument site, present time.
Sergio Bianconcini, photographer.

82. Marcus Aurelius Arch.
Courtesy of Sergio Bianconcini, photographer.

left down and a bit, there sits a man who's bought fruit and vegetables
for his family."

Theaters and Cinemas

Alhambra Cinema. The Alhambra cinema was built in 1938 over
the ruins of a funduq. It was designed by Giovanni Pellegrini and
incorporated the most advanced technology of the time. With 1,300
seats, it was one of the two important theaters in Tripoli, together
with the Miramare. The coffee shop in the elegant lobby was managed
by the Jewish Pariente family.

Odeon. This cinema house was designed by Umberto Di Segni in
the late 1940s and is arguably his last project in Libya before his immigration to Israel. It featured dubbed Hollywood movies distributed
by the Dear Film Company of the Haggiag brothers. The building is
still standing to this day.

Arena Giardino was an open-air movie theater, located in Zenghet
Hassuna Pasha, under the management of the Barda family.

83. Alhambra Theater.
Courtesy of Sergio Bian-
concini, photographer.

84. Odeon Cinema in
the 1950s. Courtesy of
private collection.

The Politeama movie theater at Suq Al Turk was established under
early Italian rule on the premises of the Funduq Al Pasha and hosted
plays by visiting actors and film screenings. The Jewish and Muslim
communities also used it for performances. The Politeama lost importance after the opening of the Miramare, but reportedly it is still in
operation under the name of the Al-Nasr cinema.

85. Odeon Cinema, present time. Courtesy of Sergio Bianconcini, photographer.

86. Politeama Theater. Courtesy of OSA, Or Shalom Archives, Bat Yam, Israel.

87. Politeama Theater. Courtesy of OSA, Or Shalom Archives, Bat Yam, Israel.

88. Miramare Theater. Postcard. Courtesy of private collection.

89. Miramare Theater interior. Photo by A. Costa. Courtesy of private collection.

In the same hall: an Arab audience (ill. 86) and a Jewish audience (ill. 87) with a banner for a show of Achille Majeroni, a famous Italian actor on tour.

Miramare Theater—Tripoli

Berenice Theater—Benghazi. The first theater hall in Benghazi, the Sala Italia, was opened in December 1926, followed by the Risorgimento, hosting artists coming from Italy. The big change was made with the establishment of a theater society under Halfalla Nahum and

90. Berenice Theater. Courtesy of OSA, Or Shalom Archives, Bat Yam, Israel.

91. Berenice Theater. Courtesy of OSA, Or Shalom Archives, Bat Yam, Israel.

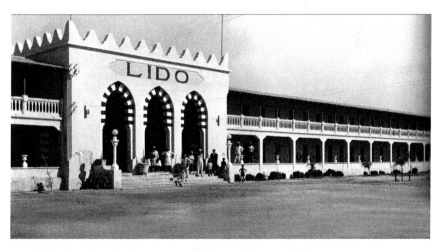

92. Lido Beach club. Courtesy of Hamos Guetta Collection.

93. Uaddan Hotel and Casino. Courtesy of MOJL, Museum of Libyan Jews, Or Yehuda, Israel.

94. Uaddan Hotel and Casino. Courtesy of MOJL, Museum of Libyan Jews, Or Yehuda, Israel.

Leone Cohen. This society started the construction of a new modern complex designed by the famous architect Piacentini. The new Berenice Theater was inaugurated on October 30, 1932, with a gala event including a filmed greeting from Il Duce.

Public Baths

Public baths include Al Hammam Al Kabir, Al Hammam Al Saghir, and Al Hammam Al Nissa (the women's bath) in the old city and later the Hammam in the Uaddan complex.

Bakers

Among others, bakers included Qushat Zenghet Sidi Umran, Qushat Al Saffar, and Qusha Sidi Umran. The bakers' services were much used by the Jewish community, and on the eves of holidays it was customary to see young Jews carrying to the oven marked baking

95. Hammam Al Kabir. Source: *Guide of Historical Landmarks of Old City* (Tripoli: n.p., 2010).

trays with bread or other food, to be retrieved before sunset. Before Passover, some of the bakeries were koshered for baking matzah and *fterah.*

Cafes and Eateries

Because of respect for dietary laws, eating out in restaurants was not a custom of the Libyan Jews. However, when the Italian side of Tripoli expanded, creating a café society culture, Jews started patronizing fashionable locales for social or business meetings.

Some of the most popular venues were the Caffè Corso, Caffè Sordi (later Caffé delle Poste), and the Caffè Commercio. The Caffè Gambrinus was under Jewish management.

The Campi Patisserie was much appreciated for its excellent marzipan and cakes. In the 1950s, Jewish patrons conveniently forgot that, at the time of the Fascist racial laws, Signor Campi had put out a sign unwelcoming Jews and dogs.

96. Caffé delle Poste. Courtesy of AIRL, Associazione Italiani Rimpatriati dalla Libia.

An interesting venue was the Akropol, a Greek ouzeria owned by the Georgiadis family, where Jews gathered for mezedes and libations of *boukha*, *lagbi*, and local Oea beer. In homage to their patrons, the cordial owners went as far as koshering their kitchen for Passover.

The Bascetta ice cream parlor (under the awning in the picture) was very popular with the Jewish community. It was not far from the Bet El synagogue and adjacent to the Lancia and Vespa showroom belonging to the Jewish Platero family.

Another accessible place was the Latteria Triestina, a dairy establishment where light dairy meals and fabulous milkshakes were served by a smiling attendant.

In the period of the British protectorate, an Italian restaurant of some repute was opened on the Corso by a gentleman called Aldo Nahum (nicknamed "Carnera" because of his resemblance to a known boxer of the time). Aldo closed the restaurant in 1950 and made Aliyah, opening another Italian restaurant, the Gondola, in Tel Aviv.

Jews in the *hara* were more strictly observant in terms of food, but one popular custom during the month of Ramadan was to join the Muslim faithful in a predawn breakfast of *sfenz* at the local fritter house.

97. Cathedral Square. Courtesy of MOJL, Museum of Libyan Jews, Or Yehuda, Israel.

98. Bascetta Gelateria. With thanks to AIRL, Associazione Italiani Rimpatriati dalla Libia.

99. Lancia and Vespa showroom. Courtesy of AIRL, Associazione Italiani Rimpatriati dalla Libia.

101. *Sfenz* stall. Courtesy of private collection.

100. *Sfenz* stall. Courtesy of private collection.

102. Brothel sign. Courtesy of Sergio Bianconcini, photographer.

Brothels

With the influx of Italian troops in the city, brothels were in demand and a number of "European-quality" establishments operated, mostly on or around the Ippolito Nievo Street near the Tripoli fairgrounds. For this purpose, a number of young professionals were brought in from the mainland and reinforced by enrollment of natives, and they became patronized by members of the community.

Industrial Construction

Manifattura tabacchi (The tobacco factory). The employees in this factory were predominantly Jewish women, for whom the proximity to their homes in the Hara was convenient. This fact was mentioned in a letter from Governor Italo Balbo on January 19, 1939, in response

103. Tobacco factory. Old postcard. Courtesy of OSA, Or Shalom Archives, Bat Yam, Israel.

to Mussolini who was urging the application of the racial laws by firing all Jewish workers: "Monopoly industries whose main factories are in Tripoli largely use trained Jewish female workers, especially for the manufacture of cigars and cigarettes. . . . It is not possible to find in Libya Italian nationals who are both skilled and willing to accept the same modest wages." The factory was then relocated in Tigrinna, near the plantations, and also there employed workers from the local Jewish community.

Architects of Jewish Origin Operating in Libya

Umberto Di Segni (b. 1892–d. 1958)
Enrico Lattes (b. 1904–d. 1934)
Carlo Enrico Rava (b. 1903–d. 1986)
Vittorio Morpurgo (b. 1890–d. 1966)

Photo Sources

Museum of Libyan Jewry, Or Yehuda, Israel
Museum Or Shalom, Bat Yam, Israel
Private Collections

Bibliography

Abramsky-Bligh, I. *Pinkas Hakehilot.* Jerusalem: Yad Vashem, 1997.
Arbib, A. R. *Memorie.* Rome: Maccabi, n.d.
Arbib, J. *L'ombra e la luce.* Nola: il Laboratorio, 2010.
Balbo, I. *La Centuria Alata.* Milan: Mondadori, 1934.

Capresi, V. *The Built Utopia*. Bologna: Bologna University Press, 2009.

Cresti, F. *Oasi di italianità*. Turin: SEI, 1996.

Culotta, P. *Città di fondazione*. Bologna: Compositori, 2007.

De Felice, R. *Jews in an Arab Land*. Trans. J. Roumani. Austin: University of Texas Press, 1985.

De Seta, C. *La cultura architettonica italiana tra due guerre*. Bari: Laterza, 1972.

Fuller, M. *Moderns Abroad*. New York: Routledge, 2007.

Godoli, E., and M. Giacomelli. *Architetti e Ingegnieri italiani dal Levante al Magreb*. Florence: Maschietto, 2005.

Guide for the Historical Landmarks of the Old City of Tripoli. Tripoli: Government of Libya, 2010.

Haggiag-Lilluf, Y. *Storia degli ebrei di Libia*. Or Yehuda: MOJL, 2005.

Labanca, N. *Oltremare*. Bologna: Il Mulino, 2002.

McLaren, B. *Architecture and Tourism in Italian Colonial Libya*. Seattle: University of Washington Press, 2006.

Nunes-Vais, R. *Reminiscenze tripoline*. Rome: Uaddan, 1982.

Piccioli, A. *La nuova Italia d'Oltremare*. Milan: Mondadori, 1933.

Pizzi, D. *Metaphysical Cities*. Milan: Skira, 2005.

Saadoun, H. *Libya*. Jerusalem: Ben-Zvi Institute, 2007.

Salerno, E. *Uccideteli tutti*. Milan: Il Saggiatore, 2008.

Santoianni, V. *Il razionalismo nelle colonie italiane, 1928–1943*. Florence: Tassinari, 2007.

Segre, C. *Fourth Shore*. Chicago: University of Chicago Press, 1974.

TCI. *Guida d'Italia: Libia*. Milan: Touring Club Italiano, 1937.

———. *Guida di Tripoli e dintorni*. Milan: Treves, 1925.

♦ ♦ ♦

PART THREE

Women

RACHEL SIMON and Gheula Canarutto Nemni and Judith Roumani
provide studies of Libyan Jewish women in two distinct periods and
three places: the late Ottoman and Italian colonial period in Libya and
the more recent years of Libyan Jewish life in Israel and Italy.

In the first of these two chapters, we find Libyan Jewish women
living in a society where gender roles were strictly separated, and the
worlds of work, formal education, and other spheres were not open
to women. Their roles lay within the home, where they allocated the
resources provided by their husbands for the benefit of the family,
especially the children. They devoted much of their time to cooking and maintaining the home, but within this limited sphere created a rich environment of women's crafts, social life, and especially
songs in Judeo-Arabic to celebrate life-cycle events. There was much
labor to be performed, such as gathering wood; spinning and weaving; sewing; grinding wheat, coffee, and spices; and of course cooking
labor-intensive dishes. The early education of boys and all the education of girls was their responsibility. Religious education was rarely
provided for girls, but instead they received practical, skill-oriented
training for their role in the home. Women's religion was based on
emotion and faith rather than knowledge, but their commitment was
very intense. By the late Ottoman and Italian period, though, some
girls in Tripoli were going to school, and girls in wealthy families were
receiving a European secular education. This led to some eventually

becoming teachers and nurses. The Zionist-oriented agricultural and summer camps offered mainly traditional roles for girls, and none of these developments allowed women opportunities for official positions of authority. They were marginalized, but insofar as they seized opportunities when available, they were a vanguard for the following generations.

The second chapter studies Libyan Jewish women who moved to Israel from about 1950 or fled to Italy with their families around 1967. In Italy, as pillars of the family, many turned out to be very resourceful in finding opportunities in the new environment. While some husbands, having lost almost everything, succumbed to despair and ill health in the new country, their wives opened shops and found ways to support the family, discovering new strengths. At the same time the older women continued to maintain traditional customs, religious observance, and especially food. The intermediate and younger generations have integrated fully into Italian life, and cuisine is perhaps the main surviving trait of Libyan Jewish life besides religious observance. The younger women do have a tendency to return to their Libyan traditions as they grow older. Thus religious observance is strong as well, Libyan Jews having brought new vigor to Italian Jewish life. Libyan Jewish women in Italy and Israel, Nemni and Roumani show us, have found their horizons vastly expanded but have continued to be strong and respected pillars of their families.

7

• ◆ •

Libyan Jewish Women as a Marginalized Vanguard in the Late Nineteenth and Early Twentieth Centuries

RACHEL SIMON

The daily life of Jewish women in Libya was shaped by Jewish law, multifaceted local traditions, and outside influences. Thus, in addition to specific Jewish components, their status was also influenced by the surrounding Muslim society, external Jewish factors, and a growing European presence. The status of Jewish women was neither static nor identical across Libya and depended on socioeconomic factors, geography, and time. This essay examines how the status of Jewish women evolved from the late Ottoman period in the late nineteenth century to their departure from Libya as part of the mass Jewish emigration to Israel and Italy starting in the late 1940s.

Traditionally, the roles of Jewish community members were gender-based. Men were expected to participate in formal religious life actively, provide for their families economically, and lead the community religiously and temporally. Women, on the other hand, were not expected to do any of the above: they were destined to take care of their family's needs from inside the home, based on provisions supplied by men. Different gender roles required different training, aimed at suitable qualifications, and consequently, from a tender age, boys and girls were treated differently.

In order to actively participate in the synagogue service, men had to be able to read Hebrew and Aramaic texts of the Bible and prayer books. For that purpose, fathers had to ensure that their sons acquired the basic skills of reading texts in the Hebrew alphabet. Some fathers took on this task themselves or hired tutors to teach their sons at home, but it was usually the community that was charged with the formal education of boys.[1] This often took place in the synagogue, where boys in mixed-age groups (usually between the ages of four and ten) were taught to read the Hebrew alphabet, gradually advancing to recite complete texts. Since the spoken language of most community members was Judeo-Arabic, boys usually did not understand what they read. This kind of education was basic for the majority of men during most of this period; only a few continued in more advanced Jewish studies as preparation for becoming religious functionaries. The community also provided for continuing education for men, which was conducted mostly in the evening, on the Sabbath, and on holidays in the form of listening to readings of religious texts, such as the Psalms and the Zohar. Yet, once again, most men did not understand these recitations because they were in Hebrew or Aramaic. Thus, although most men acquired an important tool for intellectual growth, they were in fact functionally illiterate because they did not understand the texts they recited or listened to. Another result of this situation was that most Jewish men in Libya could not contribute to Jewish studies and culture, and there were very few Libyan Jews who wrote rabbinic books (such as commentaries and exegeses) or poetry.[2] Their poetry was in Hebrew (and thus understood only by a few) or Judeo-Arabic. These works were relatively few, but since they were composed by renowned authors and at times written down (although rarely published), these texts were kept and preserved in their original

1. Rachel Simon, *Change within Tradition among Jewish Women in Libya* (Seattle: University of Washington Press, 1992), 109; Simon, "Between the Family and the Outside World: Jewish Girls in the Modern Middle East and North Africa," *Jewish Social Studies* 7, no. 1 (2000): 87–88.

2. Other forms of belles-lettres were developed only later.

form. Men also had folk poetry, mostly in Judeo-Arabic, but this was less prestigious and often lost.[3]

Women were not supposed to actively participate in the synagogue service or serve as members of the religious court or communal leadership. Consequently, girls were prepared for their role in life differently from boys. Traditionally, girls did not learn to read and could speak only Judeo-Arabic. Theirs was an experience-based education: they were trained by their mothers and older female relatives, who often lived close by. First and foremost, they learned how to run a Jewish home, namely, how to apply Jewish laws and local traditions to everyday life, such as Jewish dietary laws (*kashrut*) for every day with special rules for Passover, as well as laws regarding work and rest and activities during the week, the Sabbath, and holidays. Thus, although women could not read the laws and regulations that they had to follow, they knew how to execute them properly.[4]

Being illiterate and excluded from formal religious life does not mean that women were deprived of spiritual growth, expression, and creativity. Their spiritual life, however, greatly differed from that of men and did not follow strict formal constructions: some was verbal, some was physical. A major component of female spirituality was oral poetry,[5] in which they were not only listeners but also performers and at times even contributors. Women's poetry, which was in the local Judeo-Arabic dialect, dealt with daily and life-cycle events, Jewish festivals, the Torah, work, and specific women's issues. Many songs had a known structure and text, but they were also flexible, and individuals

---

3. Esika Marks and Edwin Seroussi, "The Musical Tradition of Libyan Jewry," in *Libya*, ed. Haim Saadoun (Jerusalem: Ben-Zvi Institute, 2007), 170–71.

4. Simon, "Between the Family," 81–82, 88–89.

5. For discussion about and examples of female poetry, see Marks and Seroussi, "Musical Tradition," 171–72; Frigia Zuaretz et al., eds., *Yahadut Luv* (Tel Aviv: Va'ad Qehilot Luv be-Yiśra'el, 1982), 387–89; Zevulun Buaron, *Meqor ha-Semaḥot: Minhage Ḥatunah bi-Qehilot Luv* (Netanya: Hafatsat Moreshet Yisra'el, 1994), 10–15, 27–28; Simon, "Between the Family," 89–90.

could insert personal contributions as fitting to the occasion. Some women were renowned for their fine singing and contributions as well as leading group songs; still, this was not based on learning, status, or age but on individual ability, which theoretically each woman could fulfill. Singing took place while in groups or alone and was open to all women.

Women had numerous chores to perform, but nonetheless they managed to find time to socialize while still multitasking. Thus, when they met, while chatting, exchanging news and opinions about daily events, and often being occupied in some handicraft, they also sang. A special socializing date was the first of the Jewish month of Ṭevet during the festival of Hanukkah, which was referred to as "The New Month of the Girls" (*rosh ḥodesh l'banat*). On this day women did not work and they visited one another, ate, and enjoyed themselves together—and sang.[6]

Numerous songs dealt with life-cycle events: birth, circumcision, marriage, and death. There were special songs in honor of mothers and their newborn babies, usually in praise of a baby boy.[7] During preparations for the circumcision ceremony on the day preceding the event, special women singers, referred to as *zamzamat*, ground spices and performed songs related to the occasion.[8] Marriage was also an opportunity calling for numerous special women's songs. Those were performed during the festivities preceding the wedding ceremony, such as the henna ceremony, the farewell party of the bride and her female friends and relatives, the "Sabbath of the Girls" (*Shabat l'banat*), and the parade bringing the bride to her bridegroom's house. The wedding ceremony itself and the festivities following it were also

6. Yaacov Haggiag-Lilluf, *Toldot Yehude Luv* (History of the Jews of Libya) (Or Yehuda: World Organization of Libyan Jews, 2000), 300; Zuaretz. *Yahadut Luv,* 373.

7. Marks and Seroussi, "Musical Tradition," 171 (including an example).

8. *Storia degli Ebrei di Libia* (Or Yehudah: Centro di Studi sull'Ebraismo Libico, 2000), 324; Zuaretz, *Yahadut Luv,* 386–88 (including several songs).

occasions for performing women's songs.[9] Of unique character were songs related to death, when special women mourners, with a set of mourning songs, sang loudly, shrieking, and hurting themselves.[10] All these various performances were understood by all, and in principle every woman could contribute to them.

Other songs were work-related, performed in the rural regions of Libya. Some songs were sung individually while at home. A typical occasion was at predawn on work days, when women sat grinding wheat, and their singing was heard all over the village.[11] Singing eased the burden of their hard work, but also it was a clear sign that a woman was not lazy: she was awake and hard at work.

Special songs were related to the Torah and saints.[12] Although women did not participate in the formal service in the synagogue, they greatly venerated religious artifacts, especially those related to the Torah. Thus, they used to clean the synagogue once a week,[13] accompanied by special songs related to the "Book," namely, the Torah. Women also had songs praising the saints venerated by Libyan Jews.

Women's creativity was reflected as well in their handicrafts. Some of this work was created while participating in leisure-time meetings of women, whose hands were kept busy knitting and embroidering while they talked and sang. They also wove at home for the family needs and at times had surplus goods for sale.[14] These handicrafts followed traditional patterns but could also have unique, personal nuances.

---

9. Harvey E. Goldberg, "The Jewish Wedding in Tripolitania: a Study in Cultural Sources," *Maghreb Review* 3, no. 9 (1978): 1–6; *Storia*, 334–40; Marks and Seroussi, "Musical Tradition," 172.

10. *Storia*, 341–42; Marks and Seroussi, "Musical Tradition," 172.

11. Marks and Seroussi, "Musical Tradition," 172; Simon, *Change within Tradition*, 86.

12. Zuaretz, *Yahadut Luv*, 388–89 (including examples in praise of Moses and Sabbetai Tzevi); Simon, *Change within Tradition*, 160.

13. For a vivid description of this, see the chapter in this volume by Hamos Guetta.

14. Simon, *Change within Tradition*, 88, 91–92.

104. Woman working. Courtesy of Hamos Guetta Collection.

While the preparation of food was a daily routine task, it still could enable women to express some creativity. Thus, for the festival of Shavuot, women baked a special kind of pretzels (*kak*) in various symbolic forms: although following traditional patterns, some room was left for individuality. These pretzels were often worn by their children during the holiday.[15]

Most girls were home-trained, but some also received more formal education, similar to that of boys. Thus, when a girl had no brothers, at times her father taught her to read, in addition to the training she received from her female relatives. Other girls, whose brothers were tutored at home, could listen in to these lessons and learn together with the boys. In a few instances, girls actually attended formal classes arranged by the community for boys.[16] Nonetheless, girls still had to perform all their traditional female tasks at home. It was, thus, very

15. Haggiag-Lilluf, *Toldot*, 314–16 (with illustrations); Zuaretz, *Yahadut Luv*, 380.

16. Simon, *Change within Tradition*, 109.

105. Women working in a factory. *La Rinascita della Tripolitania: Memorie e Studi sui Quattro Anni di Governo del Conte Volpi Misurata*, ed. Giuseppe Volpi (Milan: Mondadori, 1926).

rare that girls, usually in the urban centers, received a basic Jewish formal education similar to that of the boys. But just as was the case for boys, this formal education did not enable girls to further their spiritual growth. Women who could read were even ridiculed at times by the community: in the Dar Barukh synagogue in Tripoli, which was mainly attended by Jews with European nationality, some women followed the service in their prayer books and were mocked by the indigenous ones,[17] apparently because they were perceived as pretending to be able to perform functions reserved for men.

Before Jewish schools for girls were established in the late nineteenth century, some girls in Tripoli received formal education in non-Jewish institutions. These girls, usually from families with economic and social connections with Europe, studied in a Christian school run by nuns and were instructed in a foreign language, receiving no Jewish education.[18] A major change in Jewish girls' education took place when an Italian girls' school was established in Tripoli in 1877.[19] This followed an Italian boys' school, which opened in 1876 at the initiative of members of the Jewish community who wanted to prepare

17. Ibid., 110, 155.
18. Ibid., 109.
19. For the development of Italian education in Libya, see Ariel Paggi and Judith Roumani, "From Pitigliano to Tripoli, via Livorno: The Pedagogical Odyssey of Giannetto Paggi," *Sephardic Horizons* 2, no. 4 (2014): n.p.; Simon, *Change within Tradition*, 111–14, 127–30.

their sons to join them in their commercial interactions with Italy and be better prepared for social contacts with Europeans. In order to achieve this, an Italian Jewish educator, Giannetto Paggi, was invited to Tripoli to develop an Italian educational system, which during the Ottoman period was mainly attended by Jews. It soon became apparent that, for improving the social and economic relations of Jewish men with Italy, a similar institution for girls was required, and Barolina Nunes-Vais was brought to Tripoli to run an Italian girls' school. Here again, most students were Jewish, more often than not from upper-middle-class and wealthy families, whose parents wanted them to acquire skills that would facilitate their social connections with Italians. Studies were conducted in Italian, following much of the Italian school curriculum, to which training in certain European-style handicrafts was added, not for economic purposes but as part of creating a well-rounded personality. Jewish-related subjects were of marginal importance. The network grew fast, and after the 1911 Italian occupation, the official state educational network in which Jews participated was Italian; Muslims had their own schools. Consequently, until a local Jewish network open to women was established in the 1930s, most Jewish girls who attended school received Italian education.

The Italian schools that operated in Libya since 1876 were complemented in 1890 with the French-Jewish schools established by the Alliance Israélite Universelle (AIU).[20] This French-based organization, which was founded in Paris in 1860 in order to improve the condition of Jews worldwide and advance them culturally, was based on the French model. To achieve its goals, the AIU established numerous schools in the Middle East and North Africa, usually following requests from the local community. Most teachers were trained in special institutions in Paris, many of them coming from the Ottoman

20. On the AIU in general and its schools in Libya, see Aron Rodrigue, *Images of Sephardi and Eastern Jewries in Transition: The Teachers of the Alliance Israélite Universelle, 1860–1939* (Seattle: University of Washington Press, 1993); Simon, *Change within Tradition,* 114–26.

Empire and Morocco, which already had a veteran AIU network. These schools followed a strict curriculum, developed by the AIU, composed of French-specific subjects (such as language, literature, history, and geography) complemented by Jewish topics. The latter were the less prestigious ones, often taught by local rabbis. The AIU schools also offered professional training, mostly taught by local teachers. This was meant to attract lower-class students, who wanted to acquire professional skills in order to improve their chances to find profitable jobs. Most students in the AIU schools in Libya had been from the lower middle class and the poor. A boys' school was established in Tripoli in 1890 and a girls' school followed in 1896. Girls attended this school for four years at the most: there was no opportunity for postprimary education, which the Italian schools offered following the Italian occupation. The AIU continued to operate under Italian rule, but since the official state language was Italian, and the common language at home was Judeo-Arabic, gradually complemented with Italian, the cultural impact of the AIU schools was secondary. Consequently, although several hundred Jewish girls acquired the basics of French culture, it could not become a major foundation of their spiritual life.

The education provided by the Italian and AIU schools was immersed in Italian and French culture and geared toward different goals than those of the community. It provided graduates with some qualifications that benefited them economically, such as foreign languages and modern professions, but also created high expectations that could not easily be met, because individuals changed faster than the society at large, which remained reluctant to accept changes in women's role in society.[21]

Community-based formal education for girls started only in the 1930s at the initiative of young local Zionist men who wanted to make Hebrew the primary language of the community. These men were the product of traditional and European education who taught themselves

21. Simon, "Between the Family," 91–92.

modern spoken Hebrew, at times with the help of a Hebrew teacher from Palestine. They also subscribed to Hebrew periodicals from abroad, thus enriching their knowledge of Hebrew and developments in the Jewish world. In 1931 they formed the Ben-Yehudah Society to spread modern Hebrew in the community.[22] The teachers, all volunteers, started with small afternoon and evening classes for boys and men. Relatively soon they felt the need to include girls and women as well, believing that the role of women as the initial primary educators of the new generation was imperative in order to transform the community to a Hebrew-speaking one. Toward the end of 1931, the Ben-Yehudah Society established an afternoon school, Ha-Tiqvah (the name of the Zionist/Israeli anthem, meaning "hope"), to teach modern Hebrew and Jewish studies to those members of the community who had not had the opportunity to study them previously. Thanks to the success of these classes, the Ben-Yehudah Society became the official Education Department of the Tripoli community in 1932. Special classes for women witnessed a growing number of students (reaching 498 in 1935–1936), outnumbering the men (369 in 1935–1936) who had other options to learn Hebrew. Contrary to boys who could learn Hebrew in the traditional schools in a manner that basically left them functionally illiterate, girls studied Hebrew only in a modern way, which aimed to enable them to comprehend, speak, and write modern Hebrew within a national, comprehensive framework. Girls were at first instructed by men, but pretty soon female graduates acquired teaching experience and started teaching girls and older women. Thus, in a short period of time girls were taught subjects that had been traditionally exclusive for boys and even advanced to a prestigious profession: teaching, which was reserved for men.

All Jewish education—educational institutions and Jews attending state schools—suffered greatly during World War II following the

22. On the activities of the Ben-Yehudah Society, named after Eliezer Ben-Yehudah, one of the major advocates for the revival of the Hebrew language, see Simon, *Change within Tradition*, 131–38.

Italian anti-Semitic racial legislation. While attempts were made to continue some form of education, most Jewish children were deprived of formal education during this period. A huge change followed the Italian surrender and the British military occupation of Libya in 1942–1943. In addition to the state schools that were once again open to Jews and the traditional Jewish schools that reopened, the character of Jewish education was transformed due to the initiative of Jewish Palestinian soldiers in the British Army.[23] Starting in Benghazi, which was the first major concentration of Jews that the British encountered on their military advance from Egypt, the Jewish soldiers established a Hebrew school for both genders with a curriculum based on the one common in Palestine, thus changing the character of the school. Although at the beginning the soldiers who taught in Benghazi were not professional teachers, other military units could later provide experienced teachers. Later on, Hebrew schools opened also in Tripoli and elsewhere, many by local initiative and without outside teachers, although they often asked and received teaching materials from Palestine. Some local teachers were involved in this enterprise from the beginning, mostly consisting of Ben-Yehudah Society graduates and instructors, but the soldiers felt the need to prepare local teachers to replace themselves in the event of troop movements to Europe. In addition, British commanders started to prohibit Jewish soldiers from getting involved in community affairs, including teaching.

Consequently, the soldiers provided some teacher training for both men and women, and the number of Jewish female teachers increased. Later on, during the period of mass emigration to Israel in the early 1950s, when representatives from Israel were officially present in Libya, several of them conducted teacher training courses in Tripoli for both men and women. As a result, by the early 1950s, there were quite a few women teachers who joined the newly established Jewish teachers' union. In addition to the regular curriculum, the schools also organized various extracurricular activities, including

23. Simon, *Change within Tradition*, 138–53.

106. Woman and men at the beach. Courtesy of Hamos Guetta Collection.

theater performances. These were mostly in Hebrew on historical and national subjects, and among the actors and singers were girls and women.[24] This was another break from tradition, since women used to perform only among other women—the moral standing of women who performed before men was suspect—and theater performances were a complete innovation.

Youth movements had started to operate in Libya in the early 1920s, but they really came to the fore after the mid-1940s, following the involvement of Jewish emissaries from Palestine, one of whose goals was to create a Zionist "New Jew." In order to achieve this they targeted the youth of both genders, and over time several youth movements were established in Libya, mainly in Tripoli. While many

24. Joseph Ben David Gian (Gi'an), "Theatre in the Zionist Movement in Libya," in *Libya*, ed. Haim Saadoun (Jerusalem: Ben-Zvi Institute, 2007), 180–82.

107. Erminia Tammam, elementary school teacher, Benghazi, ca. 1950. The two boys on the left are Samuele Zarrugh and Jacques Roumani. With thanks to Erminia Tammam and Ari Tammam.

activities were gender-based, some were mixed, and gradually young adults of both genders became counselors. Moreover, to better prepare the youth for productive communal agricultural life in a kibbutz in Palestine, some communal training camps (*hakhsharot*) were established for both genders. The number of women there was small, since parents were often reluctant to let their unmarried daughters live in proximity with men, even in separate dwellings; nevertheless, some women stayed in the camp, usually when a brother was also a member there. Women did, however, perform mainly traditional female tasks, such as cooking and cleaning, and were less involved if at all in agricultural activities.[25]

During most of the period under review, Jewish women worked at home or in home-related tasks, which in the rural regions were

25. Simon, *Change within Tradition*, 169–88; Simon, "Between the Family," 93–94.

more broadly defined than in town.[26] Few women were wage earners, and those who were usually held women-related jobs, like mid-
wives and cosmeticians.[27] The latter attended also to Muslim women,
especially in preparation for weddings. Some women were occupied
in commerce,[28] mostly of agricultural products or handicrafts produced at home, but this was not common. A few others were maids,
usually in Jewish homes, and only until they got married. With the
deterioration of economic conditions in the late nineteenth century, a
growing number of women became wage earners. Part of this increase
was in traditional women-related tasks, performed by maids. Others
took advantage of newly offered economic and training opportunities. The AIU girls' school offered from the start some vocational
training for its students.[29] In addition, workshops for processing ostrich feathers for export to Europe employed women, mostly Jewish,
in an all-women environment.[30] During the twentieth century, many
Jewish women became nurses,[31] usually trained on the job. Others
became clerks in various businesses and factory workers, mainly in
the tobacco industry.[32] These jobs did not offer any opportunity for
growth: women remained in low production and employment levels. Despite the growing number of women teachers, most remained
at the bottom: girls' school principals originated from Europe, few
women were on the boards of the Education Department and the
Jewish teachers' union,[33] and women's salaries were usually lower than
those of their male colleagues.[34] Some higher-class women organized
in order to improve the working conditions of women, and for that

26. Simon, "Between the Family," 84–87.
27. Simon, *Change Within Tradition*, 92; 85, 91–92.
28. Ibid., 91–93.
29. Ibid., 114–23.
30. Ibid., 98–99.
31. Ibid., 101–2, 168.
32. Ibid., 102, 182.
33. Ibid., 150, 198–99.
34. Ibid., 103–4.

purpose they established in Tripoli in 1923 a society, the Associazione Donne Ebree d'Italia (ADEI). Later on, in 1934, ADEI established with the Ben-Yehudah Society the workshop "Mofet" in order to provide vocational training for some 150 girls, combined with the study of Hebrew and Jewish studies.[35] Thus, the number of working wage-earning women grew, but there was not a rise in their status.

Women's educational and professional progress did not basically change their status in the community. They seldom achieved any leadership positions: communal leadership remained the domain of men, not only in the religious sphere but also in the secular one. Despite the high number of women teachers, few women were on the board of the teachers' union.[36] They progressed as long as it depended on personal achievement within a field in which their services were required, but once the issue of leadership was raised, traditional concepts of who deserves to lead came to the fore and women were left behind; at the most they became secretaries, preparing the ground for the men. In the youth movements, too, women could become counselors (usually of younger girls) or secretaries, but they did not reach higher positions.[37] As for the training camps, not only did women not reach senior positions but also it was explicitly pointed out that they were in charge of traditional women's tasks.[38] Regarding spiritual growth and contribution, women were also stuck: since they did not study Jewish religious subjects in depth, they were unable to contribute in this field. As for literature, while they could speak Hebrew and became teachers, they produced very little new material. A rare example relates to students in the Hebrew schools, who were encouraged by the local Hebrew youth periodicals to contribute Hebrew poems, which the periodicals later published, and

35. Yaacov Haggiag-Liluf, "The Jews in the Local Economy," in *Libya*, ed. Haim Saadoun (Jerusalem: Ben-Zvi Institute, 2007), 45–46.

36. Simon, *Change within Tradition*, 150, 198–99.

37. Ibid., 170, 179, 182, 187.

38. Ibid., 181–83.

some of the contributors were girls.[39] The impact of modernization and Zionism was somewhat reflected in women's songs, and they created new songs on the situation before the emigration, the foundation of the state of Israel, and absorption in Israel and current affairs,[40] but this did not match women's earlier involvement with female poetry in Judeo-Arabic.

Since the late nineteenth century, all formal education that Jewish girls received in Libya was modern, in contrast to boys, many of whom continued to receive only traditional Jewish education (although a growing number of them also received modern education). The level of education that Jewish women received and their involvement in the economic field were still in the initial stages. As long as progress depended on individual capacity, women showed real progress. The level of modern education that they received, however, did not enable them yet to be creative spiritually as they had been with regard to traditional female poetry in Judeo-Arabic. Moreover, societal concepts were slower to change than individual transformation, and thus, although women were often in the vanguard, they continued to be marginalized.

Bibliography

Ben'atiyah, Pedahtsur. *Shiru lanu mi-shire Tsiyon.* [In Heb.] Bat-Yam: Or Shalom Center, 2001.

Ben David Gian (Gi'an), Joseph "Theatre in the Zionist Movement in Libya." [In Heb.] In *Libya*, edited by Haim Saadoun, 173–82. Jerusalem: Ben-Zvi Institute, 2007.

Goldberg, Harvey E. "The Jewish Wedding in Tripolitania: A Study in Cultural Sources." *Maghreb Review* 3, no. 9 (1978): 1–6.

Haggiag-Lilluf, Yaacov. "The Jews in the Local Economy." [In Heb.] In *Libya*, edited by Haim Saadoun, 33–46. Jerusalem: Ben-Zvi Institute, 2007.

39. For an example of a poem written by a young girl in 1934, see Pedahtsur Ben'atiyah, *Shiru lanu mi-shire Tsiyon* (Bat-Yam: Or Shalom Center, 2001), 52.

40. Marks and Seroussi, "Musical Tradition," 172.

————. *Toldot Yehude Luv* (History of the Jews of Libya). [In Heb.] Or Yehudah: World Organization of Libyan Jews, 2000.

Marks, Esika, and Edwin Seroussi. "The Musical Tradition of Libyan Jewry." [In Heb.] In *Libya*, edited by Haim Saadoun, 159–72. Jerusalem: Ben-Zvi Institute, 2007.

Paggi, Ariel, and Judith Roumani. "From Pitigliano to Tripoli, via Livorno: The Pedagogical Odyssey of Giannetto Paggi." *Sephardic Horizons* 2, no. 4 (2014). http://www.sephardichorizons.org/Volume2/Issue4/paggi.html.

Rodrigue, Aron. *Images of Sephardi and Eastern Jewries in Transition: The Teachers of the Alliance Israélite Universelle, 1860–1939.* Seattle: University of Washington Press, 1993.

Simon, Rachel. "Between the Family and the Outside World: Jewish Girls in the Modem Middle East and North Africa." *Jewish Social Studies* 7, no. 1 (Fall 2000): 81–109.

————. *Change within Tradition among Jewish Women in Libya.* Seattle: University of Washington Press, 1992.

Storia degli Ebrei di Libia. [In Heb.] Or Yehuda: Centro di Studi sull'Ebraismo Libico, 2000.

Zuaretz, Frigia, et al. Eds. *Yahadut Luv.* [In Heb.] Tel Aviv: Va'ad Qehilot Luv be-Yiśra'el, 1982.

8

• ◆ •

Libyan Jewish Women in Italy and Israel Today

GHEULA CANARUTTO NEMNI
AND JUDITH ROUMANI

Libyan Jewish Women in Italy Today

The world of Libyan Jewish women is a very particular one. These women, though belonging until the last years of the sixties to an Arab society, have their own specific and unique features.

In order to get a picture of these women and their position in their own families and society, we have built a statistical sample. It was conceived in such as way as to be able to draw a complete picture.

We chose to divide our sample into three different groups, according to their age:

Age 70 and up (Group 1)
Ages 50 to 70 (Group 2)
Below age 50 (Group 3)

Nine women were interviewed, three for each age group. The women were promised strict anonymity.

The questions we asked are:

1. What was the woman's position in Jewish society when Jews lived in Libya? And now in Italy?

2. Was the position of Jewish women different from the women in Arab society? And now in Italian society?

3. Did women enjoy freedom then? And now?

4. Were Jewish women educated then? And now?

5. Would you define Jewish Libyan society as matriarchal or patriarchal? Has it changed during recent years?

6. How did Jewish women deal with the escape from Libya?

7. Did social position influence the level of freedom women could enjoy?

8. At what age did women get married? At what age do women get married now?

9. Was there such a figure as a single woman? Was she accepted? And now?

10. Were they considered heirs like their brothers? And now?

11. Did they practice sports? And now?

12. What was their relationship to music?

13. Could they work? And now?

14. What was, and is now, the role of women?

15. Would you consider being a woman a minus or a plus?

108. Young women on the beach, 1940s. Courtesy of Hamos Guetta Collection.

General Overview

The first thing that emerges in the interviews is the dramatic change Jewish women faced once they left Libya.

Group 1 members, who lived for many years in Libya, talk about women who enjoy freedom, who are free to go and do whatever they like, but who, in the end, stay home. These women were all born in Libya, a country where Arab and Western cultures were mixed up together. This peculiar atmosphere can be felt in all the interviews when these now elderly women recall those times.

All the women interviewed attended school, most of them only until the age of fourteen. A few of them even attended high school, and one graduated from university.

Group 1 is the group that has been least contaminated by the escape to Europe and Israel. These women have fought to keep alive all the traditions, the language, and the food they had in Libya. Group 2 shows a lifestyle and a mentality that is still strongly marked by the Libyan style but already adheres to a Western lifestyle in many respects.

Group 3 is already European. Tradition is kept mainly through food.

Women in Jewish Libyan culture and tradition are held in great respect. They represent, for all the groups in the same way, pillars of the family and the home. It seems that, without women, this culture and tradition could be hardly be transmitted.

And yes, food had and still has a crucial, determining role.

Who Are Libyan Jewish Women?

The older women were all born in Libya. They grew up in a mixture of Arab and Italian culture, contaminated by French, British, and American nuances. This is due to the presence of foreign occupying forces during World War II and subsequent British and American connections with Libya.

The common characteristic of these women is their strong personality. When they describe those days, some of them feel very nostalgic.

Others feel as if, arriving in Europe, they were freed of the heavy and dangerous burden of the Arab culture.

When a girl was born to a Jewish family, the common reaction was to wish to the new parents, "May you have a boy!" This sentence, which may seem very antifeminist to Western ears, actually has its own meaning. It was said not because of the inferior status of Jewish women, but in acknowledgment of the fact that women always have to face a harder life.

Work for women was considered something that only poor families had to face.

In wealthy families, women stayed home and took care of the house, mostly with the help of Arab maids and servants, and cared for their children.

They cooked a lot. And cooking often became a moment for socializing with friends and their children. Couscous preparation could turn into a real social gathering.[1]

This aspect is viewed as being a consequence of the Arab influence. And, as we can see further, it changed with the arrival of these families in Italy.

Despite their primary role in the home, Jewish women in Libya were important and were seen as fundamental partners for their husbands. All the women declare that every decision in their family was taken in common agreement with their husbands.

When the moment came to leave Libya, it was husbands and wives together who took the decision to leave the country, though they were leaving all their possessions behind.

The main thing that changed when these families arrived in Italy is that many women went to work, opening, for example, shops in Rome. And this participation in the household finances was not felt as a negative issue anymore. Jewish Libyan women revealed themselves to be very capable businesswomen.

---

1. See especially the chapter by Hamos Guetta in this volume.

Once they arrived in Italy, some of the women lost their husbands (it seems in most cases that these premature deaths were a consequence of the traumatic escape from their own country, where all possessions were left behind and it consequently became necessary to start earning a livelihood from scratch).

Many of these women came from wealthy families and had never had to work when living in Libya. Once they arrived in Italy, however, they did their very best to contribute to the family's income, showing an amazing capacity of adapting themselves to the new country and the new system of living.

Jewish women in Libya enjoyed much more freedom than Arab women. They could go out, they went to the beach, they wore bikinis!

There were female basketball teams, and girls had a very rich sports and social life. These sports teams were composed of only Jewish players.

None of the interviewed women complained about the lack of freedom. There is a lot of research on the status of Jewish women in Sephardic society and it seems to suggest that Sephardic women lacked freedom.

From these interviews we can deduce exactly the opposite. Maybe Jewish Libyan society was a very unique society.

Jewish Libyan society, according to Group 1 (as well as Groups 2 and 3), accorded freedom, respect, and a primary role to women.

All the women interviewed feel very proud and honored to belong to this society.

They all talk about how the husbands, in front of their children and relatives, and of course in their private sphere, gave and still give an impressive degree of honor to their wives.

The women interviewed explained why it could seem, from an external viewpoint, that women enjoyed only limited freedom.

The outer society was Arab and Muslim. All these women recall the fact that a woman walking alone in the streets of Tripoli exposed herself to the risk of being annoyed, or worse, by Arab men.

It was not the Jewish society itself that limited women's freedom. It was the outer society that caused this.

The same case holds for marriages.

Women married generally at a young age, and this was done on purpose, due to the danger that Arabs could kidnap them to make them their wives.

There were many exceptions to early marriage, though. Some of the women got married very late, at the age of thirty, and others at twenty-four. There was no specific rule about this issue.

Jewish women were not very well educated. Most of them stopped studying at the age of fourteen. It must be borne in mind that Libya was an Italian colony, and racial laws arrived there too. These racial laws prevented Jews from going to school in the years 1938–45. In some cases, Jews organized themselves to go on providing education to youngsters in a privately based system.

But there are instances of women receiving education. One of the women interviewed studied Jewish subjects and taught children until the age of thirty, when she got married and then had to escape to Italy. Until now she is a very respected woman, and many of her ex-students refer to her as Mora Rina, "Teacher Rina."

In other cases daughters were exhorted to study by their own parents, especially the father. There is a specific story that is well worth a digression.

The woman's father had a dream: he wished to see his daughters' names published in the local newspaper. Names of graduates were published every year. His daughters studied with the hope of fulfilling their father's dreams. One of these women left for London, where she studied English, and when she came back to Libya she started working for an international oil company. Her father was always very proud of her.

Most of the interviewed women define Jewish Libyan society as officially patriarchal. But they all say that this was only formally, as an external image. Actually this Jewish society was very matriarchal. One woman, Group 2, defines men as being the minor partners of women, in Jewish society.

Women as mothers and grandmothers were, and still are, the main pillar of the family, the glue that kept and still keeps all the family together.

109. Two generations of Libyan Jewish women, Elisa Roumani and Vivienne Roumani, 1950s. Source: Vivienne Roumani-Denn; permission: Maurice M. Roumani personal collection, with thanks.

Even from a religious point of view, women had a primary role. Women did not go to the synagogue; it seems there was no place for women. This went on until a new synagogue was built and there, in the new one, women had a place too, and they went there on Friday night and Saturday morning. But this does not diminish their primary role in the religious education of their children.

Fathers traveled a lot for business or stayed the whole day in their shops. Education, and especially Jewish education, was in the mother's hands. And it is thanks to these women that Judaism never was lost in Libya.[2]

An interesting theme emerges with Groups 2 and 3. When these women get older, even the most emancipated, and those who have

2. These opinions of Libyan Jewish women today should be contrasted with the findings in the previous chapter by Rachel Simon, who examines the community in the past.

attempted earlier in their lives to get rid of Jewish and Sephardic elements, try to renew their ties with Libyan tradition. They are eager to belong to a strong and positive identity and find it in their Libyan origins.

As far as regards inheritance, most of the women say that men and women had the exact same rights. There was no such thing as men inheriting more than women, or that the firstborn inherited more than the other heirs. There was a practice, in more traditional families, to give girls in the family their portion while the parents were still alive. In this way there were no disparities during the inheritance process.

Conclusions

The Jewish Libyan world is very respectful and guarantees freedom to women.

Women were, and still are, the pillar of family and society.

In the passage from Libya to Europe and Israel, this society lost some of its features (such as the habit of not expecting women to work and of considering work for women as something that belonged only to indigent families) and acquired modern traits.

In the new generation of these women, most of them are graduates in career paths and have had the total support of their family and husbands in becoming professionals.

The role of women, even today, is fundamental for Libyan society. The family is built around the female figure and women are still, as they used to be in Libya, the most important component of society.

All the women who were interviewed when we arrived at the last question answered with a very strong answer, leaving no space for any doubts about the positive role women had and have in this society.

"Would you consider being a woman a minus or a plus?" A plus, they all answer, without any doubt.

Gheula Canarutto Nemni

Three Generations of Libyan Jewish Women in Israel

This is, rather than a survey, a portrait or series of portraits of people I have observed over the decades and with whom I have had many conversations. The genre of "Portraits" was invented, or revived for modern times, by Albert Memmi, the Tunisian Jewish writer who participated in several overlapping identities, as he would put it. He produced the portrait of the colonizer (which he is not) and the portrait of the colonized (which applied to himself, but partially, because he is also Jewish); these and the portraits of the Jew and the decolonized are all based on his close familiarity with the situations and people he describes. The genre bridges psychology, sociology, philosophy, and politics and, if the writer can avoid stereotypes and generalizations, seems to speak to readers. Thus, as an outsider (British-born but married to a Libyan Jew), I follow Memmi's example and submit this portrait of the women of a Libyan Jewish family that has been in Israel since about 1949.

They were moved to relocate to Israel in the state's very early years partly out of lack of confidence in their future in Libya and partly out of idealism. The family was torn at the time: a beloved daughter, her husband, and her young children promised to join them soon, and even packed up suitcases and crates for the move. According to those who were children at the time, the suitcases hung around in the apartment in Benghazi for a long time. Letters came back from Israel (there were still postal services between the two countries) trying to dissuade them: streetless tent cities languished in the mud of an Israeli winter; jobs, food, and everything else was scarce; there was no butter, only margarine to eat. Come later when the time of scarcity is over, they said. Perhaps they also mentioned prejudice against themselves. In the face of all these obstacles, the father, once a prosperous merchant in Benghazi, had to take a job delivering milk. With all the hardships, his health gave out, and he died the following year. Under the care of their widowed mother, the teenaged and young adult children remembered an easier life, with servants, back in Benghazi. Finding their Italian schooling useless, they must have acquired Hebrew very quickly, practically forgetting their Italian, though their Judeo-Arabic was retained. They had to live in the tent city from 1949 until 1960. Originally settling in Petach Tiqva, the mother acquired (or perhaps rented) a small house with a surrounding garden of lemon and olive trees. Her children, whom we shall call the "first generation," settled in the coastal cities of Petach Tiqva and Netanya; other relatives of the extended family settled on the coast in Bat Yam and Holon, and there they have stayed. The Mediterranean Sea is the same sea they had grown up with in Benghazi, though seen from a different angle. The only Libyan Jews who moved to inland Jerusalem were the mountain Jews from the Jebel (maintaining their special customs and *nusach* until the early 1990s).

Though still missing the comforts and pleasures of Benghazi, this older generation, still young when they arrived, forged ahead valiantly, looking for opportunities in Israel. While the men managed to find factory and office work, the enterprising women did things such as opening a fruit shop or a canteen in a factory, drawing on their culinary skills. Money was tight, and apartments were rudimentary and tiny. Netanya did not develop fast: despite the grandiose modernistic design of Umberto Di Segni, the Libyan Jewish architect who had had great success in colonial Libya (and as a top architect might have expected similar success in Israel before he fell ill there with Parkinson's disease), the main avenue of Netanya, Sderot Weizmann, was lined by a hotchpotch of buildings and its sidewalks remained paved only with sand for many decades.[3]

It is natural for the first generation to fail to advance in the face of language issues, prejudice, and other obstacles, but the next generation of women (as well as men) fared little better. Despite intelligence and talents at least as great as the other family members who eventually moved to America, Italy, or the United Kingdom, the members of this generation encountered a deficient educational system in the *ma'abarot* (temporary tent cities) and their neighborhoods in the smaller towns on the coast. The men were pulled away from their religious traditions, though they did not abandon them; and the women were undereducated in religion and adopted modern secular dress,

---

3. See Jack Arbib, *L'Ombra e la luce: Note su Umberto Di Segni, architetto* (Nola: Il Laboratorio, 2010), 60–61.

though they have never entirely abandoned their respect for Jewish religion. They continue the Libyan tradition of observance of practical aspects such as Shabbat at home and revering certain synagogues (e.g., in Netanya or Moshav Zeitan near Tel Aviv) that house rare and precious Torah scrolls brought from Libya. A member of this intermediate generation told us that she would gladly attend religious classes with rabbis, but there were hardly any clothes in her wardrobe that would be acceptable to wear to a rabbi's class, and in any case she was usually too tired to change. She would observe Shabbat in a quiet way, after preparing and serving to her family all the range of Libyan dishes, by lying on the beach, possibly a difficult self-discipline for such an energetic person. By dint of great struggle and ingenuity, this generation achieved slightly better apartments, eventually even labor-saving appliances, but money was always tight.

The third generation has not yet had the chance for a better education, though there must have been some improvements over the decades. So while all three generations of Libyan Jewish women as a matter of survival have been working in Israel, their economic status has not advanced much beyond that of their parents. One hears today of some Libyan Jewish professional women, but there are very few. However, one can be very successful at life without achieving economic success. Though some participate, for example, in the pharmaceutical industry, or work at banks, those with a low level of education are still stuck in clerical jobs. The glass ceiling here seems to be made of steel rather than glass. One cannot deny, though, that lack of upward (or horizontal) mobility has a positive side: one witnesses a family closeness, that most important of values, which may have eluded Libyan Jews who moved to Europe or the United States. Those in Israel do not complain; they maintain a very engaging social life, travel now frequently to Europe for vacations, and have always been loyal and enthusiastic citizens of their new home. In a word, they are happy.

Judith Roumani

PART FOUR

Voices

COLLECTIVE MEMORY is preserved through its retelling, and so the stories that Libyan Jews tell of their past have an important place in this volume. Over meals of couscous and its accompaniments, syrupy sweet tea with peanuts or pine nuts, in reconstituted homes around the world, Libyan Jews talk of the past and the future. Vivienne Roumani-Denn has interviewed many, and thus she brings us the flavor of lives that have seen dramatic moments. Though traumatizing, these events in Libyan Jewish history have strengthened the resolve of many Libyan Jews to survive and succeed in their new homes in Israel, Europe, or the new world. Pride in their unique traditions, strong family cohesion, and overt expression of love (in the evocative sounds of Libyan Judeo-Arabic) are like talismans that enable them to confront new situations with great confidence. The desperation of new immigrants who have nothing to lose has also contributed at times.

Jacques Roumani has interviewed Samuele Zarrugh, a successful businessman in Livorno and a three-term president of the Jewish Community of that historic city. Originating from Benghazi, he highlights some cultural differences between Jews of Benghazi and those of Tripoli, the two major communities. In this smaller, more conservative town (one of the centers of the Sanusiya order whose head, Idris, became King Idris who ruled Libya from 1951 to 1969), the Jews of Benghazi had closer relations with the local Muslims and were somewhat less assimilated to Italian colonial culture. Samuele Zarrugh attended Muslim high school and the University of Benghazi, and he was prevented from graduating only by the events of 1967. He emphasizes the close relations of neighbors, mutual invitations to weddings, and the need for Jews to ensure that they were respected in order to maintain peaceful relations. Benghazi Jews in his generation spoke the local Arabic, whereas those from Tripoli had disassociated themselves and forgotten it. His family's Jewish culture and commitment remained very strong, though, as shown by their subsequent revival of Jewish life in the old Sephardic community of Livorno.

9

• ◆ •

Life Interrupted

Interviews with Jews of Libyan Origin

VIVIENNE ROUMANI-DENN

Lahaddarni, inejik u twal ghamrik, ya rohe, ya kabdi, ya bniytchi, ya waldi. Ya ghazi, tchagla anaya, tebbutni, tubbutni, farrahni byk.

These are precious words, untranslatable terms of endearment that touched the hearts of all who heard them when they were young, the sound being as important as the sense. Do these words make a difference in a person's life? If you are a Jew from Libya, have these words inspired you or given you self-confidence when facing the challenges in your new life?

Historical Background

Jews have lived in the region of North Africa that now constitutes the modern nation of Libya for more than 2,300 years, initially under Phoenician, Greek, and then Roman rule, some 400 years before the destruction of the Second Temple in Jerusalem and a full millennium before the rise of Islam in Arabia. The eastern (Cyrenaica) and western (Tripolitania) regions of Libya found themselves conquered by tribes

I am grateful to the Librarians Association of the University of California (LAUC) for the research grant that enabled me to initiate this project with twenty-eight interviews completed in 1998–1999. It has since grown to around fifty.

from the Arabian Peninsula in the mid-seventh century CE during their invasion of North Africa and mostly ruled under various Muslim caliphates thereafter. Ottoman Turkish rule came to Tripoli in 1551 and somewhat later to Benghazi, sometimes with direct rule from Constantinople, but more commonly through local pashas. Italy invaded and conquered Libya from the Ottomans in 1911, and it remained an Italian colony until the defeat of the World War II Axis powers in North Africa in 1943, when Tripolitania and Cyrenaica fell under British administration. (A third region, Fezzan in the south, was under French administration.) The three administrative regions, with different tribal loyalties, united into an independent kingdom in 1951. King Idris was deposed in 1969 in an army coup led by Muammar Qadhafi. With major centers in the ports of Tripoli in the west and Benghazi in the east, Libya's Jewish Ottoman and post-Ottoman population at its peak was about 38,000, with 21,000 in Tripoli, 4,500 in Benghazi, and the remainder in smaller cities and villages. More than 90 percent of the Jewish Community left between 1948 and 1951, leaving 2,500 in Tripoli and 400 in Benghazi, and Jewish life essentially came to an end in 1967, prior to the coup. Most of the Community went to Israel, where there are now an estimated 120,000 Jews from Libya and their descendants, with some 3,000 in Rome and smaller numbers elsewhere.

The fact that Jews had lived in Libya was mostly unknown to the general public until the first oral history website on the subject, www.jewsoflibya.com, was built in 1997, although scholarly books and articles predated the website. Young Libyan Arabs who accessed the website refused to believe what they read and wrote that we were trying to "steal their heritage"; some ultimately consulted with living aged relatives, who fondly remembered life "with the Jews." Their recollections were confirmed in some recent interviews with Libyan Arabs who grew up in the 1950s and 1960s. The history of Jews in Libya is treated in depth in books by Renzo de Felice, Harvey Goldberg, and Maurice Roumani, and there are some personal memoirs of twentieth-century Jewish life. There are no Jews in Libya today.

Oral History

This chapter is based on oral histories of Jews from Libya. Some of them lived in Libya into their adult lives, and others left Libya as children. I conducted these interviews over a period of eighteen years in Israel, Italy, and other countries. In Israel, I traveled up and down the country, visiting urban environments, small towns, and rural farming communities (moshavim) in which immigrants from the same country were grouped together after their arrival in Israel. One of the latter, Dalton, has a winery that produces excellent wine, named for the moshav where it is made. Others are less prosperous. Oral history is a useful complement to traditional document-based history, because orality retains feelings that provide an added layer that is often lost in traditional historical writing. Linguistic shifts, for example, can reflect important emotional connections. As Alessandro Portelli notes in "What Makes Oral History Different," "Our awe of writing has distorted our perception of language and communication to the point where we no longer understand either the orality or the nature of writing itself: written and oral sources are not mutually exclusive."[1] On the other hand, there is a potential down side to oral interviews: because of the interaction between the oral historian and the person offering the oral testimony, there is always the possibility of what in the physical sciences is known as the "observer effect," wherein the act of measurement itself changes the value of the quantity being measured.

I was born in Benghazi, but I left at age twelve. Having left at that age turned out to be an advantage in conducting oral histories. I understood the culture; I spoke all the languages of the communities living in Italy, Israel, and elsewhere; and I knew the cuisine. In a sense, I was an "insider." But being a true insider could have been a handicap in talking with elderly members of the Community, whose attitude

---

1. Alessandro Portelli, "What Makes Oral History Different," in *Oral History, Oral Culture, and Italian Americans*, ed. Luisa Del Giudice (New York: Palgrave Macmillan, 2009), 21–30.

110. Libyan Jewish women taking tea in Benghazi. Source and permission: Vivienne Roumani-Denn, Collection of Vivienne Roumani-Denn.

might have been, "Why are you asking me? You already know" (i.e., a strong observer effect). But, since it was recognized that I had the memories of a twelve-year-old, the prevalent attitude was "I'm not sure you remember, so let me explain," which led to long and fruitful recollections.

Hospitality was a complicating factor in conducting many of the interviews, because one does not engage in any serious discussion in a traditional Libyan Jewish home without first exchanging pleasantries over food and drink, and the food was usually classic Libyan cooking in copious amounts. To decline would have been an insult. If there were three interviews scheduled in a community on the same day, there were three large meals to be eaten. Many interviewees saw our interaction as a conversation, and they often invited family members to participate, which sometimes added clarity but also led to digressions. It was sometimes difficult to get background televisions or mobile phones turned off.

These interactions encompass three of what I call the "Four Fs" that characterize the Libyan Jewish experience in the mid-twentieth century: food, family, faith, and fear.

The Good Days

Most testimonies focused on good memories: the beautiful cities, the sea, family life, entertainment, friends. Vittoria Duani, who left for Israel in the late 1940s, summed up the pre–World War life (speaking in Hebrew): "There were good times with the Italians. It's unfortunate that they allied themselves with the Germans [Arabic curses]. The Italians . . . they left Benghazi a paradise."

111. Children's Seder. Source: Vivienne Roumani-Denn; permission: Maurice M. Roumani collection, with thanks.

To have been an urban Jew in Libya in the twentieth century was to have experienced extraordinary cultural diversity in a cosmopolitan environment and to have become proficient in intercultural communication. As I explain to my friends in the United States, I lived a committed Jewish life at home in Benghazi in the 1950s; went daily to the De la Salle Catholic School, because the government closed the Jewish schools after 1951; and resided in a Muslim country. My best friend at school was Greek. We were constantly aware of the observance of three Sabbaths: Friday (Muslim), Saturday (Jewish), and Sunday (Christian). The Mediterranean Sea, both for bathing and for strolling along the Lungomare, was a constant in our lives. Being multilingual was essential: all Jews spoke at least Italian and Judeo-Arabic (I spoke Italian with my mother and Arabic with my father), and many spoke additional languages as well. Hebrew was taught in the Talmud Torah. The interviews I have collected confirm that my upbringing was typical. For example, Shlomo Gean recalls, "In our youth [in Benghazi] we went to the coffee shop, we went to play bowling there, billiards, or to the movies, or went for long walks along the sea, the Lungomare. The walk along the sea was very beautiful. There was the harbor, on Saturday we used to go there along the sea, watching the harbor, looking at the ships' passengers boarding, disembarking." Roger Abravanel similarly noted the uniqueness of growing up in Tripoli in such an environment as "a true melting pot. You had ethnic mixing: Arabs, Jews, Italians, French, Americans. We had Wheelus Airforce Base, the largest base outside the U.S. at the time. . . . As kids we knew people from all over the world." Mario Platero recalled that life in Tripoli was pleasant, marked by sunny days, the fragrance of orange blossoms, walking with his mother along the Lungomare, and playing sports with Italian and Jewish friends at school and in clubs. But things changed dramatically with the onset of the Six Day War in 1967, when riots broke out.

A few whom I interviewed reflected the attitude of Saul Legziel, the head of the Benghazi Community at the time of the Aliyah, who said emphatically in 1997, long before the chaos following the Arab Spring, that he would never return to Libya because there was nothing to go back to: no loved one to visit, not even a grave.[2] For Jojo Naim, "Non mi sento libico, mai accetto di essere libico" ("I do not feel Libyan, nor do I ever accept that I am Libyan"). Golda Halfon echoed my own mother, who asked, "What do you miss about Libya? That you had no rights? No freedom? You could not go out in the streets unaccompanied?" Yossi Sucary's grandmother, on the other hand, would have liked to return to Libya, even to be buried there. Even "Lydia" (Lydia is not her real name), who experienced profound traumas in Libya during the pogroms, recalled, "My heart aches. I say, why didn't we fight? This was our country. . . . Look how much they fight, and we left everything." For those who knew Libya at first hand, there seemed to be no in-between: some loved it, others would have chosen a different birthplace had it been possible.

Fear

Jews in Libya always lived with fear. They celebrated two uniquely Libyan "Purims," Purim Sherif and Purim Burghul, commemorating their deliverance from oppressive Ottoman rulers Ibraham Sherif (1705) and Ali Burghul (1795). One respondent noted, "We lived in a constant fear. And the fear basically was that we were in the hands of the Arabs, and they could do anything with us at any time in any

2. Graves were destroyed and paved over after 1967, some covered by highways.

place."[3] Yet, there were instances of individual Arabs providing support and safety during difficult times. "But an Arab saved us" was a common theme in testimonies in the context of both the Nazis during World War II and the postwar Arab pogroms. Indeed, the dichotomy of responses about feelings for Libya usually seemed to stem from Arab-Jewish relationships as they were experienced by each person or family and depended more on the personal relationships they had with individual Arabs than on the broader communal issues.

The Jews of Benghazi welcomed the British army in 1941 during the first of the seesaw battles between the British and the Germans and Italians in the eastern Libyan desert, and they suffered severely in the (Italian-led) riots that followed the subsequent British withdrawal. Benghazi Jews with British passports were sent to an internment camp in Italy and subsequently to Bergen-Belsen and Innsbruck-Reichenau by the Germans after Mussolini fell. Those with French and Tunisian passports were sent to Tunisia, where some did forced labor, and they were caught up in the closing battles of the North African campaign in 1943; thirteen members of my father's family died during one bombing raid in Tunisia. Those without foreign passports were sent to Giado, a camp in western Libya, where more than five hundred died of disease. Giora Roumani described the treatment at Giado as follows: "One day they took us to this big place, they put us in a circle. They were going to kill us. After fifteen minutes a call came from the Italian authorities. They said 'make them suffer but don't kill them.' The marshal took the elders—the rabbis, the *hakhamim*—and told them to sweep the floors with their beards, and that's what they did, on their stomachs on the floor."

Yossi Sucary recalls, "My mother until now wakes up during the night and says 'i Tedeschi are coming' in Arabic and Italian." (An

Arab neighbor risked his own life by hiding the family when the Nazis came.) "I'll tell you a story: When I was nine years old, I grew up in a very Ashkenazi neighborhood in North Tel Aviv, and on one of the memorial days of the Holocaust, the teacher talked about the Holocaust, and I said that my family was in the Holocaust as well. [They were among those sent to Bergen-Belsen.] I was the only Sephardic pupil in the class. She told me it's not true, that only the European Jews were in the Holocaust. So I went to the principal of the school, and I told him I knew from my mother and grandmother that they had been in the Holocaust. He told me that the teacher was right. . . . For two and a half years I thought that my mother and grandmother had lied to me. It was amazing, it was a difficult experience, that's why I wrote [the book] *Benghazi—Bergen-Belsen*."

In 1945 there was a pogrom in Tripoli and nearby towns in which 129 Jews were killed. Jacob Sasson recalls, "We lived in a building not far from the *hara* [Jewish quarter]. There were non-Jewish people who worked on the ground floor who protected us. They prevented the Arab Muslims from attacking our family. But my aunt was killed, with two of her children." Shalom Saada Saar recalled that an Arab saved his father's life during the pogrom, after which "I stopped painting the world [with a] broad brush." Lydia's description of this event in Amrus is horrifying, even when heavily edited. Most of her testimony is too graphic to repeat here. "Then at night we hear screaming, from every house, screaming, screaming, screaming, everyone screaming . . . there was a little boy [she is crying], they gouged his eyes. . . . In front of his mother . . . they rolled her in a straw carpet, she and her mother, they poured gas on her and burned her. I saw all of them. I cannot forget."

There was another pogrom in 1948, but this time the community was prepared, in part with training from members of the Palestine Brigade, the British army unit of Jews from Palestine who fought in the war in North Africa and subsequently in Europe. Lillo Arbib, who was head of the Tripoli Community at the time, describes the preparation: "Men and women, they were armed. All of them were armed. . . . A cousin of Pedi Ben'atiyah bought the arms . . . they go to Tunisia, they buy the arms from the Arabs." Eighteen Jews and ninety-two Arabs were killed during the 1948 pogrom.

The situation was relatively stable after Libyan independence in 1951, a movement that was supported by the remaining Jewish Community, but more riots occurred during the 1956 Suez War. I vividly recall my mother in 1956 turning out the lights and cautioning us to remain quiet as a shouting mob roamed through the streets of Benghazi.

Jojo Naim recalls that "we were always third league. Not even second league. Always *dhimmis*." (*Dhimmi* law gave monotheistic minorities a "protected" status that imposed special taxes amid other, harsher discriminatory rules.) "Always threatened. Maybe the previous [prewar] generation was better." Jojo left Libya alone at age fourteen because he was threatened by Arab children, who falsely accused him of spitting at one of them; this put his life in such jeopardy that even an Arab policeman, a family friend, could not protect him. He was sent to a friend of his father in Naples, a Christian who insisted that he attend synagogue on Friday night; he subsequently went to Venezuela, where various members of his family followed at different times.

The End

The 1967 Six Day War brought more riots and threats to Jews. Roger Abravanel, reflecting what I heard in many oral histories, said, "Hate was always there, but it exploded with the Six Day War." Jews were taken to camps in Benghazi and Tripoli. Judith Roumani Saphra, who was in Benghazi, recalls, "We heard that it was war between Israel and Arab countries. Everyone was saying come out, that's it, because we can't take care of you, we take you to the *caserma* [barracks]. We stayed there. . . . They started pulling and pushing, and then the noise, and the Arabs they wanted to kill us. Then one day . . . they came and said 'if you want to leave, we can't take care of you anymore. You are not safe enough here.' And in three planes, I remember, we went." (The planes were sent by the Italian government.)

Jacob Sasson recalled that "at the outbreak of the riots of '67 my father was at work [in Tripoli], and from there was taken by the police and interned in a camp . . . [according to the government] to protect us. . . . We lived there until we left Libya." They were allowed to leave for Italy with fifty Libyan pounds and one suitcase of clothing each, no valuables, no souvenirs. Also, they were permitted no Libyan documents that would enable them to return, just a *laisser-passer*. Two families, Luzon and Raccah, thirteen people in all, were told that they were being taken to the camp but were instead slaughtered.

Mario Platero's family lived away from the Tripoli *hara* and followed the progress of the war in hiding through a very weak TV signal from Italy. After the war was over, his father organized a convoy to the airport with support from Arab workers in his business, giving the appearance of protection although they did not have armed guards.

Daniel Buaron was alone with his father in Tripoli in 1967, while his brother Roberto was in Milan studying engineering. "I told my father I had to stay another ten days to finish my final exams or I would have lost two years of studying . . . we stayed locked in our home, and when an Arab friend who brought us food was threatened and stopped, we had to go to the Italian ambassador, Pierluigi Alverra, who was a friend. His influence allowed me to take the exam early, and we left in a diplomatic car to the airport. The ambassador told us not to take anything with us because 'if you do they will take you to customs and I cannot follow you there,' so without anything we got on the plane and we left."

They all left everything behind. The Roman Jewish Community, the Italian government, and the American Joint Distribution Committee provided assistance to the refugees, but they had to start their lives over. About one-third remained in Italy, while most of the others continued on to Israel. Jacob Sasson notes, "In Tripoli I ran a company of 120 employees, and when I came to Italy I had to survive by selling encyclopedias door-to-door." Daniel Buaron recalls, "It was very hard for my father, who never recovered. He was a person well known and liked by everybody, an important person in Tripoli. For him it was devastating. As for me, I never realized that we had lost all our money." And Roger Abravanel: "We lost everything. Father had to start from scratch and I had to do everything on my own. . . . We Jews have to rely on our own strength. We cannot count on anyone."

Faith

Sephardim do not have denominations. There is a single Libyan liturgy, similar to that of other North African communities, but with distinctive features. Some Jews in Libya were more observant than others, but there were no denominations: there was a single synagogue for all. (Arab children were known to call out *wald l'Ahram* (son of sins) to those who were on the streets during prayer times.) Shabbat was a special day, with Friday spent preparing special dishes for Shabbat dinner and lunch. Food for Saturday lunch was warmed in communal ovens operated by Arabs; even Jews who claimed to be totally secular said without exception that their families never used fire on Shabbat. (Exod. 35:3: "You shall kindle no fire throughout your habitations upon the Sabbath day.") This refusal to use fire on Shabbat, regardless of other practices, was true in all the interviews I conducted: "Aish [fire]? Never!"

In the documentary *The Last Jews of Libya*, my brother Maurice recalled going to morning prayer in Benghazi with our father: "We used to get down from our apartment, and still it's dark at night, five o'clock in the morning, and I hear next door the coffee shop still putting the chairs around and so on, and they put the radio to hear the Quran. Papa and I are going to *Bet Ha-Kneset*, and as we approach *Bet Ha-Kneset* we hear [liturgical music]." Hai Saada, Shalom Saada Saar's father, was a leader of the Bet Din (Jewish court) in Benghazi. After making Aliyah, the family lived in a *ma'abara* (refugee camp) before moving to Ashkelon. This is Shalom's memory as a five-year-old, strikingly similar to Maurice's: "The trucks had to pick them up very early, at 6 o'clock. In those days there were no alarm clocks and no buses, so my father would wake me up at 3:30, he would hold my hand—I can still feel the warmth of his hand—and I would walk from house to house knocking on the door to wake people up for *Shachrit*. . . . I still remember '*Moshe, Moshe, kom kom, haya nmshiyu al sla'* [Moshe, Moshe, wake up, let's go to synagogue]. I'd hear '*Rebbi, Rebbi edkhel, tasa qahwa'* [Rebbi, Rebbi, come in, a cup of coffee]." Robert Abravanel, who describes himself as mildly observant, recalls, "My father took me to synagogue every Friday evening and holidays. I maintain tradition, but all these things are for the family, to make sure they pick up as much as possible. Jewish education is important, and Israel more than anything. I go to Israel once a month. I teach my boys."

The Libyan refugees who came to Italy in 1967 had a strong influence on Jewish practice there, and in fact the chief rabbi of Milan, Alfonso Pedatzur Arbib, was born in Tripoli, as was the chief rabbi of Venice, Scialom Bahbout. The Libyan liturgy, which is very different from the traditional Italian liturgy, is followed in at least three Roman synagogues; the Beth El synagogue, established with the Libyan *nusach* under the leadership of Shalom Tsciuba, has over seven hundred members, and Shalom Tsciuba has led the Community in charitable activities such as obtaining and packaging food for Pesach at controlled prices and establishing Jewish lineage for those wishing to make Aliyah. There was one kosher butcher in Rome in 1967; now there are more than ten, as well as thirty-six kosher restaurants, some of which specialize in Libyan cuisine.

Memory

Two of Jacob Sasson's children now live in New York. David Sasson, Jacob's son, who was born in Rome, says, "When you see a Jew from Libya, even if you never met, you feel like family. Small in number, they are very warm people, very humble, and they like to connect with each other." David has been instrumental in building a *sla* (Libyan Judeo-Arabic for congregation) in Manhattan. "It is stressful," he notes, "but it helps preserve our traditions and liturgy. This is the push . . . keeping the traditions." David chants the weekly Torah portion in the Libyan *nusach* (cantillation).

The continuity with the past for those Jews from Libya who reached adulthood after leaving, or were born after their parents left Libya, is reflected to the greatest extent in close family relations. Most felt that intense love and acceptance was a characteristic that their parents brought with them, with especially strong mothers. Yossi Sucary notes that "my [grandmother] was extremely smart and analytical, and knew many languages, and very, very feminist," and he believes that his book *Emilia or The Salt of the Earth*, in which Emilia is a Libyan Jewish grandmother in Israel, marked the first time that the Sephardic woman was properly described in Hebrew literature.[4] For Walter Arbib, "Mother was the captain of the ship. . . . She was very warm and pretty liberal." Shalom Saada Saar described "bottomless love. We grew up very poor. My mother used to have the key to lock the refrigerator, because with seven kids, by the time she comes home from work and opens the refrigerator to cook there would be nothing left. . . . We never felt poverty, because of the love they showered on us. There were boundaries and responsibilities that we never considered crossing. Even our success is a way to give back to our parents all that they gave us. . . . It was not a silent love, the tragedy of introversion, but an expressed love. You get saturated, so you grow up with this strong self-confidence." Jacob Sasson's daughter Monique recalls a balance of love and responsibility. "We never felt too much pressure. The loving factor was calming. One counteracts the other. We were not spoiled. We were never given a gift without occasion. It is a good lesson, builds structure, responsibility, hard work, with unconditional affection." The Libyan Jewish mother was not just the "captain of the ship"; she felt the future and worked to facilitate the best for each child, without manipulation but with love.

Einat Sarouf grew up hearing how life was simple in Libya. They didn't have "money, but lots of joy. The grandma, the grandpa, and the kids, it was so small, and they had one kitchen for everybody, and the women used to cook together so they joked together, they were singing, they had a very good life. Today we have good quality of life but not like they had it. Everyone was together all the time. They were lucky because they had more intimacy, and everybody helped each other, and the friendship was very, very strong."

4. Yossi Sucary, *Emiliyah u melah ha-Arets: Vidui* [Emiliyah and the Salt of the Earth: Confession] [in Heb.] (Tel Aviv: Bavel, 2002).

One way that Einat saw her family "combine their culture with other cultures without losing their own" is in the cuisine. "When we go to my mother we eat couscous, *mafrum*, like they made it a hundred years ago, even my granddaughter likes it. . . . We were taught you are here, you are in Israel, but don't forget where you came from. . . . One of my daughters is a doctor, another a lawyer, and she studies in Wharton, and she can still make you a good couscous." Roger Abravanel, in Milan, celebrates with his cousins, the Buarons, with the two mothers. It is "family that continues—like any Jew. *Mafrum*. My ninety-three-year-old aunt makes it." Shalom Saada Saar passes on the cuisine to his daughters: "I cook, I have a book with all my mother's dishes." And Daniel Buaron leaves it to the original experts: "My mother still cooks Jewish Libyan food. My sister knows how to do all this and is teaching her children, and they will teach my children."

Music is another way in which memory is preserved, and the Libyan Jewish Community has produced some distinguished musical interpreters. Shlomit Bucknik, born in Israel to a Libyan father who was both a barber and a singer, "Sappar ve Zamaar," grew up singing at family gatherings, sitting with her mother and aunt in a circle on the floor, interweaving songs and storytelling, as the women used to do around their chores in Libya, creating stories about family, friends, and life cycles. Her mastery of Judeo-Arabic and folk style drew the attention of audiences in Israel and the Arab world alike. She grew up "soaked in singing popular songs in the authentic Tripoli Judeo-Arabic," upholding and expanding on a unique and forgotten Jewish Libyan and North African tradition of women singers.

Einat Sarouf's father, Ben Zion Halfon, born in Tripoli, fought with the Palmach in Israel's War of Independence and later became a member of the Israeli Knesset and served as deputy minister of agriculture. The archaeological museum in Nitzana is named for him. Einat says, "I grew up [hearing] Arabic music [and] the music of when Israel was being built," and she sings songs from that period in her worldwide performances.

Miriam Meghnagi, born in Tripoli, is descended on her mother's side from Shimon Labi, the sixteenth-century Kabbalist who composed the song "Bar Yochai." She now lives in Rome and travels the world, performing programs such as *From Tripoli to Tel Aviv*. She recalls that "my parents loved singing, and so did my [six] brothers, and songs inhabited our childhood, resounding and running from one room to the other." Miriam is passionate "to give voice to the absent ones and the absence. To save the memory of songs and to give life to the sounds that have been forgotten before it becomes too late . . . to return to the colors and fragrances and languages of Tripoli, my birthplace," as well as the music of other Jewish communities.

Entrepreneurship

Shalom Saada Saar believes that Libyan Jews are great entrepreneurs. "I think it's the bottomless love that the parents gave us, which creates such a secure environment in which we were not afraid . . . Libyan Jews lack fear, they are not afraid . . . to take risks." Similarly, from Walter Arbib, who founded the Skylink Group for international emergency rescue: "When you are an immigrant you take risks . . . if it goes well, good. If it doesn't go well we have nothing to lose." Shalom believes that Jews of Libya "are initiators, very much initiators, in science, industry, art, construction." He believes that leadership is the only sustainable competitive advantage, which is a notion at the core of his seminar/lecture program "Know Thyself: Everyone Has the Capacity to Lead." Looking back is only to recall our roots in order to sustain the energy to move forward.

Roberto and Daniel Buaron developed careers in finance and real estate, respectively, creating the First Atlantic companies in Italy and the United States. Daniel simply "rented an office, a telephone and a desk," and that was the birth of First Atlantic in Italy. "I never thought about obstacles." Roberto Buaron feels their successes are easily understood by the fact that the Jews of Libya are latecomers: "In the last fifty years we may have enjoyed more successes than others because we didn't have the same opportunities in Arab countries. When we came to Europe or the US we had the same opportunities as anyone else and had more drive because we were new. The others had been in Europe forever. We were the new guys. . . . Our family created for us incredible strength. It is the strongest thing we have. We are like one person."

Roger Abravanel's books are about meritocracy. "I thank Libya and Qadhafi, who made us lose everything, and I thank my father who made me understand that given that situation and being Jewish we had to carve our own way. . . . Praise should also go to the Italian schools, which gave us a good education and emphasized excellence. It is the root of our DNA, excellence." Walter Arbib continues, "Our tradition is different. We went to Italian schools, we lived in a more cosmopolitan environment. Yet we held on to traditions." And for Jojo Naim and his brother Moises, it is an immigrant story with struggles, successes, losses, and gains. In Venezuela in earlier decades they felt religious, political, and social freedom, and their businesses prospered. Moises became minister of trade and industry for Venezuela and eventually an executive director of the World Bank and editor-in-chief of the journal *Foreign Policy.* His influence extends internationally from his position as a fellow at the Carnegie Endowment for International Peace through his writings, winning him a number of awards. "Whether or not it is in our DNA, excellence, not wasting a precious moment, *shtara,* wakefulness, and risk-taking in any situation was highly valued. As our own father used to say [to encourage us children], *Yakun 'asad u akal li,* be a lion even at the risk of eating me."

Concluding Remarks

I want to thank all those whom I interviewed, now and in the past. I could fill the entire book with their stories, more from those whom I have mentioned, and so much from equally impressive people whom I had to leave out. I do want to mention here one special Jew from Libya who would certainly have had a place in this story had he not died prematurely, and who should be remembered by our community: my cousin Yossi Romano, an Olympic weightlifter who heroically tried to stop the terrorists at the Munich Olympics of 1972 and was brutally murdered.

Whatever the experiences that the Jews of Libya had with their Arab neighbors, they took with them a love for the simplicity of life there, the simplicity of religious observance, the moving beauty of their ancient liturgy, and the flavorful sensations of their unique cuisine, all of which they have worked to pass on to the generation that followed. Jews from Libya have integrated into the broader communities in both Israel and Rome, and those born there tend to think of themselves as Israelis or Italian Jews: conscious of their Libyan heritage, but distanced from it. Monique Sasson is a typical Libyan-Jewish mother, but she thinks of herself as Italian. Moshe Kahlon, the Israeli minister of finance and head of the Kulanu Party, whose parents came from Tripoli, was unwilling to be interviewed because he considers himself [fully] Israeli. Explicit Libyan Jewish identity may be preserved in the long term largely through the cuisine and liturgy.

I was barely a teen when I came to Boston from Benghazi. As a number of people quoted herein have observed, we were brought up with the expectation that we would behave responsibly and with honor and contribute to the family and Community; this was accompanied by "bottomless" love and by a background of the *finezza* rules of *Il Galateo*. I wanted to raise my children with those principles. Raising them to be responsible, but with much affection, the feeling of love, strength, and protection, would help them overcome all obstacles as first-generation Americans, at the same time as they might continue their heritage with pride. My major obstacle? *Amore, Tesoro,* Sweetheart, Love—OK. But how can one convey, in Italian or English, the comforting sense of

> *Lahaddarni, neggik u twal ghamrik, ya rohe, ya kabdi, ya bniytchi, ya waldi. Ya ghazi, tchagla anaya, tebbutni, tubbutni, farrahni byk.*

Bibliography

De Felice, Renzo. *Ebrei in un paese arabo: Gli Ebrei tra colonialismo, nazionalismo arabo e sionismo.* Bologna: Il Mulino. 1978. Translated by Judith Roumani. *Jews in an Arab Land: Libya, 1835–1970.* Annotated translation from Italian with translator's introduction. Austin: University of Texas Press, 1985; paperback and Kindle editions, 2014.

El Saiegh, Meir. *Racconti Bengasini.* www.libronelcassetto.it. N.d.

Goldberg, Harvey. *Jewish Life in Muslim Libya: Rivals and Relatives.* Chicago: University of Chicago Press, 1990.

Hesse, Isabelle. *The Politics of Jewishness in World Literature.* London: Bloomsbury Academic Press, 2016.

Lilluf, Yaacov. *Toldot yehude luv.* Or Yehudah: World Organization of Jews from Libya, 2000.

Luzon, Raphael. *Libyan Twilight: The Story of an Arab Jew.* Translated by Gaia Luzon. London: Darf, 2017.

Melman, Yossi. *Don't Shoot, I'm the Good Guy: The Life and Times of Walter Arbib.* Toronto: Malcolm Lester, 2016.

Portelli, Alessandro. "What Makes Oral History Different." In *Oral History, Oral Culture, and Italian Americans,* edited by Luisa Del Giudice, 21–30. New York: Palgrave Macmillan, 2009.

Roumani, Maurice. *The Jews of Libya: Coexistence, Persecution, Resettlement.* Eastbourne: Sussex Academic Press, 2008.

Roumani-Denn, Vivienne. Dir. *The Last Jews of Libya.* Documentary film, 2007. Reedited jubilee edition (with Hebrew and Italian subtitles), *The Last Jews of Libya Revisited,* 2017.

———. n.d. http://www.jewsoflibya.com. Website.

Sucary, Yossi. *Benghazi—Bergen-Belsen: The Lost Story of the Holocaust of North African Jews.* Translated by Yardenne Greenspan. San Bernadino: Createspace, 2016.

10

• • •

Growing Up Jewish in Benghazi

An Interview with Samuele Zarrugh

JACQUES ROUMANI

JR: This interview is being conducted in Rome, October 23, 2011, with Mr. Samuele Zarrugh, the president of the Jewish Community of Livorno.

JR: Good morning, *buon giorno*, Mr. Zarrugh.

SZ: Good morning.

JR: Mr. Zarrugh, you and your family came originally from Libya, specifically from Benghazi. Could you tell us a little about how you came to Livorno?

SZ: We came to Livorno after the Six Day War, the war of 1967, having gone through everything that the Jews of Libya, both the Jews of Tripoli and those of Benghazi, suffered during that time. We stayed for over a month, more or less, in a camp, for our own protection, then they gave us permission to leave Libya. We arrived first at a refugee camp in southern Italy, at Capua, and from there my family chose to come to Livorno.

JR: How did you come to be elected president of the Jewish Community? It is a very important job, since Livorno is a city of great historical importance in the Mediterranean Jewish world.

SZ: I started my career as an adviser to the Jewish Community of Livorno in 1970, when I was twenty-five years old. I was appointed by the chief rabbi and by the head of the Community. I succeeded in becoming a member of the council, then I was appointed vice president, then in 1998, and over the course of the next ten years, I won in three elections.

JR: *Auguri*, congratulations! Can you tell us something about your life in Libya? Your family was perhaps unique in Benghazi, and even in Libya,

112. Samuele Zarrugh,
Rome, 2011. Courtesy
of Samuele Zarrugh.

in that you had close relations with the Arab population, and you all knew Arabic very well. Unlike most Jews of Libya who tended to speak Italian, you read Arabic, you attended Arabic-language schools, and I think that you yourself are a graduate of the university. Tell us a little about the way things were.

sz: Well, we attended the Jewish school until 1953, but then it was closed because of lack of funds and also a lack of pupils. We decided then to attend the Arab school. Our Jewish friends decided to go to the Italian school [Scuola dei Fratelli Cristiani]. We [my brothers and I] decided to go to the Arab school because it would lead up to the university, whereas the Italian school only went up to the third year of middle school [la Terza Media]. We attended the Arab school, and also lived in an Arab neighborhood, so we came to know Arab culture. We knew the Arab culture from the market, from the street, and from playing together as children. I studied, I finished high school. And at the university I majored in the economics of business, I did not receive a degree because just on the day when I was supposed to take the exam in Civil Law, the Six Day War broke out. At that point our lives were at risk, and we came to Italy.

JR: Then your lives were at risk. . . . But before the Six Day War, how would you describe relations between Arabs and Jews in a neighborhood like yours, where you were the neighbors of Arabs?

SZ: Well, this is how it often is: in an Arab neighborhood, the families that count, when a Jew chooses to live among them, they have, you might say, an obligation to provide some protection, because he has chosen to live among them. This goes for the families that count, not for the masses. Life was not particularly difficult. It was not all roses and flowers, there were some scuffles from time to time, but it was generally positive.

JR: Yes, but the relations of your parents, of your father with his colleagues of the same age, were they the same as your relations with those of your own generation? Was there already a difference?

SZ: There was a lot of difference, because the new generation was somewhat influenced by the propaganda coming from Syria and Egypt. I think today living together would be much more difficult because of nationalism.

JR: After the Italian occupation ended, in the fifties and sixties, being able to speak Arabic must have helped a lot: did you have a specific coffee bar where you met, or were Arab friends invited to your home, or did you invite them during the religious holiday, did this happen?

SZ: Yes, certainly this happened. What happened was an exchange of courtesies, especially when there was a funeral, giving condolences, readings from the Quran. I remember when my father used to go and give *taazia* [condolences (Ar.)]. It was necessary to do this. And also there were people who were dear to us and I and my brother continued this. We would be invited to attend weddings, and we always went. And there were the games that the boys played in the street, for example soccer games, snooker games, we always played together.

JR: So there were friendly relations between you and Arabs?

SZ: The relationship existed, but it also had to be cultivated, in my opinion. With the Libyan Arabs, and I am talking specifically about those of Cyrenaica, you shouldn't patronize them, nor should you be submissive. It should be a relationship of equals, with dignity, and if you know how to maintain your own dignity, they definitely respect you.

JR: Was there a difference between the social relationship in Cyrenaica and Benghazi, and the relationship in Tripoli?

SZ: There was a big difference. Because Tripoli still had a big Italian presence, and the Jews of Tripoli were greatly influenced by this and by Italian culture. In contrast, the Jews of Cyrenaica were much more integrated into the fabric of Cyrenaica and Benghazi. There was also the language itself. The Jews of Benghazi spoke the Arabic spoken by the Arab masses, who were Bedouins. The Jews of Tripoli spoke a Judeo-Arabic that was much closer to Tunisian Arabic and different from what the Libyan Arabs speak.

JR: Was this written Arabic or only spoken?

SZ: It was written as well, for example the Haggadah of Passover was written in the Judeo-Arabic that was spoken in Djerba and Tunisia.

JR: Did you say that with the Arabs you spoke Judeo-Arabic or what we might call Classical Arabic?

SZ: We definitely spoke Classical Arabic, because it came to us very spontaneously, naturally, it wasn't a case of showing off. When I spoke with an Arab, it came to me automatically to speak the same way. When I visited Libya recently, in 2004, with the delegation [of Libyan Jews] to meet their then-leader, Muammar Qadhafi [the delegation never did meet with Qadhafi], and we spoke in Tripoli with the Arabs of Tripoli, they [other members of the Jewish delegation, originally from Tripoli] were amazed that we [Jews of Benghazi] spoke the same Arabic and used the same expressions as the Arabs, because they [Jews of Tripoli] understood but didn't speak spontaneously.

JR: In the school, you and your brothers were perhaps the only Jews in the school.

ZS: Yes, in the beginning. A few others came afterwards, but quit immediately.

JR: How did you manage?

ZS: I think, to be honest, perhaps because I knew how to accommodate. Our relations at school went well, not badly, and also without a great degree of closeness. They considered me like one of them, I joined in the games, I also took part in the classes on Islamic religion, I studied Quran, I studied the *Hadith*, and I was even perhaps one of the best in the class.

JR: You have also said that you really liked poetry.

SZ: Yes.

JR: Can you recite any poems that have stayed in your memory?

SZ: Well, for example, for me one of the great poets is the poet from Benghazi, Ahmed Rafik al-Mahdawi, who has written a lot. When he talks about a game of backgammon, he says, "Yalab annardu / Habibi binibugh wamahara" [My Beloved plays backgammon with intelligence and mastery].

Ahmed Rafik wrote poems of patriotism and poems of sensuality. Other poets I remember and enjoyed are Ahmad Shawqi [an Egyptian], Nazar Kasbani [a Syrian], and Elia Abumadi [a Lebanese poet who lived and died in the United States].

JR: Besides the poetry, do you remember other things you learned in school?

SZ: Yes, I remember the national anthem, which went "Ya biladi, ya biladi, Libya, Libya, Libya" [My Homeland, My Homeland, Libya] [sings].

JR: Very interesting, is this the national anthem that the [Arab Spring] Revolution has revived?

SZ: The Qadhafi Revolution canceled it, has canceled this one since September 1, 1969.

JR: They have taken the flag of the monarchy, the revolutionaries of today. Do you know whether they have revived the national anthem also?

SZ: I haven't heard. They do refer a lot to the movement of the Sanusi, of King Idris. I don't know how long this will last. We will have to see whether the Islamic faction prevails.

JR: For you who know the Arab world as a whole, and North Africa, could you compare the behavior of the Jews of Libya vis-à-vis the Arabs with those of Egypt or Tunisia?

SZ: A comparison can be made. In Egypt, in the time of King Farouk, some Jews occupied key positions, even in ministries. There were a few men, such as Rabbi Nahum, who was made a member of Egypt's al-Majma Allugaui, which, like the academy for the Italian language in Italy [Accademia della Crusca], was the highest language authority and had the responsibility to correct the Arabic language. Once in Florence I met a Jewish lady, she was very distinguished, and her husband, Yusuf Wahba, in the time of King Farouk had been governor of the Bank of Egypt. There have been other Jews, too, in important positions in Egypt. All of these were Egyptian Jews. But no Libyan Jew had ever occupied any high position, even in the time of the monarchy. In Morocco it was the same as in Egypt: in Morocco Jews occupied important positions, even today the king has a Jewish adviser, and there were some Jewish representatives in parliament. In Libya there was never any Jewish representative or Jewish government official.

JR: But during the colonial period, how had the Jews been treated?

SZ: In Cyrenaica, when the Italians arrived, the Jews saw in them a civilization that would treat them better than had the Turks. Afterwards, when the Fascist racial laws came, the Jews, exactly like the Arabs, suffered under these laws. The Jews were taken to the Giado camp, and many died from cholera and typhus. Thus the Jews suffered in Libya just as the Arab and Muslim citizens did, under Fascism. There were Jews in Cyrenaica who helped the movement of Omar al-Mukhtar because they hoped for liberation from the Fascist regime.

JR: So, has this role of the Jews been recognized in Libyan history?

SZ: This has been recognized on an individual level, never on the collective level. But no individual Jew ever received any award or recognition [*benemerenza*] for this.

JR: In 1969 the monarchy was overthrown by the Qadhafi regime. Have you had any relations with the Qadhafi regime?

SZ: With the regime no, with Arabs who went back and forth, yes. Mostly economic relations. . . . From the regime there were occasional declarations, for the consumption of the press—sporadic declarations in order for the regime to look good. There was no real opening [toward the Jews]. The Jewish community of Cyrenaica goes back to the time of the First Temple, and the Jewish community of Tripoli goes back to the Spanish period (1510–1530) and beyond.

JR: Has there been interest among the Jews of Italy in the situation of the Libyan Jews?

SZ: There has been interest, certainly, insofar as the Libyan Jews have suffered. Any opening up by the regime interested us, of course. A person can never forget the country where he was born. We have suffered, some have even been killed, not only in 1967 but also before that, in 1945 and 1948, but when we hear someone trying to make fun of our country of origin, we never appreciate it and we feel offended.

JR: Libyan culture, Libyan food, the prayers etc.—are they being forgotten?

SZ: No, thank God, Jews from Libya, especially the majority from Tripoli, who are in Rome, have opened their own synagogues and follow their own way of praying [*riti*]. Obviously the dominant culture has an influence, to some extent. In Livorno we have managed to introduce and preserve the Benghazi customs within the Jewish community of Livorno.

JR: So it is something that has been integrated into Italian Jewish life?

SZ: Yes, now in Rome there are so many kosher butchers, kosher restaurants, so much return in *teshuva* [greater religious observance, Heb.] because now the Roman Jews see the Jews of Tripoli and follow what they do. There are intermarriages between the two communities, and things are going in the most positive direction possible.

JR: And now that Libya has liberated itself from the Qadhafi regime, just today they are celebrating the liberation, we hope for a period of freedom and more openness. What do you think are the prospects and what are your hopes for the new Libya? What do you think can be done on a formal level to promote relations between Jews and the new Libya?

SZ: I believe that freedom will not come quickly, because Libya has always consisted of a series of large tribes, who have been at war with each other in the past, and thus this transition will not be easy. I hope there will be an opening, I hope Libya will become a democratic republic, secular, and one day the Libyan Jews will also have a right to vote, like Italians who live abroad and who can vote for the Italian parliament. But this is a hope, for the distant future, and perhaps we ourselves will not see it happen. I hope above all that Libya will not turn toward Islamic fundamentalism.

JR: This is a Jewish community that goes back to Roman times.

SZ: Absolutely. I am thinking of founding an association of the Jews of Cyrenaica, which would not be against anyone but would have a program of telling our children and grandchildren about the history of their parents and grandparents. What the history was of the Jews of Cyrenaica, about the revolt against the Romans, what the Jews experienced during the whole period of Islam. What Jews did for the independence of Libya, and afterwards, up to the 1967 expulsion. And I'd like to teach them about our liturgy and prayers, which are a little different from those of Tripoli. Maybe our liturgy has been less influenced from the outside. Obviously it has been somewhat influenced by that of Tunisia, and the Island of Djerba. Thus when we speak we should speak with some collective authority. We need to form an association so that when a representative speaks, he speaks in the name of the collective. This has not happened so far and this lack [of responsible representatives] has caused damage and problems.

JR: The story of your family and community is really fascinating, and I am looking forward to reading something written by your own hand that will expand on this, and we wish you great success with your projects, and *hazak ubaruch* [may you be strengthened and blessed]!

SZ: Thank you, and I am also counting on you.

◆ ◆ ◆

PART FIVE

Sufferings

THE FINAL SECTION of this volume focuses on certain unfortunate events that have befallen Libyan Jews and their reactions to these events. Harvey E. Goldberg delves back into history and shows how memory is partially preserved. Two traumatic events that endangered the Jews of Libya are commemorated in special Purims and recounted in Libyan *piyyutim*. Such a phenomenon has been discovered elsewhere as well. Even in the Israel of today, these threatening events in Libya are still partially commemorated, as Goldberg documents.

Judith Roumani looks at more modern traumas as portrayed in literature. During World War II, Libyan Jews suffered grievously at the hands of the Fascist government, allies of the Nazis, which decided to expel the Jews of Cyrenaica, who were suspected of collaborating with the enemy. Different groups had to confront different fates, depending on the passports that they held. Those with French documents were deported to Tunisia, where they were subject to Allied bombings. Those with Italian passports were sent to Italy and often interned there. Those without foreign passports were sent to inhuman camps in the desert of Tripolitania, where starvation and disease killed hundreds. Those with British papers were sent to the Nazi camp of Bergen-Belsen, a fate recounted in the novel *Benghazi—Bergen-Belsen* by the Israeli Yossi Sucary.

David Meghnagi recounts in detail the final exodus, or more accurately the expulsion, of Jews from Libya. As the Six Day War and the threat to destroy Israel loomed in 1967, local Muslims threatened Jews and made their age-old life in Libya untenable. Jews hid in their homes for weeks. The weakened king maintained that he could no longer protect the Jews and, threatened by mobs, they were first interned and then taken to the airports en masse. Two entire families were kidnapped by Libyan police and killed. The survivors' fear during those days has marked them for life. Despite these traumas, Libyan Jews cherish and remember their old way of life, as they have embarked on new careers in Italy, Israel and elsewhere. Their zest and vigor mean a high outward success rate, but the pain of uprooting and the nostalgia still follow them and live within them.

11

◆ ◆ ◆

Violence and the Liturgical/Literary Tradition

Joining the Chorus while Retaining Your Voice

HARVEY E. GOLDBERG

And why, Rabbi Avraham, have you forgotten some places?
The city of El-Hama, and also Qafsa and Djerba you did not
    remember.
Their end was utter exile, and you skipped over their chastisement.
The dismayed congregation of Zorman, and the community of
    Mesallata
And you forgot the dismayed community of Misurata,
Whose punishment was very great, and their tongue was silenced[?],
And heavy taxes and hard work were placed upon them.
Some of them fled and still wander,
And some exiled themselves to Djerba, the city you ignored.
Others went to Zorman, as if left in the wild.
Depressed all their days, their eyes and souls exhausted,
Yearning for some respite, and the relief that has not come,
[Until?] the day the son of Jesse comes, and also the son of
    Ephraim.

Anonymous
Verses added to Ibn Ezra's "Elegy"

These verses were composed by an anonymous North African
poet who appended them to a twelfth-century elegy by Abraham ibn
Ezra. Ibn Ezra's poem ("Elegy") memorialized Jewish communities that were destroyed with the expansion of the Almohad Empire

and its policies of forced conversion and exile.[1] The appended verses take "Rabbi Abraham" to task for overlooking some of the towns in the eastern Maghrib. They also condense a leitmotif of the current essay—the lack of knowledge regarding, and lack of attention to, these communities. This parallel, which bridges centuries, reflects the basic geography of the region.

Our present notion of Africa stems from the period when European ships regularly sailed around the southern tip of that continent. The Arab place name "Ifriqiya," derived from antiquity, referred to a region that today includes Tunisia and Tripolitania, the western province of Libya. They formed the easternmost stretches of the Maghrib—the Arab West with its large populations in Morocco and Algeria—and could easily be viewed as the end of "the" world—or at least of "a" world.

To Europeans and Americans, these marginal areas appeared as lands of trouble: a lair of corsairs challenging Mediterranean shipping, the territory across which Erwin Rommel advanced toward Egypt during World War II, and the base of the rogue regime of Muammar Qadhafi that provoked the West for two generations. Jews were not major players in these dramas, but neither were they absent from them. Jewish merchants trafficked in the goods stolen by Tripoli corsairs, and they ransomed coreligionists who were brought to that port. During World War II, the Fascist government sent some Jews in Tripoli to labor camps, while Mussolini exiled over 2,500 Cyrenaican Jews to a concentration camp in Tripolitania after the Jews had welcomed British forces the first and second times they entered the city. And it was a year after Qadhafi's seizure of power that the last few remnants of the community received the news of a law that seized all of their property, the coup de grâce for Jewish life in Libya.

At times Jews in Libya were isolated from other Jewish centers, but at other periods there was regular—if not intensive—contact with

---

1. Translation from Hebrew by Harvey E. Goldberg. The verses added to Ibn Ezra's "Elegy" (אהה ירד עלי ספרד רע מן השמים) were published in Nahum Slouschz, *Travels in North Africa* (Philadelphia: JPS, 1927), 222.

them. Much of their history has passed unrecorded and unnoticed by other Jews, but that which has come down to us shows interesting twists and also dilemmas. Violence erupted in their lives in diverse forms: in the eighteenth century when Tripoli was a quasi-independent regency; and in the mid-twentieth century when Jews in Libya faced Fascist persecution, a pogrom by Muslim rioters under the British Military Administration (BMA), and participation in Israel's War of Independence. In each case, Jews in and from Libya had recourse to genres of expression familiar from other Jewish groups while adopting them to their own communal exigencies.

Tripoli and Local Purims

In the early and late eighteenth century, Jews in Tripoli instituted two local Purim holidays. These marked episodes wherein they escaped, or received respite from, violence. The first was in 1705, when the bey of Tunisia laid siege to Tripoli. His troops, however, were thrown back. This brought relief to the city, as well as its Jews, who had been drafted to strengthen the town's defenses. A religious poem or *piyyut* of the subgenre called *Mi Khamokha*, modeled after a poem by Yehudah Halevi (1075–1141) to be recited on the Sabbath preceding Purim,[2] was composed later in the eighteenth century, giving details

---

2. *Shabbat Zakhor*. The phrase *mi khamokha* (who is like unto Thee?) is taken from Moses' song of deliverance after the biblical episode at the Red Sea (Exod. 15:11). Many medieval hymns of praise were composed with *mi khamokha* as the opening phrase, and utilized liturgically on various occasions. One of the most famous was a hymn (*piyyut*) authored by Yehudah Halevi (1075–1141), a Spanish Hebrew poet and religious philosopher, for the Sabbath of *Zakhor*. This is the Sabbath on which the biblical passage known as *zakhor* (Deut. 25: 17–19) is read, enjoining the people of Israel to remember Amaleq, the eponymous ancestor of Haman. That reading precedes the feast of Purim each year. See Israel Davidson, *Thesaurus of Mediaeval Hebrew Poetry* [Heb.], vol. 3 (New York: Jewish Theological Seminary of America, 1930), 121–125; and Efraim Hazan, "The Transformation of a Piyyut: the Way of the 'Mi Kamokha' from Spain to the Orient and North Africa" [Heb.], in *Culture and History: Ino Sciacky Memorial Volume*, ed. Joseph Dan (Jerusalem: Misgav Yerushalayim, 1987), 67–76.

of the events. This commemorative composition also made a claim to be incorporated into the local liturgy.[3]

This followed the form of local Purims elsewhere. The anniversary of the event—the 23rd of Tevet— became a day on which work ceased, feasting was in order, gifts were sent to friends, and alms were given to the poor (see Esther 9:22). The daily prayer of supplication (*nefilat apayyim*) was not recited, as in the case of other festivals. The day was called Purim Ashrif, after the name of the defeated bey, and the *Mi Khamokha* hymn was read on the Sabbath preceding Purim Ashrif. Not much is known about the period in general, but a striking aspect of the *piyyut* is its full identification with the city and its duress. The poet refers to the Muslim defenders of Tripoli as *hayyalenu*, "our soldiers" (I now translate the last Hebrew lines):

> And as the war drew near *our* soldiers scattered
> And *our* soldiers fell before his troops
> And *we* heard and *our heart* melted.

Jews did not take part in the battle, but the *piyyut* presents them as part of the collective engaged in the confrontation.

There is a fuller record of the events leading to the creation of Purim Burghul in the last decade of the century. An armed battle erupted between factions led by two rival brothers seeking leadership of the Regency. The sultan authorized a corsair nicknamed "Ali Burghul" to take control of the region. He landed in Tripoli in 1793 and assumed the position of pasha.

Burghul began what a later observer called a "reign of terror."[4] He pressed taxation heavily, particularly on the Jews. Notables suspected of loyalty to the previous regime were executed, and several Jews were implicated in a plot against him. Among them was a son of Rabbi Avraham Khalfon, who had been head of the Jewish

3. H. Z. Hirschberg, *History of the Jews of North Africa*, vol. 2, *From the Ottoman Conquests to the Present Time* (Leiden: Brill, 1981), 151–53.

4. N. Slouschz, *Travels in North Africa* (Philadelphia: Jewish Publication Society, 1927), 25. (This English edition consists of only one volume.)

community for a while. His son David, also a prominent communal figure, was condemned and burned alive. Later, with the aid of the bey of Tunisia, members of the previous dynasty drove Burghul out in January 1795.[5] The Jews were once again redeemed, and another *Mi Khamokha piyyut* was composed, this time by Avraham Khalfon. He also, separately, penned an elegy for his son.[6] A second local Purim known as Purim Burghul was established (the 29th of Tevet), and Khalfon's poem was incorporated into the liturgy.[7] Both hymns cited were written in Hebrew, and they fit easily into the local liturgy. With regard to Purim Burghul, another poem in the *Mi Khamokha* style, but written in Judeo-Arabic, has been discovered.[8] Its liturgical function is not clear; perhaps it was aimed at the nonlearned members of the community, including women.

The details of these compositions show that Jews in Tripoli, while officially defined as *dhimmis* under Muslim rule, were taken up in the political life of the town. The city's well-being was their well-being, and they shared in, sometimes more than others, Tripoli's travails. Ali

5. Hirschberg, *History*, 153–55; Mordekhai Ha-Kohen, *Higgid Mordekhay: Histoire de la Libye et de ses Juifs, lieux d'habitation et coutumes* [Heb.], ed. Harvey Goldberg (Jerusalem: Ben-Zvi Institute, 1978), 101–7.

6. See Slouschz, *Masa'ai*, vol. 2, 53–55; Hirschberg, *History*, 154, 180.

7. Hirschberg, *History*, 180ff; the two hymns were published together in a small hymn book titled *Mi Khamokha* (Tripoli: N.p., 1923). They also appear in F. Zuaretz, A. Guweta, Ts. Shaked, G. Arbib, and F. Tayar, eds., *Yahadut Luv* [Heb.] (Tel Aviv: Vaad Kahalat Luv beIsrael, 1982), 47–52. Most recently, they also were included in a hymn book for the Jews of Tripoli compiled by F. Zuaretz and F. Tayar, *Seu Zimrah* (Tel Aviv: self-published, 1972), 197–206.

8. See Y. Tobi, "An Unknown *Piyyut* by R. Yitzaq Luzon on Burjil Purim (Tripoli, 1795)" [Heb.], in *Studies on the Culture of the Jews of North Africa*, ed. Issachar Ben-Ami (Jerusalem: Va'ad 'Adat ha-Ma'araviyim bi-Yerushalayim, 1991), 75–82. This hymn (*piyyut*), written by R. Yitzhaq Luzon, appears at the end of a book, *Derekh ha-hayim* [The Way of Life] (Livorno: Eliyahu Ben Amozeg and Partners, 1860), by R. Hai Maimon, which was published together with another book by the same author, *Mayim Hayim*. In the Jewish National Library record, "Derekh ha-hayim" by Ya'akov ben Hai Maimon is listed as an additional title (*kotar nosaf*), with a special title page bound with *Mayim Hayim*.

Burghul's downfall resulted from the efforts of Muslim leaders, but Jews found it appropriate to phrase their experience in tropes taken from their own tradition of Purim. But reference to the Purim paradigm did not entail a wedge between them and all non-Jews; it focused on the tyrants who oppressed them.

It is worth asking how Muslims perceived the position of Jews with regard to these conflicts, or, perhaps, more precisely, what was the Jews' sense of the Muslims' perception of their place in the broader community? Purim Burghul, along with the shared experience of Jews and Muslims that it expresses, may also reflect an ambivalence with which the wider populace viewed the Jews.

The Jews were an old population in Tripoli and engaged in its affairs, but there were constant reminders of their status as *dhimmi*. One sign of their outsiderness was that European consuls in the city resided in or near the Jewish quarters. By the end of the eighteenth century, European pressure against the Tripoli corsairs was growing, and Jews at times appeared symbolically associated with the threatening Europeans.[9] To the extent that Jews sensed the ambivalence of Muslim perceptions, they had reason to stress their local loyalties. Perhaps the insertion of the *piyyutim* into the synagogue liturgy also sent a message to the Muslims that Jews were concerned with the well-being of the city. On a day-to-day basis, Muslims were not overtly interested in Jewish religious practices, but authorities were not totally indifferent to events in synagogues. Just as, in times of instability, the name of the Muslim ruler pronounced in a mosque resonated with political meaning, so the liturgical recital of Tripoli's victories in the synagogue may have reasserted the place of the Jews in the city. Through their special Purims, Jews reaffirmed ties to local residents and to Muslim authority, while evoking a metastory that has accompanied them in many lands.

9. H. E. Goldberg, *Jewish Life in Muslim Libya* (Chicago: University of Chicago Press, 1990), 29–33.

Regarding the content of the *Mi Khamokha* hymns, they recall specific acts of violence, but the overall theme is to celebrate God's redemption. Couplets of Khalfon's *piyyut* mention the heavy taxes, death by burning, and the prevention of children from studying Torah, as well as suffering by the general populace. But what is emphasized is not the fact of violence—the hymn mentions death by burning in general, while Khalfon separately penned verses mourning his son— but rather the salvation that ended it. As a vulnerable minority, violence—and apprehension over violence—was not novel for Jews. Biblical verses provided tools for expressing suffering and redemption, while a classic rabbinic trope stressed the movement from the former to the latter.

I now pause in the historical sequence to raise several points and questions. The events of the two Purims were highly local, but they entered collective memory, and broader history, by mobilizing a longstanding literary model from elsewhere. We are discussing an era when written literary production was confined to elites, and one might speculate that there existed popular Judeo-Arabic songs that celebrated the respite from Ashrif Bey before the composition of the *Mi Khamokha* about a generation later. As mentioned, the *piyyut* itself declared that it should be part of the liturgy, and we should recognize the role of this genre in enshrining "history," in laying out liturgical rules, and in constituting a form of authorization that reaches a broad audience.

One also may ask: How rapidly and extensively did acceptance of these hymns within the liturgical cycle take place? Sources reaching us may be prescriptive more than descriptive. A preface to a nineteenth-century edition of the second *Mi Khamokha* states that it was accepted in Tripolitania and also in Benghazi. A friend from Benghazi, however, told me that some Jews there referred to the minor festival as Purim Kadabi, or a false Purim. Writing early in the twentieth century, Mordekhai Ha-Kohen mentions both local Purims, but also notes that their observance was waning. After the large-scale Aliyah to Israel (1949–1951), a leader of the community, Rabbi Frigia Zuaretz,

113. Jewish children in the *hara* of Tripoli. Courtesy of Hamos Guetta Collection.

turned to Israel's Sephardic chief rabbi to ask whether these practices should be maintained, and he received a positive answer. A liturgical calendar issued by a Libyan synagogue in Ramat Gan in the 1990s continued to mark off these days, but I do not know how widespread the practice was in actuality. In any event, it is clear that the move to Israel, and the historical events preceding it, presented new contexts for recounting violence.

In the mid-twentieth century, Jews in and from Libya faced violence in three phases, rapidly succeeding one another. Each story is complex, and here I will briefly point to features of each and highlight some complexities and paradoxes. Placing these against the background of the earlier episodes, I will then summarize by formulating some general issues raised by this peripheral Jewish community that at times found itself in the vortex of global currents and events.

Italian Fascism and World War II affected Jews in Libya in various ways. In 1936 Italo Balbo, governor of the colony, decided that several Jews should be flogged publicly for refusing to open up their shops, located in the new section of Tripoli, on the Sabbath. Two years later, there was a top-level decision to apply the racial laws passed in Italy to the Libyan colony, and the same Balbo resisted their implementation, claiming that the economy would be hurt by restricting the activities of Jews. The Jewish quarter of Tripoli lay close to the sea, precisely where the Italians placed anti-aircraft guns during the war, so consequent Allied bombardments wreaked havoc with that part of the city. Some Jews were hit directly, while many fled Tripoli seeking shelter outside the city. Jews witnessed Nazi military might when German forces, led by Rommel, joined the Italians and launched the move toward Egypt. After the historical turnabout in El-Alamein, the British took Benghazi but later were ousted by the Italians, and they had to recapture it a second and then a third time. Jews welcomed the British forces during the first invasion, and Mussolini decided to deport over 2,500 Jews from Cyrenaica to a concentration camp in Giado, in southern Tripolitania. Eventually, close to 600 people died there of starvation or typhus before the eventual liberation. In a different set of moves, Jews with British passports were deported to Europe, reaching Bergen-Belsen, where they were held to be exchanged for German POWs held by the British.

A second phase took place under the BMA that ruled Libya from early 1943. This was an anti-Jewish outbreak in November 1945, which, over three days of rioting by Muslims in Tripoli and smaller communities, brought death to over 130 Jews, along with the destruction of shops, homes, and synagogues. There also was rape, the desecration of Torah scrolls, and even forced conversions to Islam. Opinions vary about the causes of the riots. The British were slow in putting them down, and there are debates over whether this may have been an intentional delay. There did not appear, and still has not, a salient literary expression of these events, but there seems little doubt about the fact that the deep uncertainty arising from them fed into the emigration of close to 90 percent of Libya's 38,000 Jews to Israel when that became possible in the spring of 1949.

Only a small part of the events mentioned have entered into lasting narratives, whether internal to the community of Libyan Jews or in forms reaching wider audiences. A number of reasons can be offered. First is the rapid sequence of traumatic events within the space of a decade. The shocks surrounding World War II were hardly over when

114. Unmarked graves of forty-five Jewish victims of the pogrom of 1945 in Tripoli. The entire cemetery was razed under the Qadhafi regime and a commercial center built there. From Renzo De Felice, *Jews in an Arab Land: Libya 1835–1970* (Austin: University of Texas Press, 1985), courtesy of the late Raffaello Fellah.

the community was rocked by subsequent violence and shifts, including almost total displacement to Israel. Another set of questions concerns: who might be the intended audience of any such narrative? With regard to the 1945 riots these could include authorities (the BMA), Muslim Arab neighbors with whom Jews might have to continue to interact, a wider international community, or future generations in Israel—an option that was only vaguely envisioned immediately after the pogrom. Each of these implies a different language of expression, including local Judeo-Arabic, standard Arabic, European languages, and Hebrew. Frigia Zuaretz, born in Tripoli in 1907, penned a Hebrew poem marking the flogging of Jews who refused to open their shops on the Sabbath, but these are verses that have hardly been noticed except by members of the older generation of immigrants to Israel.

Regarding Israel itself, which became the home of the majority of Libyan Jews, one can trace an evolving growth in collective historical consciousness. Even more poignantly, one might examine factors working against the Jews from Libya giving voice to the violent traumas in their recent history. What were the silences and how long did they last? Which ideological and social factors mitigated their expression? And to what extent were there forms of co-optation that muffled the telling of their own specific story? In the space available, I provide a glimpse into some of these dilemmas.

Regarding World War II and the Holocaust, some irony is involved. The Jewish soldiers in Palestine who volunteered for the British army sought to make contact with remnant Jewish communities freed from Axis control. European Jewry was foremost in their minds, while in fact the first liberated community they contacted was in Libya. Thus a portion of the Yishuv was well aware of the World War II experience in Libya, including some well-known cultural and religious figures. With the subsequent mass immigration, and the growth of Holocaust consciousness after the Eichmann trial and the anxiety preceding the 1967 war, a warped image of the Holocaust being an "Ashkenazi affair" arose, and the experience of Libya's Jews receded from collective memory. There are accounts that members of the community offered to testify at Eichmann's trial, or sought to be included in the reparations agreements reached with West Germany, but were firmly rebuffed. Some reports are disturbing, such as a statement attributed to Nahum Goldman that the Libyan Jews were seeking to "hitchhike" (*litfos tremp*) on the Holocaust. There also are incidents recalled by school children of Libyan parents whose teachers rejected the statement that their parents were affected by the Holocaust.[10]

With time, history confirmed the full dimensions of Nazi deeds and plans, and rectifications were made. In addition, as efforts to perpetuate Holocaust awareness sought new avenues, the events in Libya and in Vichy-controlled North Africa have received increasing attention. A one-hour documentary screened in 2005 (*A Matter of Time*), which was featured on Israeli TV on Holocaust Memorial Day, tells the story of families in the Giado camp. Recently, a historical novel appeared that weaves a tale around the adventures of a young woman against the background of the travail of Benghazi Jews interred in Bergen-Belsen. Written by a native Israeli from a Benghazi family, it illustrates one way in which the specific story of Libya's Jews has slowly attracted a broader audience while resonating with widely held Israeli concerns and values (this novel is discussed in detail in chapter 12 in this volume). This trend may continue for a while. I attended a Holocaust Memorial Day event during which it was pointed out that

10. On this, see specifically the statement by Yossi Sucary in his interview with Vivienne Roumani-Denn in chapter 9 in this volume (p. 192).

the Benghazi families were in Bergen-Belsen at the same time as Anne Frank, and some may have met her.

The second violent encounter of the mid-twentieth century has had less of a narrative echo within Israeli society. This does not reflect its historical impact. Following the 1945 riots, the BMA urged Arab and Jewish leaders to repair the breach between the communities,[11] and the Jews prepared a report detailing the riots and their consequences. Under the heading "Arab-Jewish Relationships throughout the Centuries,"[12] it mentions a theatrical presentation by the Maccabee Organization, earlier in the year, of the Bible story about Joseph and his brothers, stressing that the play was in local Arabic and presented to an audience including Muslim notables and representatives of the BMA. Allusion to the play was an attempt to distance themselves from the riots. The story of Joseph, appearing in the Quran, is a favorite Muslim tale,[13] while for Jews it is the prototype of societal success in a land of exile.

These contextual factors lost relevance after emigration. While Frigia Zuaretz and other colleagues, in a Hebrew Memorbuch of Libyan Jewry published in 1960, reviewed details of the events, and also suggested that memorial prayers be recited on the anniversary of the riots, I have seen little evidence that this became common practice. The date is not marked on the Ramat Gan liturgical calendar. What has taken place in the past generation, with the development of a Libyan Jewry heritage center that regularly organizes events celebrating the community's past and promoting its continuity, is that the three violent encounters of the mid-twentieth century—World War II, the riots, and the fallen Israeli soldiers—have been grouped together in commemorative practice. The heritage center, located outside of Tel

11. Renzo De Felice, *Jews in an Arab Land: Libya, 1835–1870*, trans. Judith Roumani (Austin: University of Texas Press, 1985), 197ff.

12. Comunità Israelitica della Tripolitania, *I tumulti antiebraichi in Tripolitania: 4, 5, 6, e 7 Novembre 1945* (Tripoli: Ben-Zvi Institute Collection, 1945), 17–18.

13. Bernard Heller, "Yusuf b. Ya'kub," in *Encyclopaedia of Islam* (Leiden: Brill, 1931), 4:1178–79.

Aviv, is largely taken up by a museum that includes a room dedicated to the theme of Yizkor. In terms of explanations and texts presented, the three different episodes appear in their distinctive details but are linked together in an overarching framework, a metonymy that speaks to Israeli sensibilities.

Each year, the center has organized one memorial event and often all three violent junctures are highlighted. Emphases and format vary on each occasion, but the gestalt is maintained. This is one way in which Jews from Libya have overcome the forced choice presented to them upon immigration—between holding on to their past or becoming Israelis. Along with other groups, they have found narratives creating synergy between these identities. While in Libya they were at times wary of too much attention directed to their internal stories, in Israel they have had to strive so as not to be ignored.

12

◆ ◆ ◆

Yossi Sucary's Novel *Benghazi—Bergen-Belsen* in the Context of North African Jewish Literature of the Holocaust

JUDITH ROUMANI

Yossi Sucary, of Libyan Jewish origin but born in Israel, has produced a striking novel about how Libyan Jews holding British passports were deported to the Nazi concentration camps through the collaboration of the Italian Fascist government. Based on his mother's memoirs and his own research, he has pieced together the painful story of one family of Jews from Benghazi, telling the story through the words of a young girl who experienced much of the worst of the Holocaust, but survived to move to Israel and found her own family, even though her traumas must have left her emotionally scarred. Although it tells a history unique to one particular group of Libyan North African Jews, this novel can usefully be viewed also in the context of other works of fiction by North African Jewish writers. Like them, and most decisively, it gives the lie to the old saw that Sephardim and Mizrahim were not victimized during the Holocaust.

Sucary's novel tells but one chapter of the story of Libyan Jews during the Holocaust years. Each group found itself sent to a different destination, depending on the vagaries of the passports they held. Those holding Tunisian (*protégés français*) passports were sent to Tunisia, then under Vichy administration and Nazi occupation, while those holding Libyan passports or no passports at all (as subjects of the Italian colony of Libya) were sent to internment camps in the desert. Full Italian citizens were sent back to Italy and met various fates. The Libyan Jews who happened to hold British passports spent about two years in Fascist internment camps in Italy before being sent on to Bergen-Belsen, which was not an extermination camp but had terrible conditions that led to the deaths of many thousands of prisoners.[1] Though the experience of North African Jews in the Holocaust has not received much attention until recently, Jews undoubtedly suffered, and hundreds died, through their treatment by the Nazis, the Vichy government, and the Fascist Italian authorities, and it was only because the Axis forces were losing the war in North Africa that the aims of the Nazis' Wannsee Conference (extermination of the Jews) were not applied in North Africa. North African Jewish literature of the Holocaust has also not received much attention, and so it is well worth examining some other North African Jewish literary productions before turning to *Benghazi—Bergen-Belsen*.

Our first point of comparison is the work of the well-known Tunisian Jewish writer Albert Memmi, whose early novel, *La Statue de sel* (*Pillar of Salt*) (1953),[2] was written only a few years after the events of the Holocaust.

Although one cannot assume that novels are necessarily autobiographical, Memmi's account of his experiences under Nazi occupation in Tunisia, told by his fictional character, Alexandre Mordechai

---

1. See the online *Holocaust Encyclopedia* (Washington, DC: United States Holocaust Memorial Museum, n.d.), "Bergen-Belsen," http://www.ushmm.org/wlc /en/article.php?ModuleId=10005224. The novel under discussion is Yossi Sucary, *Benghazi—Bergen-Belsen* (Tel Aviv: Am Oved, 2013) [in Heb.]. Quotations from *Benghazi—Bergen-Belsen* are from the English translation by Yardenne Greenspan, with the author's kind permission. This translation was published in 2016 (San Bernadino: Createspace, 2016). The novel has also been turned into a play of the same title, performed by La Mama Company off-off-Broadway, March 23–April 9, 2017, directed by Michal Gamily, playwright Lahav Timor, starring Veracity Butcher as Silvana, Lily Leah Azrielant as Rebecca, and Mohammad Bakri as the father Eliyahu.

2. Albert Memmi, *La Statue de sel* (Paris: Corrêa, 1953); *Pillar of Salt*, trans. Edouard Roditi [1955, 1975] (Boston: Beacon, 1992).

115. Compagnia Lavoro: work camp for Jews in the Libyan desert, ca. 1942. From *Jews in an Arab Land: Libya 1835–1970* (Austin: University of Texas Press, 1985), courtesy of the late Raffaello Fellah.

Benillouche, is probably very close to the way things actually happened.[3] For some months in 1942–44, Tunisia was occupied by the Nazis in order to bolster the Axis defense of North Africa. They took the leaders of the Jewish community of Tunis hostage and demanded several thousand Jewish laborers, who were sent to dig trenches for the Nazi battle lines on both sides of Tunisia. The only event that somewhat contradicts the historical record in this book is Memmi's placing a pogrom during the war years in Tunis, though no such event occurred: he may perhaps, for novelistic reasons, be transposing events from Iraq (1941) or Libya (1945) to Tunisia. He is, of course, making the point that the Jew is an outsider, a stranger, neither colonizer nor colonized and thus vulnerable. In his *Portrait d'un Juif* (*Portrait of a Jew*) (1962),[4] Memmi makes the case that Jews truly belong only in

3. On the porous boundary between Sephardic autobiography and novel, see Jonathan Schorsch, "Disappearing Origins: Sephardic Autobiography Today," *Prooftexts* 27, no. 1 (Winter 2007): 82–150.

4. Albert Memmi, *Portrait d'un Juif* (Paris: Gallimard, 1962); trans. Elizabeth Abbott, *Portrait of a Jew* (New York: Orion, 1962).

their own land. On balance we see the Holocaust and his experiences of the Nazi period in Memmi's novel as just one element in the vast historical process that was uprooting indigenous North African Jews from their ancestral homelands and launching them toward Europe, the Western Hemisphere, or Israel.

The Holocaust writing of Edmond Jabès provides another point of comparison with Sucary's novel. Jabès was a Jew born in Egypt. In 1956, under Nasser's regime, the screws were tightened more and more on this most ancient of Jewish communities; some were imprisoned and almost all were expropriated, until the Egyptian Jews departed from their ancestral home almost penniless, leaving everything behind, and made a new start in Israel or Europe. Jabès was one of these, moving to Paris and gradually, with great effort, reestablishing himself. He left behind in Egypt his library (he was already a published poet) and his emotional roots. Soon after arriving in France, whose culture he had always idealized during his French education in Egypt, he discovered anti-Semitism in the form of graffiti on a wall. Somehow his individual trauma of leaving Egypt was transposed or displaced to the collective trauma of the Holocaust from which his own community had been largely spared but that was fully experienced by European Jewry. His novels are poetic, lyrical, and surrealistic, lacking most of the elements of a conventional novel such as plot, psychology, and a rational progression of events. He has, in fact, written seven volumes (*Le Livre des questions* [*The Book of Questions*], 1963, 1973)[5] that refer to the tragic relationship of a young couple who return from the camps; she has gone mad, and he is contemplating suicide. Their expressions and their plight are commented on by a sort of traditional chorus of rabbis and their students. Jabès has had broad influence on subsequent poets, philosophers, and fiction writers of the Holocaust even though much of his enigmatic writing is somewhat inaccessible

5. Edmond Jabès, *Le Livre des questions* (Paris: Gallimard, 1963–1965); *The Book of Questions,* trans. Rosemarie Waldrop (Middletown, CT: Wesleyan University Press, 1976–1977).

for those who prefer more traditional novels. The suffering, though, is raw and unadulterated.[6]

Albert Bensoussan's novel, or perhaps fictionalized autobiography, *Frimaldjézar* (1976),[7] is frankly nostalgic for an idyllic childhood world. Its lyricism, humor, and wordplay have helped set the tone for later novels in the same idiom. It describes the childhood of a middle-class Jewish boy growing up in Algiers during the colonial period, World War II, the Allied victory, and Algerian independence. Since this childhood world is lost forever, the novelist, from his new home in misty, chilly Brittany, refers to it as Nineveh, the city to which the prophet announces its doom. Like Nineveh, the city in the novel is not destroyed but rather transformed. Its way of life becomes less carefree, and its multicultural population of colonial times has given way to a much more homogeneous one in the postindependence period. But the parallel with Nineveh of a population of joyful insouciance, unaware of what destiny may hold, seems an apt image for colonial Algiers, at least for the Jews. The name *Frimaldjézar* is related to the word *frime*—show or fun—and much of the happiness of life in this beautiful suburb perched on a hill above the sea comes from enjoyment of superficial, trivial things, such as the smells of spices, the pleasant confusion of the markets, the noisy prayer of the synagogue, and particularly the facile glories of the local opera playing before a public easily delighted.

The child (so we are told) saw the essential unreality of the colonial society, for which the opera constituted its heart. Unlike adults, the child found his world too new, too marvelous, to be taken for granted. Beneath his joy lurked what turned out to be a realistic fear of losing that world.

---

6. See http://www.sephardichorizons.org/Volume4/Issue2/Roumani.html #sthash.RcjOS15D.dpuf.

7. Albert Bensoussan, *Frimaldjézar* (Paris: Calman-Lévy, 1976). Subsequent page numbers quoted in the text refer to this edition. This work won the Prix de l'Afrique méditerranéenne in 1976.

Bensoussan does refer also to the ability of his community to return to the villages in times of danger.[8] He describes a Jewish shepherd perfectly at home in the hinterland and shows the filtered impressions of world war and the Holocaust. Jews with remote connections to Algeria, or none at all, were coming to take refuge there, bringing rumors of boxcars and crematoria. His home became a stopping place for Jews on their way to hide in the countryside: "Il y avait foule à la maison, base de transit pour le retour aux villages" [There were crowds of people in our home, which had become a base of transit to the countryside] (55).[9] North Africa had thus over the centuries constituted a refuge for Jews in times of danger. The centuries spent in North Africa have become another chapter in the history of the exile of the Sephardim and their migration from one country to another around the Mediterranean basin:

> Notre passage en Isbilia, simple péripatie. Aprés Tolède, après l'Espagne, et notre séculaire enracinement en terres maugrèbes, et notre long déhanchement d'un part à l'autre de Méditerranée, adieu Frimaldjézar. (185)

8. Ami Bouganim, of Morocco and now Israel, refers in *Récits du Mellah* (Paris: Lattès, 1981), 26, to a tendency for Jews in time of plague to take refuge in the countryside. Such an option implies the maintaining of a whole network of relationships with non-Jewish, Arab, or Berber villagers, on a permanent basis, ready to be activated. See also the book and documentary film by Robert Satloff: *Among the Righteous: Lost Stories from the Holocaust's Long Reach into Arab Lands* (New York: Public Affairs, 2007), discussing cases of Jews who were rescued or hidden by Muslims during the Vichy/Nazi/Fascist period; the film title is *Among the Righteous: Lost Stories from the Holocaust in Arab Lands* (dir. Robert Satloff, produced in partnership with MacNeil-Lehrer Productions, 2010); see https://www.pbs.org/newshour/spc/among-the-righteous/index.html.

9. Since the time of the defeated Jewish revolt against the Romans in Cyrene, 115–117 CE, Jews have taken refuge in the interior of North Africa (the Sahara). See Renzo De Felice, *Jews in an Arab Land: Libya 1835–1970*, trans. Judith Roumani (Austin: University of Texas Press, 1985, 2014); and Jacob Oliel, *Les Juifs au Sahara: le Touat au Moyen Age* (Paris: CNRS, 1994).

[Our passing through Isbilia had been just a detour. After Toledo, after Spain, and our centuries-long rootedness in Maghrebian lands, and our long loping from one side of the Mediterranean to the other, farewell Frimaldjézar.]

As with other writers, in Bensoussan's novel the Holocaust merges with the more recent trauma of the exile of Jews from North Africa.

For some writers in this intermediate generation, the Holocaust became mainly a plot motif in historical novels. The Tunisian-French novelist Nine Moati's *La passagère sans étoile* (Passenger without a Star, 1989)[10] tells of an assimilated Frenchwoman of Livornese-Tunisian origin (*gorni*, in Tunisian Judeo-Arabic) who escapes from the Nazis via a circuitous route, eventually returning to Paris only to witness her mother's arrest. She then joins the Resistance and participates in the rescue of Jewish children from France. The novel has a cinematic quality, with much action and changes of scene, and the heroine goes through a series of improbable coincidences managing to witness many major events of the war. Moati has her characters meet (and of course admire) the characters from the film *Casablanca*, while she figures in a novel by a famous English novelist. These fictional ploys undermine the apparent factualness of this historical novel and serve to distance the Holocaust.

A few recent Sephardic writers take steps toward bringing back a more direct approach to the Holocaust. Gini Alhadeff's *The Sun at Midday: Tales of a Mediterranean Family* (1997), an English-language memoir by an author born in Alexandria after the Holocaust, seems to be one of those Alexandrian novels celebrating a lost era of Mediterraneaness. Alhadeff's parents had the whole family converted to Catholicism and she did not know she had Jewish roots until the age of twenty. Thereafter she has been assiduously in search of identity:

10. Nine Moati, *La Passagère sans étoile* (Paris: Seuil, 1989). The title is obviously a double entendre on the heroine's not wearing her Jewish star and on not having a guide or destination for her travels, except that she is drawn back to Paris and her mother, though this is one of the most dangerous places for her to be.

a search that includes the specter of Auschwitz as chronicled in her uncle's newly discovered memoir, which occupies forty-five pages of her book. The identity she fixes on by the end entails total self-determination: she does not want to identify as Jewish just because Hitler would have considered her so.[11]

These other North African Jewish writers can all provide points of comparison, of similarity or contrast, with the novel of the Israeli writer Yossi Sucary, *Benghazi—Bergen-Belsen*. Published a few years ago (2013), it won a prestigious prize in Israel, and has been translated into English.[12]

This novel, like Sucary's previous fiction, focuses on characters closely resembling his mother and grandmother. Sucary's earlier confessional novel, *Emiliyah*,[13] dramatizes the first-person narrator's relationship with his grandmother, who emigrated to Israel from Benghazi, Libya. Such a vivid and engaging character manages to control her grandson's life even from beyond the tomb. Emiliyah and many

---

11. Gini Alhadeff, *The Sun at Midday: Tales of a Mediterranean Family* (New York: Pantheon, 1997), 102–47, the uncle's account of being a prisoner at Auschwitz. For an approach to other relevant Sephardic and Mizrahi writers, see my "Sephardic Literary Responses to the Holocaust," in Alan Rosen, ed., *Literature of the Holocaust* (Cambridge: Cambridge University Press, 2013), 225–37.

12. The Brenner Prize. It is interesting that some Libyan Muslim writers of short stories have taken note of the presence of Jews in Libya up to 1967, characterizing Jews in a not necessarily negative way. See Ethan Chorin, *Translating Libya: The Modern Libyan Short Story* (London: London Middle East Institute at SOAS, 2008), esp. story by Kamel Magur, 159–76, and analysis, 206–8. The Maronite Christian novelist of Benghazi, Alessandro Spina, who wrote a nineteenth-century-style vast psychological panorama of Libyan life in Italian, does not to my knowledge portray Jews in Libya in his novel, though he does examine interfaith (Muslim-Christian) relations in Cyrenaica in the Italian colonial period. His emphasis is on the moral limitations of the Italian rulers (specifically the army officers) stationed in Benghazi, and the despair and desperation of the Muslim nationalists, portrayed in one of his main characters.

13. Yossi Sucary, *Emiliyah u melah ha-Arets: Vidui* (Tel Aviv: Bavel, 2002). Also published in French translation: *Emilia et le sel de la terre: Une confession*, trans. Ziva Avran (Paris: Actes Sud, 2006).

of her fellow-migrants from Libya live in Pardes Katz, a neglected and depressing almost-suburb of Tel Aviv. Such neighborhoods have in the past bred delinquency and disaffection. Emiliyah regrets moving to Israel and wishes to be buried in her hometown, Benghazi. The narrator, whose relationship with the author may be questionable, likewise establishes his personal version of observing Israel's Memorial Day (Yom Hazikaron) when a siren sounds for Israelis to mark their respect for the memory of those who have died defending Israel. The narrator observes the two minutes of silence in memory of his grandmother, destroyed he believes by the State of Israel. The rest of the book relates to his psychological journey in search of identity, through yoga, French philosophy, German philosophy, American philosophy, a brief return to the religious belief of his ancestors, and finally to his opening a summer camp for the children of Pardes Katz—his issues with Israel and himself still unresolved. This book seems designed to shock, and therefore one turns to the next one with perhaps a certain trepidation.

Benghazi—Bergen-Belsen deals with the mother, more than the grandmother, but earlier in her life, and confronts issues of an earlier time that are entirely different. The resentment toward Israel does not come into being in this novel: Israel did not yet exist. The focus is on a young girl, here called Silvana, caught up in the events of the Holocaust as they affected her Libyan Jewish family between 1942 and 1945. She is a headstrong young girl who knows her own mind. Sucary tells the story sensitively and with restraint, but since this is a Holocaust story, readers know that we will eventually have to confront events "beyond the limit-experience."[14] In a postscript to the novel, Sucary thanks both an expert on Libyan Jewish culture, the historian Yaakov Haggiag-Lilluf, who shared his expertise about World War II and his fascinating knowledge regarding the fate of Libyan Jews, and

14. Title of a book by Gary Mole, *Beyond the Limit-Experience: French Poetry of the Deportation, 1940–1945* (New York: P. Lang, 2002).

Sucary's mother, who shared her story "sparing no detail, even if it caused her indescribable pain" (318).

The events of the novel take place in three different countries, Libya, Italy, and Germany, everything being filtered through Silvana's consciousness in this first-person narrative. The narrative is linear, as a Holocaust memoir often is, without confusing flashbacks or interruptions in the order of events. We understand Silvana's relations with each member of her family—mother, father, and sister Toni—and perceive how they evolve in each situation. We also see the constraints on a young woman in a Muslim country in the 1940s, even when it was a colony of Italy.[15] We understand her family's economic and social situation and learn that they have acquired British passports by living for a while in Egypt. The prized British citizenship, though, once the British army had twice been driven out of Benghazi, turned these indigenous Jews into enemies of the returning Fascist authorities and thus subject to reprisal. Silvana describes her father as a wealthy notable of the Jewish community, who may have been closer than many other Jews to the Muslims, and this seems to have given him a certain prestige. Silvana certainly has an immense love for her city of birth, Benghazi, for the Libyan Desert, and for the sea and beaches. She muses poetically that "just as the desert was a warm blanket that had covered her since childhood, the sea was the bed on which she lay. Its smell always healed her exhaustion. The sight of its waves washed away all hardships, distress and aches" (6).

During the initial part of the book, though, the family's close relations with Muslims change. We see the Muslims drawing back when these Jews are in danger from the Fascist/Nazi troops occupying Benghazi. Silvana's first encounter with a German is with a soldier who has a "vulture" on his cap. Her fears are soon realized as she is

15. Silvana's father, who is apparently quite liberal, tells her she can go anywhere she likes, but her mother tries to restrict her movements, especially forbidding her to go near the mosque. Silvana loves to go to the beach, but hides among the rocks, away from the eyes of the Muslim, Jewish, and Italian men.

arrested and imprisoned in the Italian school, and later she finds her family has been brought there too. They are allowed to return home, but a few months later, after the British once more attack and are driven off again, all the Jews are again arrested in reprisal. Just after they have been released from their first arrest, they see a tent nearby and realize it belongs to the son of a friend of Eliyahu the father, this friend being the head of one of the most important Muslim tribes in Cyrenaica. The son provides warm and respectful hospitality and arranges for the Jewish family to be transported back to Benghazi.

As punishment for collaborating with the enemy, most of the Jews of Benghazi are either imprisoned or deported. This time these British Libyan Jews are loaded onto trucks and transported across Libya to Tripoli. During the long journey, Silvana's father distinguishes himself. As the prisoner convoy halts for the night, somewhere along the road running parallel to the Gulf of Syrte (Ajdabiya), food, water, and shelter are not to be found either for the Italian soldiers, the Nazi guard and officer, or their prisoners. The father Eliyahu takes the initiative, requesting shelter and food from an Arab notable (another one of his contacts), owner of the best house in the village. The Jews receive the warmest and most lavish hospitality imaginable and the best room in the house. Their Italian and Nazi guards are also fed, and housed, but they have to sleep outside in the corridor. Thus, briefly, the old relations and mutual respect of Jewish and Muslim Libyans in the Ottoman era are reasserted, giving the somewhat depressed father a psychological boost. The family feels immense pride in him: "Silvana's father wasn't seen as a man who retrieved his authority with force, but as authority itself, returning to its natural dwelling following a period of forced exile" (102).

Soon, though, the prisoners become prisoners again. There are no righteous Muslims who hide the Jews from the Nazis and Fascists in this book, though Silvana imagines, and persuades her sister, that when they get to Tripoli, they will first go and stay with their Muslim friends and then return to Benghazi. There are, though, sympathetic and hospitable Muslims, as we have just seen. Silvana's father has no other ideas up his sleeve, and the convoy arrives in Tripoli, where the

Jews are hustled onto a boat (not a ferry boat but a cargo boat where they have to stay in the hold), which takes them to Naples. Fear sets in again and Silvana herself begins to show her leadership qualities, encouraging and animating where the older people seem incapable of doing so. All had dreamed of visiting Italy but not under such circumstances.

The second part of the novel covers the Benghazi Jews' imprisonment in Italy. Transported by truck from Naples, they are driven north to a castle in the hills of central Italy, a place called Civitella del Tronto, where after climbing a hill they are imprisoned in a building that had been used as a hospital, terribly hot in summer and terribly cold in winter. The two years of imprisonment take a psychological and physical toll on them. All are underfed, though they are allowed to send one person off to the village to buy some food to supplement their meager rations. At one point the men are sent off for forced labor, and Nino, the same young man who had been purchasing the rations, previously a religious and idealistic person, becomes a sort of kapo, betraying the others and incurring their hatred, all for the sake of better rations. Silvana and her sister spend months plotting an escape, but then the menfolk return; suddenly they are sent on to the transit camp of Fossoli in northern Italy, and shortly thereafter loaded onto a sealed transport to Bergen-Belsen. In all these moves, they are never told their destination, and not knowing this adds to their fear. There is a harrowing narrative of the experience on the train, eight days of agony until they arrive in Bergen-Belsen. Nino commits suicide on the train, and there is another death as well.

Despite the unbearable conditions, no one wants to leave the perceived safety of the train when they arrive at Bergen-Belsen. They do not know what sort of camp this is, and whether they are about to be murdered on the spot. Bergen-Belsen was actually a camp for supposedly privileged prisoners, such as these British citizens, but nevertheless thousands died from disease, starvation, or harsh punishment, as the horrifying pictures and accounts from its ultimate liberation attest.

At Bergen-Belsen, the debilitated and semistarving Libyan Jews are put to work. Families stay together, but the Libyan Jews suffer not only from Nazi oppression and punishment but also from prejudice from Ashkenazim, who call them "black Jews." After many months of suffering, the British subjects are suddenly removed to another camp, and so Silvana's family (except for the father, who had died) is saved. Silvana, however, is left behind, because she had spent the night in the barracks of an Ashkenazi friend. The book ends with the shooting execution of this friend by a sadistic guard, and a harrowing rape scene, just prior to Silvana's salvation by the arrival of the British. Silvana recovers in a hospital tent, then joins survivors in singing "Hatikvah." The dramatic aspects of the story have led a producer to stage a version of this novel in New York.

Sucary tries throughout to show a sense of solidarity among the Libyan Jewish women, especially within the family, and Silvana's close solidarity with her Ashkenazi friend, Rebecca, who gives her a reason to hope and to try to stay alive. The tragic death of the friend is because the guard imprisons them both for some minor infraction (stealing water) and gives the two friends an hour to make the terrible choice of which one of them should die. Rebecca has no more will to live, whereas Silvana wants to live, so the two of them make the decision together. After Rebecca's death, Silvana's rape by Dutch Ashkenazi male inmates shows that this female solidarity had been well-founded. The menfolk of the Libyan Jewish families also come off less well than the women, as we see their authority within the family gradually being eroded. Silvana's father, in particular, becomes less and less able to cope. The women are stoical, better able to deal with adversity, and more resourceful. There is a hint that men's relationships with each other are more fragile than women's, due to the men's inherent competitiveness. Silvana's father becomes depressed and eventually dies, perhaps of a heart attack, at roll-call time in Bergen-Belsen.

Silvana's own personality, her sister's, and her mother's all evolve and mature during the course of the book. From a rather reckless and what might be viewed as an irresponsible young woman, still not married at the age of twenty in Benghazi, she evolves into a mature and courageous leader of her people. She does not find a husband, as the traditionalists would have wished, but the way she relates to her times, and her evolving worldview, are portrayed with great insight and sympathy. She is very often conflicted in her emotions. Silvana also describes how her sister Toni (who had been a rather spoiled child who always took the route of comfort and expected others to cater to her needs), in the face of danger, showed a new determination and earned Silvana's respect for the first time. The mother does what little she can to help her family, masks her suffering under a blank face, and endures in silence. When she is beaten upon arrival at Bergen-Belsen, she does not even cry out. Silvana is always alert to her mother's expressions and moods, though, and is elated whenever her mother's face briefly is not suppressing pain. Silvana yearns for her support, taking her mother's hand and caressing her own hair with it, but the onus shifts to the daughter to be the moral support of the family. At one point in Bergen-Belsen, Silvana and her sister sense that the mother has given up and is likely to die of starvation and fatigue, and they decide never to leave her alone. The mother and sister are both saved by their transfer out of Bergen-Belsen to another, less arduous camp.

Unusually for a Holocaust novel, Silvana (or rather the author through her thoughts) discusses her sexual needs quite frankly. She conceives a passion for a Jewish soldier from the Palestine Brigade whom she saw at a community event in Benghazi when the Allies briefly controlled the city. The arrival of the Jewish soldiers from Palestine fighting with the British was a major community event, commemorated in many photographs of the time. She constantly hopes to find him again, and even hopes he has been taken prisoner so she can meet him in some prisoner of war camp. There are references to the sexual lives of prisoners even within Bergen-Belsen. It is a part of Silvana's personality that she is quite "forward" for her time and location, whether for her good or for her detriment, and the very discussion of such topics marks this novel as a twenty-first-century literary production rather than one of the time it describes.

Though this is a novel, there is no need to doubt its historical accuracy. It is generally thought that no Libyan Jews had died in Bergen-Belsen, which after all was not officially an extermination camp (though the conditions of starvation, maltreatment, and punishment were so harsh that thousands of Jews did die there). Sucary's text, nevertheless, tells us of several Libyan Jewish deaths, some of them peripheral to the camp experience. As the Libyan Jews climb up a hillside to the castle/hospital at Civitella del Tronto, their first prison, one old man passes away. The young man, Nino, accused of collaboration, commits suicide during the train journey from Fossoli to Bergen-Belsen. Eliyahu Hajaj, Silvana's father, collapses and dies at roll call, whether from exhaustion or a heart attack we do not find out. An old lady, Mama Regignano, is shot because no one in their group knows any word of Yiddish except Silvana, and she has forgotten the one word she knew. Then two others, a religious man called Meir and his sister, are shot by a Nazi guard for not moving fast enough. All the remaining Libyan Jews at Bergen-Belsen are subsequently moved to a more lenient camp for British prisoners of war at Biberach-an-der-Riss,[16] except for Silvana who is away from her tent and gets left behind. The threat of danger and death come not only from the Nazis but also from the Dutch kapos and inmates she then has to deal with, who hate and despise her as a "black Jew." It is a Dutch kapo who plays a cruel psychological game and then kills Silvana's only friend, a young Dutch girl, and several others rape Silvana. Her sufferings are thus commensurate with those of survivors who have seen the worst of the Holocaust. Primo Levi would have understood Sucary's unveiling of the "gray zone" where victims are morally contaminated by the same evil as their persecutors.

16. Biberach-an-der-Riss was a prisoner of war camp, primarily for British officers, and conditions were far better than in most Nazi camps. See *Encyclopedia of Camps and Ghettos*, ed. Geoffrey P. Megargee (Bloomington: Indiana University Press and USHMM, 2009). For historical background on Libya, see Patrick Bernhard, "Behind the Battle Lines: Italian Atrocities and the Persecution of Arabs, Berbers and Jews in North Africa during World War II," *Holocaust and Genocide Studies* 26, no. 3 (Winter 2012): 425–46.

This painful odyssey of the Benghazi Jews is enlivened through-out by Sucary's original style. As well as being realistic, his style is a lyrical or poetic one. His attempts to show how the psychological con-flicts going on in the mind and heart of Silvana lead to pure paradoxes in her expression. The more difficult her circumstances, the more she prefers to express herself in Arabic. In times of extreme violence, fear, or suffering, there is a Surrealist quality or a Cubist fracturing of real-ity. No doubt Sucary is familiar with Picasso's *Guernica* portraying the aerial bombing of a Spanish town. He is a writer who has read widely, and his other novel *Emiliyah* shows a character who is another alter ego of the author, most probably, and who likes to imagine him-self in the company of famous French writers, such as Albert Camus in Algeria, as he walks through the depressed Tel Aviv suburb where he spends much of his time. The fracturing of reality due to violence is an aesthetic technique also applied by an Algerian novelist writing at the time of the Algerian Revolution, Mohammed Dib in his *Qui se souvient de la mer* (*Who Remembers the Sea*) (1962).[17] In this novel, due to the effects of violence, the walls of the city shift, and the French soldiers resemble bulls or minotaurs. Sucary also portrays in a Picas-soesque style the dehumanization of the inmates brought about by the terrible, inhuman conditions of Bergen-Belsen:

> A doughy mass of people wandered before her; marionettes with flailing limbs, buckling knees, their skeletal arms flying in all direc-tions with no coordination, making growing and shrinking elliptic-cal shapes through the air, no direction or purpose, as if their loyal operators feared that if they paused, even for a moment, they would stop moving forever. (300)

After her mother and sister have been taken away, Silvana dreams of them, dreams that she is constantly chasing after them and unable to

---

17. Mohammed Dib, *Qui se souvient de la mer* (Paris: Les Editions du Seuil, 1962); trans. Louis Tremaine, *Who Remembers the Sea* (Washington, DC: Three Continents Press, 1985).

touch them because something like a magnetic field is repelling her from contact—an interesting image for the unbridgeable distance between them.

Whether or not Sucary has read Mohammed Dib's novel, which after all is not the only presentation of the dehumanization of war through aesthetic means, his own *Benghazi—Bergen-Belsen* portrays with great creativity and originality some important subject matter never before shown in fiction.

Silvana's ultimate decision to survive is also brought to us through a visual image, that of life as a scrambled photo album, in which one picture, that of the desert of Libya, stays in her mind and gives her the will to pull through:

> Images of her life blended before her, out of order, a photo album touched by some invisible, amused, and cruel hand that had rid it of any logical order of a life story. Silvana erased the images one by one, shaking herself out of them. One final blurry image from one of her last solitary desert excursions still flickered through her mind: the day when the desert seemed to pounce on itself like a storm, the camels galloping beyond the screen of sand, the darkness that took over the dunes, smudging them until it was pushed away by the rays of sun that sliced through it. Her desert, not far from Benghazi, the Sahara Desert, the place where the wind brought eternity and the single moment together to converge. All at once the will to live ignited within her, burning brightly. She had to stay alive. (307–8)

The unbearably painful result of these thoughts is that because of her choice Silvana has to see her friend die.

Sucary's novel recounting the sufferings of Libyan Jews during the Holocaust well deserved the literary prize it received in Israel, the Brenner Prize, and can take an honored place among North African Jewish novels of the Holocaust. Not only does it possess unique experimental aesthetic qualities and technique, as a psychological and historical novel it portrays the anguish of Sephardim/Mizrahim who were victims of the Nazis and a part of Libyan Jewish history of

116. Returning to Libya from Bergen-Belsen by train, ca. 1945. Courtesy of Yad Vashem photo archives.

which the rest of the Jewish world is hardly aware. In the last words of the novel, as Silvana sings "Ha Tikvah" with a group of other survivors after the liberation of Bergen-Belsen, she emphasizes her Arabic accent, as she says, "so they would all know: she too had been there!" (317).

13

• ◆ •

Libyan Jews between Memory and History

DAVID MEGHNAGI

*Trace the first page of the book with a red mark, because the
wound is invisible at first.*

—Edmond Jabès

Traces

It was taboo to talk during my childhood about the November 1945
pogrom. Everybody knew, nobody talked. I must have been three or
four years old. I pretend to be involved with my toys so I can listen
and understand better why there have been funerals in the dark, during the curfew, along a route protected by a cordon of armed troops
who did not intervene earlier and now were preventing the families
from following their dear ones to their last resting place. On the terrace on top of the house where I live, there is writing in white chalk:
"November 1945, the day of the *chomata*." With this term, two of my
brothers gave a name to the massacre (*pra'ot*) consisting of more than
130 verified deaths; dozens of mutilated corpses; synagogues burned
and desecrated; Torah scrolls pulled apart, torn up, and burned; pregnant women whose bellies were cut open; and children whose heads
were dashed against the walls.

Everything became enveloped in secrecy: the vivid memory of the
murders, as well as the resistance and the great exodus that involved
almost all the Jews of Libya. My parents are careful about what they
talk about when I am there. When my mother talks about it with

117. Jewish children outside the walls of Tripoli, late Ottoman or early Italian period. Courtesy of Hamos Guetta Collection.

her friends, I sharpen my ears. The older people use half phrases. I learned early to recognize the meaning of certain paraphrases and particular allusions in the conversations among older people, when the talk turned to 1945 or 1948. Sometimes, though, the veil of secrecy would lift in my mother's conversations with her friends.

The memories of the pogrom, secretly nursed, are oppressive. To lighten the anguish, I seek out the traces of another story, the Jewish self-defense effort that in 1945 fought back against the murderous crowd at the entrance to the Jewish quarter (the *hara*) and in 1948 came prepared for the next tragic appointment.

Among the many signs is the mass grave in a separate area of the cemetery, where there is a large tomb in memory of Mushi Fellah, a man of means who committed the imprudent act of confronting the murderous crowd by himself. On the occasion of a funeral, I always take the time to pause there in prayer. Twenty-two years later, in June 1967, during the weeks when we were shut up in our apartment, his nephew almost met the same fate.

My father was obsessed with the story of Giado, a place in the Jebel about 175 kilometers from Tripoli. He often talked about it with

118. Jewish archeological remains that are more than 2,000 years old, in a cave near Giado, Nafusa Mountains, Tripolitania. This photo is part of a photography project by a student from Libya, in cooperation with the World Organization of Libyan Jews. In Giado 2,600 Cyrenaican Jews were imprisoned in 1943, of whom 562 died due to Fascist maltreatment and were buried in the ancient Jewish cemetery. With thanks to the World Organization of Libyan Jews.

my mother. He did it in a roundabout way, using allusions. The Jewish community of Cyrenaica was interned in Giado on Mussolini's orders, under the accusation of sympathizing with the enemy. The crime was committed in a situation of total isolation, away from the public eye, against a defenseless population that was harshly oppressed by the racial laws and suffering from the war.

Strengthened by British support, the Sanusi brotherhood was a thorn in the side of the Italian occupying forces. Despite its violence, Italian colonialism had not been able to bring Cyrenaica to heel, and when the war broke out the brotherhood attacked Italian villages. The Jews, accused of sympathizing with the enemy, were deported en masse. More than six hundred people died from hunger, thirst, and illness—a third of the Jews of Cyrenaica. They would all have died of punishments, hunger, and maltreatment if the Allied forces had not arrived in time.

At that time, the truth about the mass exterminations was not yet in the public domain. Some people declined to use soap because of dubious rumors that the Nazis were using human fat to produce soap. Libyan Jews with British passports, about three hundred of them, were deported to Italy and from there to Germany. They were saved from extermination camps due to the fact that they were British citizens.[1] When they went home in 1945, their lives were turned upside-down again by a new pogrom.

During the war, in order to protect the population from the Allied bombings, the Jewish community built shelters at its own expense, but they were not adequate. Our house in Tripoli was destroyed by the bombings. Many Jews sought refuge in the interior of the country. Jews and Arabs shared fear and hope for a swift end to the war. My brother, who had been born only recently, fell seriously ill. Since my mother didn't have anything else, she fed him dates. "If he doesn't make it," she said to herself, "I won't leave him here in the desert. I'll take him to Tripoli and give him a Jewish burial." A mother's love, added to the newborn's will to live, triumphed. The date-based treatment was successful.

In Tripoli, the roof of a large synagogue, in which panicked people had sought refuge, collapsed on the people at prayer. A scene of carnage. It was not rebuilt, because in the meantime the Jews left Libya en masse. From the terrace roof of the Sla l'Kbira,[2] during the festivals of Rosh Hashanah and Yom Kippur, I would look inside: chairs scattered and broken, memorial lights for the deceased shattered. The sight of the Holy Ark, destroyed and empty, was shocking.

I try to counteract the thought of what has happened, and could happen again, with my imagination, by creating opposite events that relieve my anguish. In my imagination, I seek the traces of another

---

1. See the previous chapter on Yossi Sucary's novel, *Benghazi—Bergen-Belsen*.
2. The Great Synagogue of Tripoli.

history: Jewish self-defense, which in 1945 repelled the murderous crowd at the entrance to the Jewish quarter and in 1948 came
prepared.

The 1945 pogrom came unexpected, ferocious and sudden, after
the liberation, when hope had begun to pulse again and expectations
for a better life became more intense and for the country as a whole
a different and independent future became possible. For the Jews of
Tripoli, the pogrom was a fracture in time and space. After this, nothing could be the same again in Jewish-Arab relations. It was meticu-
lously prepared, with the houses and shops of Jews marked with chalk.
British troops intervened to reimpose order only on the third day,
when the worst had already happened.

What in the eyes of an outside observer would seem to be a sui-
cidal political move, casting a shadow over the future of the country
and its application for sovereignty, for Arab and Islamic nationalism
was an act of affirming identity, of questioning an entire order of values and hierarchies that the Turkish domination firstly, and Italian
colonialism secondly, had imposed. Unleashing destructive violence
against a defenseless minority is in this perverse logic an act of challenging the foreign power, its authority and legitimacy, to intervene
in relations between Muslims and Jews. It is a way of affirming the
Muslim "right" to dispose arbitrarily and freely of us Jews, who were
"guilty" of daring to challenge our "status." In the conception of
the Arab conquerors, Jews, Christians, and even Zoroastrians were
to be considered *dhimmi*, subject peoples authorized to practice their
traditions in exchange for an act of submission that entailed paying
special taxes and a juridical and moral status of inferiority. From this
condition of *dhimmi*, which at moments of crisis in the central power
would expose the Jewish community to great danger, one could only
escape by converting to Islam. The consequences would have been far
different if the uprising had turned against the British forces in the
country, who intervened only three days after the fearsome massacre
had started, after the Jewish population of the old quarter had managed to contain the attacks and repel them.

Napoleon the Jew and Sigmund Freud

I understood very soon, from my mother's accounts of the 1948 pogrom, that at that time she must have been already pregnant with me
and that the decision to call me David was not by chance. On that
warm May night, when my parents celebrated the birth of Israel by
conceiving me, in the old Jewish quarter people stayed awake until
very late. Despite fear and the certainty of a new pogrom materializing
on the horizon, which would fall on the community punctually, joy
had been reborn in people's hearts. My mother assembled my brothers
and showed them a blue and white flag, and she sang with them songs
of joy and hope.

My mother talked often about the "lost tribes." She was convinced that they were hidden in some secret part of the planet, waiting for redemption by the Messiah. "At the end of time," she would
often say, "they too will make their return to Zion." The sound of
the shofar will reverberate on Mount Zion, and according to proph-
esy the peoples will forget the art of war. Reading Isaiah, and for
me also the Song of Songs, is an inexhaustible source of thoughts,
dreams, and emotions.

On the wall of the hallway to our home my father had put the
photo of Muni el Gabbay in full view—a strong man who had died at
a young age due to many blows. His long mustache extended an aura
of protection over us all. In Tripoli we remembered him with pride,
even though when he was in prison not many people were concerned
about the fact that his mother did not have enough money to prepare
her Shabbat. The idea that Muni was related to our father reverberated
an aura of security over our fragile home. For me it was as if Muni were
still alive. He would join together with us and protect us if they tried to
break into our undefended house. The idea that the dead are engaged
in a permanent dialogue with the living has not left me, and it later became the basis of my therapy's approach to trauma and the processes of
resilience. Even when we are completely alone, we are really not alone.
Those who have preceded us, toward whom we are fully responsible,

no less than to the living, and to those who will come after, watch over us and need protection.

My father lost everything in the war. His house collapsed under the bombs. He had lost his father when he was a child, and he lost his mother during Mussolini's visit in 1938. The balcony collapsed beneath the weight of the people on it. He saw his mother say the Shema during her last moments. My father had got married shortly before, and my mother was pregnant with my brother Simone. On the wall, my father kept a prominent picture of Napoleon. Against all evidence, he maintained that Napoleon was Jewish and that he kept his identity secret in order to help his less fortunate fellow Jews. To confirm his belief, my father recalled that many Jews in Spain had concealed their true identity to protect themselves from persecution. Moreover, Napoleon had made a "Zionist" declaration in which an appeal was made to the Jews of the world to reestablish their home-land in Zion. Those were sufficient proofs for my father. It did not matter that Napoleon then forgot all about his declaration and that subsequently he did not have the problem on his mind. Ottoman troops, assisted by the British, halted Napoleon and obliged him to return to Egypt, where his ships were attacked and destroyed. After the Egyptian project, by which he had hoped to subdue Great Britain, was abandoned, and after another victory over the Turks, Napoleon quickly returned to Paris where he assumed absolute power. Instead of Napoleon, it was the British who entered Jerusalem in celebration, prefiguring what would happen a century later during World War I. Perhaps for my father. Napoleon's defeat had an explanation in his name? I would have liked to ask him, but he is no longer alive. In Hebrew, *nofel* means "to fall." Napoleon ended his life as a prisoner and in exile because, unlike the British leaders, he did not have a sense of limits.

The idea that Napoleon was Jewish has no basis. But one should not overlook the way my father used to give credit to his arguments. In his reckless thought patterns, my father had far more authorita-tive comrades. A genius like Freud, who has revolutionized our way of thinking, used similar arguments to support the idea that the

Napoleonic general Massena was allegedly of Jewish origin because of the assonance of his name with the Hebrew name Menasheh. The subject matter is different, but the procedure is similar. It goes back to the ancient Jewish custom of opening the Scriptures to new meanings. Born in the Talmudic academies, this technique had been used by Freud to analyze his own and his patients' dreams.

Between Colonialism, Fascism, and Arab Nationalism

For Jews of the Arab world, that world's encounter with European colonialism meant a chance for emancipation from centuries of oppression, insecurity, and humiliation. Because these changes did not come from within Arab society, they were overloaded with ambiguities and ambivalence. Arab nationalism was organic. The Islamic *'umma* ("community of the faithful") was now replaced by the Arab nation from which Jews were excluded. From the Mashreq to the extreme edges of the Maghreb, the mere desire to "emancipate" and be considered like any other citizen was a crime. Any jurisprudential change was regarded by the Islamic majority as an attack on the values of the *'umma*, a violation of an "immutable" social order. Liberalism in the Arab countries was kept away from the masses, trapped by the bonds with colonial and traditional power.

Only the regimes in the Arab world where traditional elites retained their power more firmly have shown tolerance toward their minorities. These are usually authoritarian monarchies with a strong religious legitimacy (Morocco is an example), which resisted the repercussions of pan-Arab radicalism and Islamic fundamentalism. As with pan-Slavist nationalism, Arab nationalism excluded Jews. As it happened in Germany at the time of the wars of liberation against the Napoleonic domination, the emancipation of the Jews gradually took on the meaning "catastrophic" for the *'umma* values, an alteration of its "natural" balance. Long before Zionism became a movement of national revival, and hostility and bias against Israel and its existence became ideology, pogroms took place in almost every area of the Arab world.

The relationship between Jews and Arabs in Libyan traditional society was characterized by constitutive ambivalence that, in times of crisis and weakness of central power, could lead to dangerous, life-threatening consequences. It is not a coincidence that in the history of the Jews from Tripoli, next to the official Purim, which tells the story of Esther and the miraculous rescue from Hamman's murderous project, there are two other Purims related to the history of the local community and its escape from mortal danger. In the more tolerant version of Islam, the Jews were the *dhimmi*, "subjugated" people entitled to "protection" in exchange for a subordinate, humiliated condition. To avoid violence and destruction, the Jews *had to stay in their place*. Regardless of the economic and social status achieved, such a condition was considered immutable. In a society where men and women were completely separate, where women could not show their face in public, the Jews were considered and perceived as "men deprived of their manhood," as "women." For this reason, unlike Muslims, in the eighteenth and nineteenth centuries Jewish peddlers could interact with Arab women for the sale of their merchandise. The specialization of the Jews in some branches of trade was also the result of this social condition.

As in the rest of the Arab world, the changes in the moral and legal enslavement of the Jews to the Arab majority were the result of events outside Arab society, first more timidly with the Ottoman conquest and then with the Italian conquest. The Arab failure to accept the changed environment, and to rework and revise it as the critical factor in reestablishing relationships with groups and individuals sharing different religious and cultural attachments, had devastating consequences.

With the Ottoman reconquest of Libya from the Qaramanlis Jews ceased to belong to the Arabs. Finally, they could rely on a centralized power to protect them from the harassment that had continually victimized them, especially in the country's interior. During the Ottoman period, the social and civil rights of Jews improved considerably compared to the preceding centuries. The hostile reaction unleashed against them because of these changes was partially mitigated by the Islamic character of the governing authorities, to whom they turned for protection.

But once the Italians arrived, other Muslims no longer dominated Arabs. Instead "infidels" now were invading the sovereignty of the *'umma*. In this new situation, Jews were doubly suspect. The Arabs interpreted Jews' improved social standing as a "sinister" development, disrupting centuries of asymmetrical relations resting on the domination and oppression of religious minorities.

This explains why, notwithstanding the violent persecution suffered by the Jews, the period of Italian rule is remembered in the collective memory as a time when their legal subjugation by the Arabs was suspended. The Fascist persecution happened during wartime. Having experienced both pain and persecution previously, it was seen as just a fact of life. According to popular perceptions, which failed to fully take into account the reality of the situation, all of this was mistakenly considered as "a consequence" of war.

Jews saw the arrival of the Italians as promising change and improved living conditions. On the other side, the new rulers initially saw the Jews as a bridge for the Italian population. But their viewpoint changed quickly, long before the regime embraced anti-Semitic and racist policies. From the very beginning, Italy's colonial policies were contradictory. First, there was a desire to quickly integrate Jews and to advance Italian policies in the Mediterranean area. But then the Italians worried about antagonizing Arabs. Following this, they sought Arab nationalist support for the Axis cause. As a consequence, Jews were becoming the paradigmatic scapegoat: on one side suspected by the Arabs for favoring Italy and on the other rejected by the colonial government, following the new anti-Semitic policies of the 1930s. They became a target for the discontent and violence arising from a fractured social order and value system once considered immutable.

What proved truly traumatic for the Jews of Tripoli was seeing how the few shopkeepers who dared challenge the colonial regime's order to remain open on Shabbat were publicly whipped in the town squares. These occurrences were not only the end of a dream but also a prelude to further tragedies and suffering.

This decision of Governor Italo Balbo reflected the policies of forced Italianization, aiming to change the customs and practices in

Libya. With the extension of the anti-Semitic laws of 1938 to Libya as well, from one day to the next Jews were forbidden to attend public schools, work for the government, or use public transportation.

In the collective Jewish memory, the contemptuous crowds of Italians and Arabs applauding triumphantly the public whippings and the newspaper headlines announcing "Tripoli is not Tel Aviv" represented a grim omen. If from one day to the next Jews could be publicly humiliated, then anything could happen. Certainly, it signaled the end of a world in which Italians had appeared to be their guardians. By disseminating seeds of hate, the Italians advanced the idea that open hostility to Jews was legitimate. These events were a prelude to the brutality that unfortunately claimed the Benghazi Jewish community, whose members were deported and confined to the Giado internment camp located south of Tripoli.

The Liberation

With the arrival of the British Army, the Jewish community shed the nightmare of the anti-Semitic laws, the deportations and the bombings, the forced labor, and the reprisals. But had the Axis offensive at El Alamein succeeded, the destruction would have affected the Yishuv as well.[3] As became known later, mobile gas chambers already tried out on the eastern front with the Soviet Union were ready in Athens. Incited by the radio broadcasts from Berlin and Bari of the Jerusalem Mufti Haj Amin al-Husseini, there were also nationalist Arabs along with Islamic irredentists who on their own account would have preceded the Germans, just as they did in Baghdad where a pro-Nazi government had been briefly installed.

The offices of the young Jewish Zionists reopened the morning after the liberation from Fascist rule. And thus began a race. Since the 1920s, Jews had wondered what were the chances of leading a mass return of Libya's Jewish community to the land of their fathers. The aspiration to return to Zion always was considered by a majority of the

3. The name for Zionist settlement in Palestine prior to the State of Israel.

Jewish population an essential element of their cultural and religious identity. In Tripoli, Zionism was experienced as a universal identity. A return to Zion would be the completion of a historical cycle rooted in both prayer and the collective dreams of an entire nation, where both the ancient and the modern converged. The rabbis were occupied in the front ranks in teaching modern Hebrew. Meanwhile the Zionists won a majority in the community elections. Meetings with Jewish soldiers of the Yishuv, who were part of the British Eighth Army, generated enthusiasm. Resuming their activity, the Jewish Zionist associations reenergized themselves. From the Maccabi to Ben Yehudah, from the Scouts to the Zofim and the youth organization Hechalutz, all were buzzing with hopeful new initiatives. They studied Hebrew with passion while also composing mystical and religious songs. They translated the most beautiful love songs from Arabic to Hebrew. Meanwhile the Yishuv organizations took care of the children, preparing them for their new life.

The Pogroms of 1945 and 1948

Following the British Army's arrival, foreign cadres returned, representing elements of Arab nationalism (red fez–wearing Syrians, Palestinians, and above all Egyptians, commonly employed by the police auxiliary services). This created a situation loaded with danger. Raising the specter of a "Zionist plot," Arab nationalism solidified the envy and frustration of the Arab street together with the material interests of the emerging economic strata. Jew hatred perversely affirmed their identity: it was a way of saying that in an independent Libya of the future there would be no room for Jews. The severing of economic ties with Italy, the drought, and the subsequent overflowing of the banks of the local *wadis* created a background scenario that shortly could have become a nightmare.

Following news of anti-Jewish riots in Cairo and Alexandria in 1945, groups of local Arabs proceeded to mark the shops and homes of Jews with chalk. This was the start to a bloody pogrom that caught the Jewish population off guard. The British Army took three days to intervene after the worst had already occurred. Meanwhile the Arab population had been led to believe by the ambiguous and often complicit police forces that the pogrom implicitly had been authorized.

After a farcical reconciliation ceremony, there were reports that the Jewish minority's absence from the Libyan independence movement would serve as a pretext for the British mandate to delay the country's independence. In a somewhat similar vein, American Jewish organizations demanded that the British presence be used as leverage to incorporate into the constitution guarantees to protect minorities in the new state.

Tensions flared to a new height three years later, in 1948, when hundreds and then thousands of Arabs arrived, all heading east to join the Arab armies in the war against the new state of Israel.

This time, however, the Jewish population was not taken by surprise. Groups of boys and girls, trained in secret in expectation of conflict, openly challenged the aggressors. Responding to their female leader's cry of "Giat al Haganah!" (The Haganah has arrived!), they were at the ready with boiling oil to pour on those forcing their way into the Jewish neighborhood, with knives and stones and some pistols and grenades. Unprepared for the Jews' response, the crowd of pogromists retreated in disorder, leaving behind their dead and wounded. Repulsed by the Jews of the old city, the aggressors tried the same thing with the Jewish families in the city's new neighborhoods.

In contrast to 1945, the army intervened almost immediately, re-establishing order. But any coexistence between the two communities had ended forever. A stream of desperate Jewish people converged on Tripoli from every direction, not wanting to return home to their small, unprotected communities. The evacuees slept on the streets, in the alleyways, and in the courtyards of the synagogues. For those who didn't have even a roof to sleep under, Israel's birth was a dream of redemption. Even for those who had never given it any thought, more than two millennia of Jewish life in Libya was reaching its end. By now it was clear that in the future Arab state there would be no room for Jews. The exile was transformed into an exodus, with a jolt of pride and redemption. The pain and suffering were sublimated.

Whoever owned anything sold it at fire sale prices, liquidating everything for almost nothing. In exchange for selling out their businesses as craftsmen, skills that had rendered Jews famous in the entire Arab world, the Jewish community and the British acting as mediators negotiated with the future Arab leaders the total divestiture of all Jewish businesses. They accepted something that in no normal country could have happened. The Jews would be able to freely leave the country while the Arabs wouldn't suffer undue harm. Following this surreal logic, the Jews would exit the country in the name of a dream, while the Arabs would get rid of them forever at no economic cost.

For Jews, their pain reflected the times, the birth of a new era. A messianic time with its labor pains at the gates (*Chevele Mashiach*). Such suffering was the price for a better and more just world, where a Jew could live freely. The oldest fears collided against hope, producing frenzied expectations that had seized their hearts. Defying the sea, hundreds of boats departed for Eretz Israel between 1945 and 1948. In their songs they invoked God's name, praying for calm seas as they risked their lives on improvised crafts. To avoid the British coastal gun emplacements, they swam to the fishing boats and cargo ships on which they booked passage. In the narrow alleyways full of refugees and in the homes they sang: "Mahla hassafra ba'd al 'id amcia l'bhar ic'nna" (How beautiful is the departure after the holidays—Pesach and Shavuot—when the seas are placid), "Li 'andu mliunin ma'mscisc l'lbalestin, imscilà kan al mskin, iqs al lim ui'esh senior" ("Those with two million won't go to Palestine; the impoverished will go there and pick oranges and will live like the rich").

For many, the most precious valuables were a blanket and some aluminum pots, some olive oil, a kitten or a small dog that they couldn't live without, a siddur (prayer book), and some geranium and saffron seeds to plant in the land of their fathers.

The fragrance of those geraniums helped make everything awaiting us less excruciatingly painful: severing ourselves from our birthplaces; rendering familiar the mythical places to which we were returning; shrinking the gap between the promises of redemption and the reality of tough Israeli life in the fifties and sixties, with its tent cities (*ma'abarot*) such as Beit Lid, Tel Litvinski, Mahane Israel, and the development town Bat Yam. Today, just as it did a half-century ago, the geranium leaf still serves to enhance the scent of our coffee and to bless the arrival of Shabbat.

The Postwar Period

On the eve of the great exodus for Israel, the community numbered about 35,000 to 40,000 Jews out of a total population of under one million. They overwhelmingly lived in Tripoli, but some also came from the interior of the country. Following the exodus of at least 36,000 between 1948 and 1951, a few more than 4,000 remained, of which about half possessed a foreign passport. The very first to leave were the poorest who had lost everything, which meant all hope of returning to their homes or to their villages if they came from the country's interior. On the other hand, of those who remained, more than a fourth were destitute.

The gathering in of the last drops of the exodus was only a question of time. Rising pan-Arabism and the intensifying Mideast crisis became ever more salient. One could also include the violent and perverse achievement of creating hatred through the politics of "identity." Moreover, wider geopolitical concerns were now a factor. Hatred of the Jews, "guilty" of violating the taboo of Omar, was about to be transferred to an entire nation collectively "guilty" of building a Jewish state on land "originally" Islamic. Half a century earlier, Muslims massacred the Armenians for having attempted to do something similar. Abandoned by a Russia convulsed by disturbances that eventually led to the tsarist regime's collapse, Armenians were left isolated and abandoned by the world to be exterminated by Turkey. Even today they are still awaiting restitution and acknowledgment.

In Tripoli during the fifties, even a simple basketball game could threaten the precarious equilibrium with the Arabs. Cheering Arab fans playing against a Jewish or Italian team could never accept losing. When we played among ourselves and one side lost, it was never a problem; we would continue to be friends and greet each other. But with the Arabs if we won there was the risk that it would end in being pummeled. That such things also happened at the stadium transformed sports into a caricature. One time during a summer tournament at the New Lido, the members of the Basketer team, captained by my brother Simon, had to flee the basketball court and stadium without changing their clothes. Infighting among Arab fans was the rule. But when it concerned a match with a foreign or Jewish team, the Arab fans suddenly united. It became a conflict over "identity." Whenever an Arab team lost, violence inside and outside the stadiums could not be excluded. As our insecurity worsened, an unwritten rule required our beloved team to lose the tournament. A Jewish victory might cost too much. The late Rahmin Fellah[4] learned this during a heated game when the Jewish team Aurora violated the unwritten rule that it must lose whenever it played the team Ittichad. Aurora, which emerged from the great and glorious Maccabi Club that was legally dissolved, had its days numbered. But even when most of its team members left to join Ahli, an Arab team, winning the tournament was still denied them.

The end of Jewish organized sports was approaching, but in the two-year period from 1959 to 1960 the coup de grâce arrived. The law forbade a team from hiring more than a certain number of "foreign" players. Even though the Jewish players were undoubtedly Libyan, they had to be assigned to multiple Arab teams to the point of becoming invisible. Retreating from the country's public life to protect their collective and personal security was becoming the most elementary precaution, a kind of Golden Rule for Jews. The Jews would never have been permitted to identify themselves using the symbols of the new Libyan nation even if they had wanted to do so. We could say we were Libyans, but never Arabs nor Muslims. Ultimately, this counted most in defining national identity.

As a boy I instinctively identified with the struggle of the Algerian people. So, violating an unwritten rule, I was unable to resist going

---

4. Raffaello Fellah, president and founder of the Association for Libyan Jewry, which represented the rights of Libyan Jews in Italy after 1967.

119. Tripoli town, 1959. Courtesy of Hamos Guetta Collection.

to an exhibit in support of the Algerian struggle, wanting to be able to understand what was going on. There I met a young Algerian who recounted his life to me. I, however, was unable to do the same. The good feelings that at the age of ten drove me to attend the exhibit encountered an immovable barrier: I was forced to add another country to the long list of countries already boycotting Israel. Of this I was certain. And in case I would have forgotten, a crowd of demonstrators was there to remind me. After having cursed France, they hurled the most violent slogans against Israel, which felt like driving blades into my heart.

Though Jews were not allowed to participate in the new oil industry, conditions indirectly improved for everyone. It reduced the number of poor families in our community to forty. Jews occupied a significant presence in Tripoli, and the many families who moved to the city's new neighborhoods highlighted this change in their social status. But as living conditions improved, so did our sense of insecurity. Those who boasted about their powerful connections and enjoyed the dubious privilege of attending some official ceremonies suffered from illusions. Our insecure position rested on a political class condemned by historical change and increasing political upheavals that would end up making us strangers and foreigners in our own country.

An Internal Migration

After independence was declared, those Jews having the right to vote were careful not to exercise it. Similarly, the Jewish community leadership refused, out of fear, to accept funds for a group of elderly and sick Jews who had neither relatives nor work and were waiting to leave for Israel. Accused of subversion, the community regretfully felt compelled to shut down the Maccabi Club. When the government suspended postal service with Israel, we still could take some comfort in using friends and acquaintances living in Italy to maintain contact. Soon afterward (1960–1961), a series of rules targeting both "non-Libyan" persons and businesses extinguished their right to buy property. Import-export agents, of whom four hundred were Jewish, were restricted to representing no more than ten clients. Moreover, in sympathy with the Algerian independence struggle, they imposed a boycott on importing French products. The discriminatory character of the regulations was most apparent in the unwritten rule of public notaries and the judicial branch to restrict Jews, whether Libyan citizens or not, from any involvement whatsoever in the petroleum industry and acquiring property.

Jews, furthermore, could not be employed in public administration. In the private sector any productive activity, including buying land, required that a Jew had to hire an Arab partner. These frontmen became the actual owners of the assets. For the Arab elite all this served to expel Jews from the country's economy. Following a ruthless logic, each step carefully prepared for the next one. Of course the bureaucracy's pervasive corruption and disorganization somewhat slowed the process.

Not satisfied with seizing only the assets of those who had fled the country, the state sought total control, evidenced by the decree of December 1958. Some two years later, in March 1961, the state placed all Jewish property belonging to those who had left in the massive exodus under its "custody." From that moment, even possession of photographs of the emigration from one decade earlier could pose a danger. Fear had become so widespread that even talking about one's relatives in Israel became taboo. In this atmosphere, my father sought to destroy any evidence whatsoever of past contacts with our relatives. Postcards needed to be burned and then flushed down the water pipes in the bathroom. We spent an entire night getting rid of photos of our Israeli relatives and letters from them; every kind of greeting card imaginable, which we had long valued as precious. For me these souvenirs served as not just memory-laden fragrances of the past but enunciated promises of a different future, which I would hear each time sirens from the port preannounced a departing ship. That siren sound of a ship setting sail still takes me back in time, to my childhood dreams, to the angst and hopes of a different life full of joy, happiness, and freedom. As a boy I spent hours at the port, hanging out and watching ships set sail. I imagined the day when I would leave my country forever and be reunited with those who had left before I was born, those who had held me in their arms when I was a child, and I was cared for every day by doctors sent by Israel to aid our community in preparation for the great exodus. Our house was not far from the port, and whenever my mother heard the siren I heard her repeat in a low voice, "Ah ya Rabbì al 'Ali smma'na has Al Maschiah" ("O omnipotent King, let us hear the Messiah's voice").

Our old *hara*, Tripoli's Jewish quarter, with its derelict houses, where going about was no longer particularly safe, was in my opinion more interesting than the city's new section with its wide boulevards and gardens. Searching for traces of a past that had been taken away, I was keeping alive hope for a different future. My mother's tears that inevitably followed the singing welcoming in the Shabbat were heartbreaking. In Israel we would have rediscovered the lost wholeness of our lives. While waiting to emigrate, I used to explore the narrow streets of the old Jewish quarter looking for pieces of the life that had been stolen from me. With its old houses of prayer, the beauty of the narrow streets and alleyways drenched with dreams surpassed that of the small Royal Palace. When I would stop to pray or study in the *hara*, it seemed as if I was with the grandparents I never knew and the angels who accompanied them to the land of our fathers, and they were with me. This was a secret I confided in no one. On Shabbat I went from one synagogue to another searching for wisdom from a distant past. Sometimes I would come in the morning and only leave at sunset, other than a break for lunch. More often I would spend Shabbat afternoon until late in the day in a synagogue where we learned Talmud. Because my grandfather had learned Talmud there, it meant a lot me.

In that synagogue I learned what it means to think freely. An elderly and revered rabbi who had been deported to Bergen-Belsen did not spend his time questioning God for His "silence" concerning Auschwitz. It was evident that speaking that way about God pained him. Clearly for him God was everything, and for this reason we turned to him like a secret friend. Those who sat around him listened in silence, both concerned and worrying whether the youngest would hear what he was saying. I understood within my deepest self that Jews can challenge God, and no matter what they wished, they couldn't avoid doing so. To protest signals the apotheosis of a faith overcoming its initial period of naiveté. Did not our patriarch Abraham plead for divine *pietas* to spare an evil city, only because of the mere possibility that a few righteous and innocent people might be living there? And didn't Jacob struggle with the Angel to gain a blessing? Had not Job shouted at God, pouring out all of his anger and pain, only in the end to earn both his attention and gratitude? A Midrash—saying far more than its authors would have realized—describes God as existing because of what man does to make his existence possible. God exists wherever a heart and a home welcome him.

How I would have liked to have been born one or two generations earlier. I could have had some great teachers with whom to study Talmud and the Zohar. In the more distant past there had been some major ones. Two were Rabbìs Shim'on Labi and Yehudah Labi. My mother, who was a Labi, often went to pray at Yehudah Labi's tomb, bringing with her food for the elderly and needy. Some said they would speak with the angels and that their memory is passed from one generation to the next. This story permeated the tales of the old women who lived near the now-deserted synagogues once attended by the old sages.

Mystics said that a chant is like a pitcher, a vessel; a chant breaks the pitcher, it then mends the crack, freeing the sparks trapped in the *kelipot*, after the Breaking of the Divine Vessels (*Shvirat Hakelim*). A well-delivered *Keter* in the *Musaf Tefillah* on Yom Kippur was an event worthy of comment, and there would be weekly comments on the delivery of the prayers, celebrating the triumph of someone who had a beautiful voice. I loved being in the synagogue, full of joyful children for the holidays, especially the festival of Shavuot (the Jewish Pentecost) when children joined the women to spray rosewater and orange blossom essence. A time to indulge in almond milk drinks (*orzata*) and almond torte (*bocca di dama*) and for judging who could best recite the Aramaic commentary to the "Song of Songs."

At fourteen, I was a recognized *hazzan*. I was overjoyed when my non-Jewish high school teacher, who treated with great respect my absences from school on Saturdays, accepted my invitation to a Jewish religious service. It meant that for him we were not invisible, since he described the scene in his published memoirs.[5]

In Tripoli, whenever someone died, the mourning period affected the entire community. To help console the family members of the deceased, the custom was to say *khla'lkm l'brakha* ("May his memory be a blessing"). Mother and father have departed, but the void has been filled with their blessing and its afterglow will affect future generations. These words accompanying bereavement helped dull the pain. On Yom Kippur, along with all of the deceased relatives, everyone remembers the community's sages. As we stand and listen in silence, the names of the giants of past generations are called out. Out of respect, as each name is called, the men kiss the tzitzit on their tallits. In that solemn moment we were not alone, we are not alone, but are joined by all of the preceding generations since the dawn of time.

---

5. A. Proia, *Impressioni di viaggio (1955–2002)* (Minturno, Latina: Caramanica, 2006), 42.

When I was a child I knew everything about Purim Shushan, the story of Esther, Mordekhai, and the evil Haman. But if I asked about the origins of our Purim Katan, Purim Sherif, and Purim Burghul—which we affectionately called *Burim G'abuni* (Mock Purim), to distinguish it from the real Purim, which provided the model, according to schemes of meaning for the most important historical event of the Diaspora—very few people could give me any enlightenment. I knew in a general way that a few generations earlier the Jews had experienced great danger but the divine hand had saved them and, for that reason, we celebrated a holiday. As for the story, understood in its modern sense, we only had a vague idea.[6] History as a discipline did not belong to my country. It was family memory that dominated. Even those of our rabbis who were most aware of this aspect backed up that story. Unfortunately the knowledge was not accessible at home or in my school, so I had to improvise.

Linguistic Games

I had developed my own system to pass from one language to another. I had noticed that sometimes it was enough to change an *s* into a *sh*, a *b* into a *v*, to find the same word. From the Arabic *shamsi* (in our dialect *sams*, sun) one could pass to the Hebrew *shemesh*, from *'abd* (servant) to *'eved*, from *f'al* (merits) to *mif'al* (enterprise, establishment). Not having much vocabulary, I began performing similar journeys from Hebrew to Aramaic: from *baruch* (blessed) I arrived at *berikh*, from *shem* (name) to *sheme*, from *'olam* (world, forever) to *'alma*. The game could also be played from Italian to English. I had noticed that in order to pass from Italian to English, in many cases it was enough just to subtract a suffix at the end. From *stazione* one could arrive at *station*, *inaugurazione* would give *inauguration*, *situazione* would yield *situation*, and so on. As I have discovered many years later, I was not alone in my linguistic games. A Syrian musician, whom I

---

6. For a historical/anthropological approach to these events, see chapter 11 by Harvey Goldberg in this volume.

met many years later in Rome, would do the same thing to get from English to Italian.

Without realizing it, I was retracing the imposing work that Jewish grammarians had done in the Middle Ages for the Hebrew language, starting from Arabic, as well as Noam Chomsky's work on transformational grammar. I discovered all of this much later when I was working on the great Tibbon family, who translated from Arabic into Hebrew, and studying the marvelous compositions of Yehuda Halevi and Ibn Gabirol, who translated from Arabic into Hebrew, full of love and nostalgia. All of this, in the mind of a teenager hungry and feverishly thirsty for knowledge, was accompanied by the belief that Adam and Eve spoke Hebrew, and that before the confusion of languages, the human race spoke one language and it was the language of the Bible; this belief is still fascinating to me. Such diverse ideas and systems, such as that by looking at a man's shadow one could know how many years he still had to live, were able to coexist in the world that I grew up in.

How to get from one language to another is a subject that could occupy me for hours. It was my oasis in which I celebrated my personal triumph over the absurdity of the world I was living in. I could pass freely between the worlds I had grown up in and the cultures in which I was being formed. In this world of mine, people did not hate each other if they spoke different languages and did not follow the same religions. I considered these differences as riches that could be exchanged.

Marriage ensured the succession of generations, the perpetuation of last names and first names, and so parents always had precedence. Kashrut was respected, but the number of people who were not ashamed to be seen in a car on the Sabbath was increasing. Except for one or two "rebels," the Jews' shops all remained closed on Saturdays, while Christians closed on Sundays. The Libyan authorities imposed the Friday afternoon closing on everyone. Marriages took place almost entirely within the religious group one belonged to, usually between persons of the same social status. It was a huge scandal if things were not like that.

The use of the Italian language was a distinctive sign of status, one that separated us in the end from the country in which we were born. Within the circle of people of European culture, our dialect was disdained. Any Jew who attended the Italian high school did everything to show himself more Italian than the Italians in mastery of the language.

Our beautiful pronunciation of the "r" was a shibboleth, and at school there were some who did everything to hide it, hoping to make their difference less obvious. There were also some who would pathetically pronounce the "r" in the French way.

In our dialect, I could decline an Italian word as if it were Arabic, and I could conjugate an Arabic verb as if it were Italian. It was an oasis in which a Jew could feel Italian or Maltese, Greek or Arab, while continuing to be Jewish. It was a great interior treasure that not everyone realized they had. In our dialect, I was free to put the Italian pronouns after Arabic words and vice versa; I could pass from one linguistic code to another or change the structure of a sentence, depending on whom I was talking to, and with the same interlocutor in certain situations. I could ask "Kif halk?" (How are you?) and hear myself answered in three different ways that reflected the deep changes going on in our lives. "Hal bai Hamdu L'lla" (I am fine thank God), "Hali buono ringraziamo Dio"; "Sto bene baruch Ha-Shem."

Arabic grammar and Italian grammar could combine randomly with English grammar. Passing from one linguistic code to another was like traveling across different continents and cultures. The letters and words of our dialect, the combinations within it, revealed our geographic and cultural journeys, the differences within a single family, the different psychic provinces that entered into contact between the family members. The letters and words that were chosen were worlds that one could pass through rapidly, and the linguistic combinations revealed our cultural history and its internal dramas. They showed in synchrony the changes that we had faced, the direction that our life was taking in the face of historical forces that we did not control and that were contributing to sealing our destiny, making us strangers and estranged in our own country, a country that we had lived in for centuries and millennia. They indicated that we were suspended between an uncertain Europeanization and a rejection that one could breathe in the very air.

In the proposition "Ringraziamo Dio," the obligation to always thank God came in a new language, which was already an indication of a cultural passage toward new linguistic codes and behavioral models. In the Hebrew version "Baruch 'Shem" (or more exactly "Baruch Ha-Shem"), we observe the basic rule never to pronounce the Name in vain: "'Hamdu L'lla' took us to the heart of the Muslim world. Thirty years later, the same people, meeting in Rome, New York, or Tel Aviv, could reformulate the same phrase, perhaps inserting an English term instead of an Italian one, a Hebrew word instead of an Arabic one. I can attest to hearing exactly that, in the following exclamations of two women from Tripoli who ran into each other in New York after almost forty years: 'Eize surprise, 'amlcili, Sono veramente frhana to meet you!'"

The two women had left Tripoli at the beginning of the 1950s, rebuilding their lives in the United States and Israel. The exclamations were a metaphor for a long stretch of time having passed and much space having been crossed. The word *eize* indicated the rebirth of a language and the reconquest of an independent national existence. The word "surprise" indicated the long cultural journey and the transformations that her internal life had faced by even the partial use of a fourth language, English, added on to Arabic dialect, Italian, and modern Hebrew. *'Amlcili*, from the Arabic *'amltili* (you gave me), was the preservation of an entire world, the tonalities of which survive in the very accent of the oldest Jewish dialect. It was the indication that something precious, which had made the psychological preservation of the person's entire identity possible, had remained intact; to paraphrase the great Russian poet Esenin, something had remained intact so that everything could change. *Sono veramente* is a trace of the profound effect the Italian language had had on the Jews of Libya and their identity. The word *frhana* (in Arabic, happy) expressed the joy of reencounter in the oldest of the languages. The English "to meet you" was highly evocative because it used the language of the country in which the meeting took place. Probably the same people, meeting in Rome or Tel Aviv, might have changed these words to *di vederti* or *lirot otakh*. In Jewish mysticism, the world of *Pleroma* is described as a complex linguistic web, vessels that communicate with each other, in which the Divinity manifests itself to itself and its energy unfolds after being restricted in order to make space for Creation. It is a large metaphor about how the innermost processes of the psyche work, and it anticipates the great psychological constructs of the twentieth century. It is a metaphor that adapts itself well to representing the image of our journey. Every word used can be considered like a *Sefirah*, in which a precious secret is mysteriously enclosed, an enigma to be deciphered, the trace of a journey undertaken, so many worlds with their stories. The apogee of this interlacing of worlds and cultures could be achieved speaking three or four languages at the same time, depending on whom one was talking to, passing from one language to another with the same person, or with several people, according to the subject. These *Sefirot* are at work even when one dreams, according to the dream, the place in which it is situated, the psychic parts that are in play. It is the lasting fruit of a painful past of removals and uprootings.

The 1960s

Of the 6,300 Jews who were officially resident in Libya in 1967 (the real number was less because the community was careful not to cancel from the lists of its members those who had left under the excuse of a tourist trip), 300 lived in Benghazi. Excluded from activities connected to processing and refining petroleum, the Jews found adequate compensation (with obvious changes in general living standards for the whole community) in business and in representing foreign companies. In less than six years, the number of poor Jews, estimated in 1957 to be about half of the community, and not holding foreign passports, fell to no more than forty families. The growing well-being was highly visible in Tripoli in the number of young Jews enrolling in the Dante Alighieri Italian high school; in the abandoning of the old Jewish quarter, by then mainly inhabited by Arabs, for the quarters of the new city; and in the intensified use of Italian instead of Arabic (in contrast, among educated young Arabs there was a contrary process of substituting Arabic dialect for classical Arabic). The growing linguistic barriers were a background to a changed scenario loaded with tensions and conflict that reached their height in the weeks preceding the outbreak of the June 1967 war.

The discovery of petroleum and the resulting increase in living standards succeeded initially in stabilizing the monarchy and the old elites in power. In this climate of relative tranquility and optimism of the early sixties, the Libyan Jews' right to citizenship was recognized again due to the petition of a group of community leaders, who already had the citizenship of a European country, together with the initiatives of American Jewish organizations vis-à-vis the United Nations.

But it was only a partial concession, limiting passport issuance to those forced to travel for business or health. And even in such cases a family member always was held behind as a hostage. In any event the authorities intentionally denied Jewish community requests to once again directly administer their religious and social welfare institutions. This meant refusing administrative approval to admit a chief rabbi from abroad to reestablish the rabbinic court or to hire teachers and obtain textbooks needed for reopening the Jewish schools.

Faced with a noticeable erosion of internal support and accusations of selfishly hoarding the Arab nation's wealth, the Sanusi regime modified its anti-Jewish laws in line with those promulgated by the most radical Arab governments. Israel no longer appeared on the schoolroom maps hung on the classroom walls; any mention of it in a foreign newspaper was removed. Even an article discussing the playoffs in Chile between Israel and Italy for the World Cup met the same fate. Day after day the list of business firms forbidden to have any commercial dealings whatsoever with Israel expanded. Despite a UNESCO protest, the Jewish school, the Alliance Israélite Universelle, was shut down.

Each time Jews sought to deal with the new situation and to protect a portion of their property either by seeking protection from higher-ups or by leveraging the inefficiency of the state bureaucracy and its corrupt officials, it sparked a new wave of hatred against them. Each Jewish émigré was seen as a potential Israeli soldier and every coin sent abroad a gain for the "Zionist entity." Caught in this grim atmosphere, the most prominent Jews were compelled to hand over money to the PLO (Palestine Liberation Organization) run by Shukeiri, whose explicit goal was the destruction of Israel. When the West German and British soccer teams paired off in the 1966 World Cup Final, the Arabs cheered for the Germans. The message transmitted was clear.

The Pogrom of 1967

The first stirrings of the 1967 pogrom came on Friday, June 2, when the mullahs in the mosques and in radio sermons called for jihad against Israel and the Jews. Almost at the same time the government, under pressure from Syria and Egypt, announced that, beginning June 5, there would be a week of propaganda activities dedicated to the Palestinian cause. Furthermore, in the name of the king, Libya declared itself to be "in a state of defensive war," committing all its resources to liberate Palestine. Everywhere radios blasted the news that any hope for the "Zionist entity" had vanished, and its inhabitants would be exterminated and then thrown into the sea.

Panicking, the Jewish leadership telegrammed its solidarity with the king, reaffirming its loyalty to him and its neutrality. The synagogues proclaimed a fast, while at home Jews lit candles to remember Rabbi Meir and Rabbi Shim'on Bar Yohai, two of the great Mishnah rabbis. According to the important Libyan Jewish mystical tradition, these two rabbis occupy a central role in the liturgy, so much so that in the moving recital of "Anenu" at Yom Kippur they are positioned between the Patriarchs and King David.

What terrorized me most during those angst-ridden weeks was the prospect of indiscriminate violence that would target the women and the aged. Above all, I feared for my sister, mother and father, and brothers. But the distress sparked by the images of Arab armies surrounding the Jewish state helped attenuate these terrifying images of what might happen around me.

The spirit of sacrifice had possessed my inner being; I had lost all interest in my own personal survival. The calm that precedes the very end had taken control of my sinews. In those days I lost the desire to live.

During those nights of darkness and silence, I repeatedly wondered what would happen if the Arab armies struck Israel first. Tel Aviv was just a few kilometers from the eastern front, and only a wire fence constituted Jerusalem's border. And here we were, trapped and cut off from the rest of the world. Sleeping armed with a knife, I thought about how I could fight valiantly for my family and myself.

When, on June 5, 1967, news came of the war's outbreak, the crowds on the street rejoiced. Radio Cairo had announced Tel Aviv's and Haifa's destruction. We were certain it was untrue. All just crude, vulgar, bloody propaganda. But the anguish was enormous. The screams from the crowds provided just a taste of what was awaiting both us and our belongings once the indiscriminate violence exploded. From the balconies of the headquarters of the PLO came calls for jihad.

During the interminable and silent moments waiting for my family and the neighbors to return home, I wondered in anguish what we would do should the crowd attempt to break down the entrance doors of the building in which we lived. My brother Isaac had managed to flee from the flames consuming his office through an inner courtyard window. As had happened before in 1945 and 1948, gangs of youth had marked the Jewish homes and stores with chalk.

Only after proclaiming a state of emergency and a curfew were the security forces able to regain control with difficulty. The turning point came on Thursday, June 8, when police confronted farmers marching to Tripoli from their nearby village (Zawia), which had supplied more volunteers to fight Israel than anywhere else.

Armed with clubs, picks, and knives, the farmers had planned to cleanse the city of any trace of foreigners and Jews. The organizers expected that the joining of the urban and rural protests would signal the beginning of a general uprising that would then involve elements of the armed forces. Fortunately, the events developed differently. Jews living in the old city were evacuated and brought by the hundreds, along with others, to newer neighborhoods where they gathered in police stations, barracks, and Camp Gurgi, located on the city's edge.

In the days that followed, reports of fighting between police and rebels were interspersed with news that the Israel Air Force was about to bomb the country. In the collective imagination, Israel had become so omnipotent that its soldiers could deploy anywhere to repay Libyans in their own coin with the brutality that they had envisaged against defenseless Jews. News that Israeli planes penetrated Egyptian airspace from the west, and not the east as had been expected, fanned the collective hysteria. Fear of suffering the same destiny as the one the Arabs had planned for the Jews produced terror and panic.

From the closed shutters at home, it was unclear what was happening. Cars and motorcycles laden with sacks of flour were heading into the country's interior in flight, apparently fearing they would be pursued. Economic activity was totally paralyzed; those who just days before were exuberant now wandered around like zombies. No longer did young combat volunteers embrace each other on the street below the headquarters of the PLO, next to trucks loaded with all the household furnishings including the tea. All of which were headed for a death trip. The exhilarating paroxysms had been transformed into the darkest despair. Heavy footsteps of the military standing guard around our homes broke the nighttime silence. Along the deserted streets the police trucks rotated and circled.

Locked inside our building, we spent endless days in front of the Buaron family's television. Nothing pointed to going back to our earlier situation. We had no information about our relatives or of my brother Simon, who seven years earlier had immigrated to Israel. We wondered what we would do if the army or the police came to take us to Camp Gurgi, where Jews from the old city had been transferred in massive numbers following the arson and plundering of their homes. And what if it were all just a trap to murder us? Who could guarantee that the military, after having loaded us on trucks promising to take us to a secure place, wouldn't then decide to kill us? My mother couldn't calm down, exhorting all of us not to follow if told to do so. Hadn't the same thing already happened with the Nazis? Hadn't Jews left their homes unaware of the Final Solution that awaited them? We were never, never to leave our homes. My brother Jacob fully agreed with this, and he was the one who made all the decisions.

My mother's fears were not unfounded. As we learned afterward, a group of soldiers had used that technique to capture and then slaughter the Raccah and Luzon families, both of whom lived on our street. The mass murder plot, put into motion initially against the Raccah and Luzon families, assassinated in Tripoli's periphery, had been blocked by the police, whose suspicions were aroused when their relatives made repeated requests for information.

Fifty-two of us shared the food that my mother managed to obtain from a black Muslim family in exchange for money and small gifts. Their sons were looters, but thanks to their mother's goodwill toward us they behaved differently from other Muslims. In order to avoid making their Arab and Palestinian neighbors suspicious, once they had returned from "going shopping" they would call for my mother, but used instead the name of their youngest daughter, "Ishà." But other families too during that time received similar help from their Christian and Muslim neighbors. On the day of our departure from Libya, Ishà's mother asked our forgiveness.

We could even say we were fortunate. We lived not far from the central police station. Every evening we got together in a neighbor's home to listen to Arrigo Levi's latest radio news bulletins. Once the worst moments had passed, some unwound by mimicking Nasser's last speech announcing the resignations of his collaborators and the telephone conversation intercepted by the Israeli Mossad between King Hussein of Jordan and the Egyptian leader.

Maliciously, someone would smile whenever the recently remarried older man would put on scent before retiring to his living quarters. Then there was another man who joyously would place biscuits in the shape of the Star of David, baked by his wife, around his neck.

In our hearts we began to feel safe. And in many homes it became a time for conceiving children.

There were contrasting images on the television screen. When a little girl sitting with us saw a Palestinian woman on screen with her son on the Allenby Bridge, she exclaimed, "Poor things!" Emotions ran high when we saw the television images of Israeli soldiers praying at the Kotel (*Kotel Hamma'ravi*) and watched them tuck messages with their prayers in the cracks of the long-suffering stones. I am however left alone with a troubling thought. Our great fear has subsided and we are celebrating Israel's salvation. But what about those who lost their sons?

Emerging from our defenseless homes, and once again hearing the dove's lost voice, confirmed that the "Little Sister" we remember each year at Rosh Hashanah (the Jewish New Year) was with us. This symbolic divine feminine image—the *Shekhinah*—that all welcome didn't abandon us in our painful exile.

Departure

The days passed slowly. We were holed up in our homes. In one apartment a telephone rang. Most of the time the telephone calls were threatening, sorely testing our nerves. A young Jew who unwisely reopened his butcher shop to deliver meat to friends was knifed to death. Another, a girl who went out to get bread, was killed on the spot, strangled with an Arab hijab. Maybe her accent betrayed her, or someone recognized her. Whoever possessed a passport had already left town. For us everything was more complicated. We needed both an exit visa and a country willing to let us continue on to Israel. There was one country: Italy. In the end, following long international negotiations, the Italian government had agreed to grant three-month tourist visas to Jews who requested them. I should have been happy, having nurtured this dream for years. Yet as this moment arrived, I was full of bitterness; and I was not the only one who felt this way. It was enough to look at the face of my brother Victor or the hidden glances of my sister and father.

The evening of June 5, across the historic Jewish quarter, flames soared high and I didn't know which of my friends were still alive. If some had fallen into depression, there were always those who gently pushed them. My brother Victor, not wanting to give up and unbeknownst to us, called his Arab officemates to say a final farewell. But they insulted him and threatened to behead him if they found out where he was. Victor was left reeling. Some, learning what just happened, laughed uncontrollably at his naiveté; but others comforted him.

While we were getting ready to depart, a sock fell out of my mother's pocket. It belonged to Simon, my brother who left the country seven years ago. How many times the authorities and the Arab neighbors had asked us to explain his absence. My mother always held on to that sock, concealing it between her pockets and her womb. Now he was on the battlefront and I didn't know if he was alive and whether he would ever come back. To myself I said, "God, let him live!"

The day to depart arrived. A police jeep waited for us. It was early morning and the air was still cool, thanks to the sea breeze sending us its kind, warm wishes. Soon it would become hot and muggy. The machine-gun-armed policeman couldn't wait to finish his thankless assignment. I felt all alone with my baggage. The dream of leaving my country forever was about to come true. I hadn't imagined leaving in this way. It was then that I began to develop the idea that the Exodus story actually had been embellished: the flight with the unleavened bread is the cold reality that the biblical text conserved with a lot of evidence. The story of the plagues that struck Egypt only existed in the minds of those who had saved themselves by fleeing. It was then that I began to see the "The Song of the Sea," and how it represents the drowning enemy, in a new light: it was an event that actually didn't happen. Rather, the Egyptian legions that perish in the water are phantoms and persecutors whom we can forever put behind us. In the solitude, trying to haphazardly arrange my thoughts, I saw an Italian Maltese friend go by. We exchanged a meaningful glance. We did not hug each other. We said "hi" as if nothing had happened.

Epilogue

For many years I lived as if my childhood experiences belonged in the past tense. An enormous watershed divided my life: before and after could not be reconciled even if only a few years separated them. A break in time. I then discovered that by looking at this problem from the standpoint of my work, my feelings are a response to a common pattern. I didn't suffer alone. Tens of thousands of other Jews forcibly expelled from Arab countries shared the same fate. These people now live in places like Rome, Paris, New York, or Tel Aviv, a thousand or more kilometers from where they forged their memories as adolescents or as young men and women. The pattern doesn't change. The break extends across time and space. With the passage of time, however, the younger generation, which had no personal experience of what happened, has cautiously begun reestablishing and renewing interest in the places and customs of their ancestors. Involved in the search for political dialogue and a peaceful solution of the Middle East conflict, the idea of returning to my home country even for a brief visit has never crossed my mind. Nothing connects me any longer to that country, and I think of myself as fortunate having gotten out alive. Fortunately, those like me were able to build new lives elsewhere in more hospitable countries, where we have preserved intergenerational family ties, linking together grandchildren to grandparents. Nevertheless, I carry in me a deep sense of unease because of the unspeakable fate suffered by others less fortunate than me. Such feelings may erupt recalling the fragrant scents of my childhood, or while simply waiting in an airport. One day, glancing at the flight information display board, I imagined seeing two distinct flight departures (Roma—Tel Aviv, Roma—Tripoli) superimposed, so that one flight destination continued on to the next destination and then vice versa.

As in a dream, I am there and I am here and elsewhere. Tripoli travels with me, part of my dreamlike world, together with the musical rhythms of the Orient, so rich and expressive. Along with the love songs and liturgical melodies of the *Birkhat levana* that I heard at home, when dreaming all of these continue to resonate in my mind. Then there are the painful memories of lost friends, of sweet fragrances and sea breezes, as well as my fantasies of watching the departing ships, imagining that I was on board, cradled and protected as if in a mother's womb.

What a joy I felt moving from Arabic to Hebrew and then from Hebrew to Arabic, and composing in Italian as if it were Latin, the result ending in writing incomprehensibly. This continued until my high school teacher, recognizing the problem, suggested, "Why don't you emulate the writers of the French Enlightenment, who wrote very clearly? If you did so, your Italian would be both improved and more elegant." The resulting changes were noticeable and rapidly produced results. For a long time I continued to be inspired by French seventeenth-century writers, up until I no longer managed to distill and break down the complex melody of the languages of my childhood. My vigilant consciousness may surrender to delightful fantasy.

Bibliography

Arbib, Lillo. "The Antisemitic Riots in Libya of June 5th, luglio 1967." Report in *American Jewish Committee Archives*, July 1967.

Carpi, Leone. "La condizione giuridica degli ebrei nel Regno Unito di Libia." *Rivista di studi politici internazionali* (January–March 1963): 87–92.

Cohen, Mordechai. *Gli Ebrei di Libia*. Giuntina: Firenze, 1994.

De Felice, Renzo. *Ebrei in un paese arabo: Gli ebrei nella Libia contemporanea tra colonialismo, nazionalismo arabo e sionismo (1885–1970)*. Il Mulino: Bologna, 1978.

Freud, Sigmund. "Lettera a Max Eitingon del 6 febbraio." In *Lettere alla fidanzata e ad altri corrispondenti Sigmund Freud*. 1938. Reprint, translated by *Mazzino Montinari* and Giuseppina Quattrocchi von Wissmann. Torino: Paolo Boringhieri, 1990.

———. "L'interpretazione dei sogni." In *Opere complete di Sigmund Freud*, Vol. 3, 1899. Reprint, Torino: Bollati Boringhieri, 2002.

———. "L'uomo Mosè e la religione monoteistica. Tre saggi (1934–1938)." In *Opere complete di Sigmund Freud*, Vol. 9, 329–453. 1934–1938. Reprint, Torino: Bollati Boringhieri, 1975, 1979, 2003.

————. "Prefazione alla traduzione ebraica." In *Opere complete di Sigmund Freud*, Vols. 7, 8–9. 1930. Reprint, Torino: Bollati Boringhieri, 1975, 2000.

Goldberg, Harvey E. *Cave Dwellers and Citrus Growers: A Jewish Community in Libya and Israel*. Cambridge: Cambridge University Press, 1972.

————. "Ecologic and Demographic Aspects of Rural Tripolitanian Jewry: 1853–1943." *International Journal of Middle East Studies* 2 (1971): 245–65.

Habib, Zachino. *Due relazioni sul pogrom del 12–13 giugno 1948*. AUCII, fasc. "Fatti di Tripoli." N.d.

————. "I tumulti anti ebraici in Tripolitania 4, 5, 6 e 7 novembre 1945, relazione aggiornata al 31 dicembre 1945." In Archivio dell'Unione delle Comunità Israelitiche Italiane, fasc. *Fatti di Tripoli* (November 4–7, 1945). Report dated December 31, 1945.

Ha-Kohen, Mordekhai. *The Book of Mordechai: A Study of the Jews of Libya: Selections from the Highid Mordekhai of Mordechai Hakohen Based on the Complete Hebrew Text*. Edited and translated (with introduction and commentaries) by Harvey E. Goldberg. London: Darf, 1993.

Jabès, Edmond. *Il libro dell'ospitalità*. Milano: Cortina, 1991.

————. *Le livre des questions*. 1963. Reprint, Paris: Gallimard, 1988.

Jones Edmond. *Vita e opere di Freud*. 3 vols. 1953–1957. Reprint, Milano: Garzanti, 1977.

La Sacra Bibbia ossia L'Antico e il Nuovo Testamento: tradotti da Giovanni Diodati. Rome: Libreria Sacre Scritture, 1981.

Meghnagi, David. *Il padre e la legge (Freud e l'ebraismo)*. 1992. Reprint, Venice: Marsilio, 3a ed. aggiornata, 2004.

————. *Ricomporre l'infranto. L'esperienza dei sopravvissuti alla Shoah*. Venice: Marsilio, n.d.

————. "Tra memoria e storia: essere ebreo in un paese arabo." In *Identità e storia degli ebrei*, edited by David Bidussa, Collotti Pischel, and R. Scardi, 237–53. Milan: Franco Angeli, 2000.

————. "Un ragazzo nel pogrom: giugno 1967." In *La cultura sefardita*, edited by David Meghnagi, D. Levi, and G. Fubini, 1:323–31. Rome: Rassegna Mensile di Israel, UCEI, 1983.

Meghnagi, David, and Mark Solms. *Freud and Judaism*. London: Karnac Books, 1993.

Nerazzini, A. 1997. "Sui giornali del 1945." *Diario* 2, no. 35 (September 10–16, 1997): 23.

Ortona, M. "Il pogrom dimenticato." *Diario* 2, no. 35 (September 10–16, 1997): 14–22.

Proia, A. *Impressioni di viaggio (1955–2002)*. Latina: Caramanica, 2006.

Satloff, R. *Tra i giusti. Storie perdute dell'Olocausto nei paesi arabi*. Venice: Marsilio, 2008.

Valensi, Lucette, and Nathan Wachtel. *Memorie ebraiche*. Edited by Alberto Cavaglion. Torino: Einaudi, 1996.

Zuaretz, Fridja, et al., eds. *Yahaduth Luv*. 1960. Reprint, Tel Aviv: Vaad Kahalat Luv be Israel, 1982.

Selected General Bibliography

♦   ♦   ♦

Interviews

♦   ♦   ♦

Contributors

♦   ♦   ♦

Index

Selected General Bibliography

Abitbol, Michel, et al. "Jews in Muslim Lands in the Modern Period: History and Historiography." In *Sephardic Jewry and Mizrahi Jews*, edited by Peter Y. Medding, 44–65. Vol. 22. Oxford: Oxford University Press, 2007.

Abramsky-Bligh, Irit. *Pinkas Hakehilot.* Jerusalem: Yad Vashem, 1997.

Alhadeff, Gini. *The Sun at Midday: Tales of a Mediterranean Family.* New York: Pantheon, 1997.

Applebaum, Shimon. "The Jewish Revolt in Cyrene and the Subsequent Recolonisation." *Journal of Jewish Studies* 4 (1951): 177–86.

———. *Jews and Greeks in Ancient Cyrene.* Leiden: Brill, 1979.

Arbib, A. R. *Memorie.* Rome: Maccabi, n.d.

Arbib, Jack. *L'ombra e la luce: note su Umberto Di Segni.* Nola: il Laboratorio, 2010.

Arbib, Lillo. *Gli Ebrei in Libia fra Idris e Gheddafi 1948–1970: Pagine di storia contemporanea.* N.p.: Arezzo: Stango Editore, 1989.

Artom, Elia. "L'Importanza dell'Elemento Ebraico nella Popolazione della Tripolitania." *Atti del Secondo Congresso di Studi Coloniali. Naples: Centro di Studi Coloniali* (October 1934): 116–27.

Balbo, Italo. *La Centuria Alata.* Milan: Mondadori, 1934.

Baldinetti, Anna. *The Origins of the Libyan Nation: Colonial Legacy, Exile and the Emergence of a New Nation-State.* Abingdon, Oxon: Routledge, 2010.

Ben'atiyah, Pedahtsur. *Shiru lanu mi-shire Tsiyon.* [In Hebrew.] Bat-Yam: Merkaz Or Shalom, 2001.

Benbassa, Esther, Jean-Christophe Attias, and Michel Abitbol. *Juifs et musulmans: une histoire partagée, un dialogue à construire.* Paris: Découverte, 2006.

Ben David Gian (Gi'an), Joseph. "Theatre in the Zionist Movement in Libya." [In Hebrew.] In *Libya*, edited by Haim Saadoun, 173–82. Jerusalem: Ben-Zvi Institute, 2007.

Benichou Gottreich, Emily, and Daniel J. Schroeter, eds. *Jewish Culture and Society in North Africa*. Bloomington: Indiana University Press, 2011.

Bensoussan, Albert. *Frimaldjézar*. Paris: Calman-Lévy, 1976.

"Bergen-Belsen." In *Holocaust Encyclopedia*. Washington, DC: United States Holocaust Memorial Museum, n.d. http://www.ushmm.org/wlc/en /article.php?ModuleId=10005224.

Bernhard, Patrick. "Behind the Battle Lines: Italian Atrocities and the Persecution of Arabs, Berbers and Jews in North Africa during World War II." *Holocaust and Genocide Studies* 26, no. 3 (Winter 2012): 425–46.

Bouganim, Ami. *Récits du Mellah*. Paris: Lattès, 1981.

Camera di Commercio Industria ed Agricoltura della Cirenaica. *Guida commerciale della Cirenaica*. Benghazi: Società Anonima Tipografica Italiana, 1926.

Capresi, Vittoria. *The Built Utopia: The Italian Rural Centers Founded in Colonial Libya (1934–1940)*. Bologna: Bologna University Press, 2009.

Carpi, Leone. "La Condizione giuridica degli ebrei nel Regno Unito di Libia." *Rivista di Studi Politici Internazionali* 30, no. 1 (1963): 87–92.

Chorin, Ethan. *Translating Libya: The Modern Libyan Short Story*. London: London Middle East Institute at SOAS, 2008.

Cohen, Giulia. "Giulia Cohen racconta." Progetto REMSHOA, http:// www.annapizzuti.it/. Ebrei stranieri internati in Italia durante il periodo bellico, n.d. https://www.youtube.com/watch?v=kh8BszVZWb4.

Cohen, Mark R., and Abraham L. Udovitch, eds. *Jews among Arabs: Contacts and Boundaries*. Princeton: Darwin Press, 1989.

Cohen/Ha-Kohen, Mordekhai, and Martino Mario Moreno. *Gli ebrei in Libia: usi e costumi*. Vol. 2. Florence: Casa Editrice Giuntina, 1994.

Comunità Israelitica della Tripolitania. "I tumulti antiebraichi in Tripolitania: 4, 5, 6 e 7 Novembre 1945." Unpublished manuscript, 1945.

Cresti, Federico. *Oasi di italianità*. Turin: SEI, 1996.

Culotta, Pasquale. *Città di fondazione*. Bologna: Compositori, 2007.

David, Eyal. "The Daily Life of Upper-Middle Class Jews in the City of Tripoli in Libya (1951–1967)." [In Hebrew.] M.A. thesis, Hebrew University of Jerusalem, 2014.

Davidson, Israel. *Thesaurus of Mediaeval Hebrew Poetry.* [In Hebrew.] Vol. 3. New York: Jewish Theological Seminary of America, 1930.

De Felice, R. *Ebrei in un paese arabo: Gli ebrei nella Libia contemporanea tra colonialismo, nazionalismo arabo e sionismo (1885–1970).* Bologna: Il Mulino, 1978.

De Felice, Renzo. *Jews in an Arab Land: Libya, 1835–1870.* Translated by Judith Roumani. Austin: University of Texas Press, 1985.

De Seta, Cesare. *La cultura architettonica italiana tra due guerre.* Bari: Laterza, 1972.

Dib, Mohammed. *Qui se souvient de la mer* [Who Remembers the Sea]. Paris: La Différence, 2016. First published 1962 by Les Editions du Seuil (Paris).

Dr. Gayed's Blog. http://dr-gayed.blogspot.com/search?updated-min=2011 -01-01. January 1, 2011.

El Saiegh, Meir. *Racconti Bengasini (2).* www.libronelcassetto.it. N.d.

Fischer, Wolfdietrich, and Otto Jastrow, eds. *Handbuch der arabischen Dialekte.* Wiesbaden: Harrassowitz, 1980.

Fuller, Mia. *Moderns Abroad: Architecture, Cities and Italian Imperialism.* New York: Routledge, 2007.

Gerbi, David. *Costruttori di Pace: Storia di un ebreo profugo della Libia.* Rome: Edizioni Appunti di Viaggio, 2003.

Godoli, Ezio, and Milva Giacomelli. *Architetti e ingegneri italiani dal Levante al Magreb, 1848–1945.* Florence: Maschietto, 2005.

Goitein, Shelomo Dov. *A Mediterranean Society: The Jewish Communities of the Arab World as Portrayed in the Documents of the Cairo Geniza.* Vol. 3, *The Family.* Berkeley: University of California Press, 1978.

Goldberg, Harvey E. *Cave Dwellers and Citrus Growers: A Jewish Community in Libya and Israel.* Cambridge: Cambridge University Press, 1972.

Goldberg, Harvey E. "Al Leshonam ve-Tarbutam shel Yehudey Tripolig taniya." *Leshonenu* 38 (1974): 137–47.

———. "Introduction." In *Sephardi and Middle Eastern Jewries: History and Culture in the Modern Era,* edited by Harvey E. Goldberg, 1–55. Bloomington: Indiana University Press, 1996.

———. *Jewish Life in Muslim Libya: Rivals and Relatives.* Chicago and London: University of Chicago Press, 1990.

———. "The Jewish Wedding in Tripolitania: A Study in Cultural Sources." *Maghreb Review* 3, no. 9 (1978):1–6.

———. "Language and Culture of the Jews of Tripolitania: A Preliminary View." *Mediterranean Language Review* 1 (1983): 85–102.

Government of Libya. *Guide for the Historical Landmarks of the Old City of Tripoli.* Tripoli: N.p., 2010.

Haggiag-Lilluf, Yaacov. "The Jews in the Local Economy." [In Hebrew.] In *Libya*, edited by Haim Saadoun, 33–46. Jerusalem: Ben-Zvi Institute, 2007.

———. *Toldot Yehude Luv* [The History of the Libyan Jews]. [In Hebrew.] Or Yehuda: World Organization of Libyan Jews, 2000.

———. *Yehude Luv ba-Shoah.* [In Hebrew.] Or Yehuda: World Organization of Libyan Jews, 2012.

Ha-Kohen, Mordekhai. *The Book of Mordechai: A Study of the Jews of Libya: Selections from the Highid Mordekhai of Mordechai Hakohen Based on the Complete Hebrew Text.* Edited and translated with introduction and commentaries by Harvey E. Goldberg. London: Darf, 1993.

———. *Higgid Mordekhay: Histoire de la Libye et de ses Juifs, lieux d'habitation et coutumes.* [In Hebrew.] Edited by Harvey E. Goldberg. Jerusalem: Ben-Zvi Institute, 1978.

Harris, Lillian Craig. *Libya: Qadhafi's Revolution and the Modern State.* Boulder: Westview Press, 1986.

Hazan, Efraim. "The Transformation of a Piyyut: The Way of the 'Mi Kamokha' from Spain to the Orient and North Africa." [In Hebrew.] In *Culture and History: Ino Sciacky Memorial Volume*, edited by Joseph Dan, 67–76. Jerusalem: Misgav Yerushalayim, 1986.

Heller, Bernard. "Yusuf b. Ya'kub." In *Encyclopaedia of Islam*, 4: 1178–79. Leiden: Brill, 1931.

Hesse, Isabelle. *The Politics of Jewishness in World Literature.* London: Bloomsbury Academic Press, 2016.

Hirschberg, Haim Z. *History of the Jews of North Africa.* Vol. 2, *From the Ottoman Conquests to the Present Time.* Leiden: Brill, 1981.

Jabès, Edmond, Antonio Prete, and Maria Gregorio. *Il libro dell'ospitalità.* Milan: Raffaello Cortina editore, 1991.

Jones, Ernest. *Vita e opere di Freud.* Milan: Garzanti, 1977.

Journo, Arthur. *Il ribelle.* Rome: Lettere, 2003.

Khalfon, Abraham. *Ma'aseh Tzaddikim.* Edited with introduction, notes, and index by Asaf Raviv. Ashkelon: Peer HaQodesh, 2009.

Khalfon, Hayyim. *Lanu u-Levanenu* [For Us and Our Children after Us: The Life of the Libyan Jewish Community]. [In Hebrew.] Netanya: published by author, 1986.

Labanca, Nicola. *Oltremare*. Bologna: Il Mulino, 2002.

Levy, Lital. "Historicizing the Concept of Arab Jews in the *Mashriq*." *Jewish Quarterly Review* 98, no. 4 (Fall 2008): 452–69.

Littman, David. "Jews under Muslim Rule in the Late Nineteenth Century." *Wiener Library Bulletin* 28 (1975): 35–36, 69–72.

Luzon, Raphael. *Tramonto libico*. Florence: Giuntina, 2015.

———. *Libyan Twilight: The Story of an Arab Jew*. Translated by Gaia Luzon. London: Darf, 2017.

Maimon, R. Ya'akov ben Hai. *Derekh ha-ayyim* [The Way of Life] and *Mayim Hayim* [The Waters of Life]. [In Hebrew.] Livorno: Eliyahu Ben Amozeg and Partners, 1860.

Marçais, William. "Comment l'Afrique du Nord a été arabisée." *Annales de l'Institut d'études orientales d'Alger* 4, no. 14 (1938): 6–17.

Marks, Esika, and Edwin Seroussi. "The Musical Tradition of Libyan Jewry." [In Hebrew.] In *Libya*, edited by Haim Saadoun, 159–72. Jerusalem: Ben-Zvi Institute, 2007.

McLaren, Brian L. *Architecture and Tourism in Italian Colonial Libya*. Seattle: University of Washington Press, 2006.

Megargee, Geoffrey P., ed. *Encyclopedia of Camps and Ghettos*. Bloomington: Indiana University Press and USHMM, 2009.

Meghnagi, David. "Il Campo di Giado." Unpublished paper, n.d.

———. *Il padre e la legge (Freud e l'ebraismo)*. 3rd ed. Venice: Marsilio, 2004.

———. *Ricomporre l'infranto: L'esperienza dei sopravvissuti alla Shoah*. Venice: Marsilio, 2005.

———. "Tra memoria e storia." In *Identità e storia degli ebrei*, edited by David Bidussa, Enrica Collotti Pischel, and Raffaella Scardi, 237–53. Milan: FrancoAngeli, 2000.

———. "Un ragazzo nel pogrom: giugno 1967." In *La cultura sefardita*, edited by David Meghnagi, D. Levi, and G. Fubini, 1:323–31. Rome: Rassegna Mensile di Israel, UCEI, 1983.

Meghnagi, David, and Mark Solms. *Freud and Judaism*. London: Karnac Books, 1993.

Melman, Yossi. *Don't Shoot, I'm the Good Guy: The Life and Times of Walter Arbib.* Toronto: Malcolm Lester, 2016.

Memmi, Albert. *The Desert: Or the Life and Adventures of Jubair Wali al-Mammi.* Translated by Judith Roumani. Syracuse: Syracuse University Press, 2015.

———. *Jews and Arabs.* Translated by Eleanor Levieux. Chicago: J. Philip O'Hara, 1975.

———. *La Statue de sel.* Paris: Corrêa, 1953. Translated by Edouard Roditi as *Pillar of Salt* (Boston: Beacon Press, 1992).

Ministero delle Colonie, Mostra Coloniale di Genova. *Le Scuole Italiane in Tripoli.* Rome: Tipografia Nazionale G. Bertoro, 1914.

Moati, Nine. *La Passagère sans étoile.* Paris: Seuil, 1989.

Mole, Gary. *Beyond the Limit-Experience: French Poetry of the Deportation, 1940–1945.* New York: P. Lan, 2002.

Nettler, Ronald L. "Early Islam, Modern Islam and Judaism: The Isra'iliyyat in Modern Islamic Thought." In *Muslim-Jewish Encounters, Intellectual Traditions and Modern Politics,* edited by Ronald L. Nettler and Suha Taji-Farouki, 1–14. Amsterdam: Overseas Publishers Association and Harwood, 1998.

Nunes-Vais, Roberto. *Reminiscenze tripoline.* Rome: Uaddan, 1982.

Paggi, Ariel, and Judith Roumani. "From Pitigliano to Tripoli, via Livorno: The Pedagogical Odyssey of Giannetto Paggi." *Sephardic Horizons* 2, no. 4 (2014). http://www.sephardichorizons.org/Volume2/Issue4/paggi .html.

Piccioli, Angelo. *La nuova Italia d'Oltremare: l'Opera del fascismo nelle colonie italiane.* Milan: Mondadori, 1934.

Pizzi, D. *Metaphysical Cities.* Milan: Skira, 2005.

Pizzuti, Anna. *L'Applicazione delle Leggi Antiebraiche Fascisti Nella Colonia Libica e l'internamento in Italia,* n.d. http://www.annapizzuti.it/public /SLIDELIBIADEF.pdf.

Portelli, Alessandro. "What Makes Oral History Different." In *Oral History, Oral Culture, and Italian Americans,* edited by Luisa Del Giudice, 21–30. New York: Palgrave Macmillan, 2009.

Proia, A. *Impressioni di viaggio (1955–2002).* Latina: Caramanica, 2006.

Rodrigue, Aron. *Images of Sephardi and Eastern Jewries in Transition: The Teachers of the Alliance Israélite Universelle, 1860–1939.* Seattle: University of Washington Press, 1993.

Romanelli, Pietro. *La Cirenaica romana*. Rome: Airoldi, 1943.

Roumani, Jacques. "The Emergence of Modern Libya." PhD diss., Princeton University, 1987.

———. "From Republic to Jamahiriyah, Libya's Search for Political Community." *Middle East Journal* 37, no. 2 (Spring 1983): 151–68.

———. "Libya and the Military Revolution." In *Man, State and Society in the Contemporary Maghrib*, edited by I. W. Zartman. New York: Praeger, 1973.

———. "Libya: Exploring Terra Incognita." *Middle East Journal* 37, no. 1 (Winter 1983): 88–93.

———. "Libya on the Brink: Insecurity, Localism, and the State Not Back In." Article, part of the Middle East-Asia Project (MAP) series on "'Civilianizing' the State in the Middle East and Asia Pacific Regions." Middle East Institute, March 12, 2014. http://www.mei.edu/content/libya-brink-insecurity-localism-and-state-not-back.

———. "Review Article based on John Wright's *Libya* and Adrian Pelt's *Libyan Independence and the United Nations*." *International Journal of Middle East Studies* 5, no. 2 (1974): 222–30.

———. "Review of *Modern Middle Eastern Jewish Thought: Writings on Identity, Politics, and Culture, 1893–1958* by Moshe Behar and Zvi Ben-Dor Benite." Sephardic Horizons 3, no. 2 (Summer 2013). www.sephardichorizons.org.

Roumani, Judith. "The Holocaust in Sephardi-Mizrahi Literature: A Review of Some Responses in Prose." *Sephardic Heritage* 4, no. 2 (2017). http://www.sephardichorizons.org/Volume4/Issue2/Roumani.html#sthash.RcjOS15D.dpuf.

———. "Sephardic Literary Responses to the Holocaust." In *Literature of the Holocaust*, edited by Alan Rosen, 225–37. Cambridge: Cambridge University Press, 2013.

Roumani, Maurice M. *Gli ebrei di Libia dalla coesistenza all'esodo*. Translated by Laura Bonifacio. Rome: Castelvecchi, 2015.

———. *The Jews of Libya: Coexistence, Persecution, Resettlement*. Brighton: Sussex Academic Press, 2008.

———. "Libya." In *Encyclopedia of Jews in the Islamic World*, edited by Norman Stillman, 249–53. Leiden: Brill, 2010.

Roumani-Denn, Vivienne. "The Last Jews of Libya," n.d. www.jewsoflibya.com.

———. "The Last Jews of Libya." Documentary film. Directed by Vivienne Roumani-Denn. Honolulu, HI: Lion Tree Productions, 2007.

———. *The Last Jews of Libya Revisited.* Documentary film. Honolulu, HI: Lion Tree Productions and VR Films LLC, 2017.

Saadoun, Haim. *Libya.* [In Hebrew.] Jerusalem: Ben Zvi Institute, 2007.

Sacra Bibbia ossia L'Antico e il Nuovo Testamento: Tradotti da Giovanni Diodati. Rome: Libreria Sacre Scritture, 1981.

Sacy, Antoine Isaac Silvestre de. *Grammaire arabe à l'usage des élèves de l'école spéciale des langues orientales vivantes: avec figures.* Paris: De Bure, 1810.

———. *Grammaire arabe à l'usage des élèves de l'ecole spéciale des langues orientales vivantes.* Vol. 2. Paris: De Bure, 1831.

Salerno, Eric. *Uccideteli tutti.* Milan: Il Saggiatore, 2008.

Santoinni Vittorio. *Il razionalismo nelle colonie italiane, 1928–1943.* Florence: Tassinari, 2008.

Satloff, Robert. *Among the Righteous: Lost Stories from the Holocaust's Long Reach into Arab Lands.* New York: Public Affairs, 2007.

———. *Tra i giusti. Storie perdute dell'Olocausto nei paesi arabi.* Venice: Marsilio, 2008.

Schorsch, Jonathan. "Disappearing Origins: Sephardic Autobiography Today." *Prooftexts* 27, no. 1 (Winter 2007): 82–150.

Segre, Claudio G. *Fourth Shore.* Chicago: University of Chicago Press, 1974.

Shenhav, Yehouda. *The Arab Jews: A Postcolonial Reading of Nationalism, Religion, and Ethnicity.* Stanford: Stanford University Press, 2006.

Simon, Rachel. "Between the Family and the Outside World: Jewish Girls in the Modern Middle East and North Africa." *Jewish Social Studies* 7, no. 1 (2000): 81–108.

———. *Change within Tradition among Jewish Women in Libya.* Seattle: University of Washington Press, 1992.

Slouschz, Nahum. *Masa'ai be-Erez Luv.* 2 vols. Tel Aviv: Va'ad Ha-Yovel, 1937–1943.

———. *Travels in North Africa.* 1927. Philadelphia: Jewish Publication Society of America, 1944.

Spina, Alessandro. *The Confines of the Shadow: In Lands Overseas.* Translated by André Naffis-Sahely. London: Darf, 2015.

———. 2006. *I Confini dell'ombra.* Brescia: Morcelliana.

Stillman, Norman. *The Jews of Arab Lands: A History and Source Book.* Philadelphia: Jewish Publication Society, 1979.

Storia degli Ebrei di Libia. [In Hebrew.] Or Yehudah: Centro di Studi sull'Ebraismo Libico, 2000.

Sucary, Yossi. *Benghazi—Bergen-Belsen*. [In Hebrew.] Tel Aviv: Am Oved, 2013.

———. *Benghazi—Bergen-Belsen*. Translated by Yardenne Greenspan. San Bernadino: Createspace, 2016.

———. *Emilia et le sel de la terre: Une confession*. Translated by Ziva Avran. Paris: Actes Sud, 2006.

———. *Emiliyah u melah ha-Arets: Vidui* [Emiliyah and the Salt of the Earth: Confession]. [In Hebrew.] Tel Aviv: Bavel, 2002.

TCI. *Guida d'Italia-Libia*. Milan: Touring Club Italiano, 1937.

———. *Guida di Tripoli e dintorni*. Milan: Treves, 1925.

Tobi, Y. "An Unknown Piyyut by R. Yitzaq Luzon on Burjil Purim (Tripoli, 1795)." [In Hebrew.] In *Meḥkarim be-tarbutam shel Yehude Tsefon-Afrikah* [Studies on the Culture of the Jews of North Africa], edited by Issachar Ben-Ami, 75–82. Jerusalem: Va'ad 'adat ha-Ma'araviyim bi-Yerushalayim, 1991.

Trevisan Semi, Emanuela, and Piera Rossetto, eds. "Memory and Forgetting among Jews from the Arab-Muslim Countries: Contested Narratives of a Shared Past." Special issue of *Quest: Issues in Contemporary Jewish History*. Journal of Fondazione CDEC 4 (November 2012). http://www.quest-cdecjournal.it/.

Valensi, Lucette, and Nathan Wachtel. *Memorie ebraiche*. Edited by Alberto Cavaglion. Torino: Einaudi, 1996.

Yoda, Sumikazu. *A Description of the Arabic Dialect of the Jews of Tripoli (Libya): Grammar, Texts and Glossary*. Wiesbaden: Harrassowitz Verlag, 2005.

Zuaretz, Frigia, and F. Tayar. *Seu Zimrah*. [In Hebrew.] Tel Aviv: self-published, 1972.

Zuaretz, Frigia, et al. *Yahadut Luv* [Libyan Jewry]. [In Hebrew.] 1960. Tel Aviv: Vaad Kahalat Luv be Israel, 1982.

◆　◆　◆

Interviews

All conducted by Vivienne Roumani-Denn, unless indicated.

Lillo Arbib, January 1998

Vittoria Duani, January 1998

"Lidya" (asked to hide her name for fear of retribution), January 1998

Shlomo Gean, February 1998

Golda Halfon, February 1998

David Peled, February 1998

Saul Legziel, March 1998

Moshe Labi, June 2003

Giora Roumani, May 2004

Samuele Zarrugh, October 2011 (conducted by Jacques Roumani)

Roger Abravanel, May 2015

Mario Platero, May 2015

Jojo Naim, June 2015

Shalom Saada Saar, June 2015

Shlomit Bucknik, July 2015

David Sasson, August 2015

Monique Sasson, August 2015

Walter Arbib, January 2016 (phone interview)

Daniel Buaron, January 2016

Miriam Meghnagi, February 2016

Jacob Sasson, May 2016

Einat Sarouf, June 2016

Roberto Buaron, September 2016

❖ ❖ ❖

Contributors

Shimon Applebaum, a British-trained archaeologist, was a sergeant in charge of antiquities in Cyrenaica in the British Military Administration of Libya. He lived in ancient Cyrene for eighteen months, 1943–1944. He earned a PhD at Oxford. He was later professor of history at Tel Aviv University and authored articles such as "The Jewish Revolt in Cyrene and the Subsequent Recolonisation," *Journal of Jewish Studies* 4 (1951): 177–86; and books, including *Jews and Greeks in Ancient Cyrene* (Brill, 1979).

Jack Arbib is an aeronautical engineer and writer on Jewish architecture and history in Libya and Italy. He has been knighted and appointed an officer of the Ordine della Stella d'Italia (2015) for his efforts in documenting the history of and restoring the Jewish heritage of Monte San Savino in Tuscany. He has published *L'ombra e la luce: note su Umberto Di Segni* (Il Laboratorio, 2010), as well as other historical studies. He is the chairman of the U. Nahon Museum of Italian Jewish Art.

Gheula Canarutto Nemni holds a doctorate in economics and is a researcher on business ethics and social responsibility. She lives in Milan. She is a novelist, Jewish Orthodox feminist, and commentator on Jewish affairs. Nemni is the author of the acclaimed novel *(Non) si può avere tutto* (Mondadori, 2015) and writes frequently for *Times of Israel*.

Harvey E. Goldberg is professor emeritus of anthropology at the Hebrew University of Jerusalem. He is the author of many articles and several books on the Jews of Libya, such as *Cave Dwellers and Citrus Growers: A Jewish Community in Libya and Israel* (Cambridge University Press, 1972) and *Jewish Life in Muslim Libya: Rivals and Relatives* (University of Chicago Press, 1990). Goldberg is editor of *Sephardi and Middle Eastern Jewries: History and Culture in the Modern Era* (Indiana University Press, 1996).

Hamos Guetta is an industrialist in Rome and a promoter of Libyan Jewish food and traditions. He writes a food blog, has a television program, and posts on YouTube about Libyan Jewish food. He has also accumulated an archive of photographs of Jewish life in Libya. Guetta expresses his gratitude to an Alitalia air hostess, Floriana Zappoli, who saved the lives of his family and many other Libyan Jews in 1967.

David Meghnagi, coeditor, is professor of Clinical Psychology and the Psychology of Religion and director of a master's program in Shoah education at La Sapienza, Roma Tre University, and author of numerous articles and books on the Shoah, Freud, Israel, the Arabs, and Libya. These include "Un ragazzo nel pogrom: giugno 1967," in *La cultura sefardita* (1983); *Freud and Judaism* (1993); *Il padre e la legge* (*Freud e l'ebraismo*, 3rd ed. (2004); and *Ricomporre l'infranto: L'esperienza dei sopravvissuti alla Shoah* (2005). Among other activities, Meghnagi is a member of the Task Force for International Cooperation on Holocaust Remembrance and Education and a performer and promoter of the Libyan Jewish musical heritage. He has recorded *Shiru Shir* (2006), a CD collection of Libyan Jewish religious songs.

Chief Editor **Jacques Roumani** earned his PhD in Politics and Middle Eastern History from Princeton University with a dissertation on Libya, *The Emergence of Modern Libya: Political Traditions and Colonial Change"* (1987), and he is the author of numerous articles on Libyan developments. He worked for many years at the World Bank and the Inter-American Development Bank, taught courses as a senior lecturer on the political economy of the Middle East at Bar-Ilan University and the University of Maryland, and initiated a joint Israeli-Palestinian Peace Project at the Truman Institute of the Hebrew University of Jerusalem.

Judith Roumani, PhD, coeditor, has published numerous articles on Sephardic literature, particularly literature of the Holocaust. She is author of *Albert Memmi* (CELFAN Editions Monographs, 1987); a journal editor (www.sephardichorizons.org); and a translator of R. De Felice's *Ebrei in un Paese Arabo* (1978), De Felice's *Jews in an Arab Land: Libya 1835–1970* (University of Texas Press, 1985), and Albert Memmi's novel *Le Désert* (Syracuse University Press, 2015).

Maurice M. Roumani is professor of Political Science and the Middle East at Ben-Gurion University of the Negev where he is the founding director of the J. R. Elyachar Center for Studies in Sephardi Heritage. He is a leading expert on Libyan Jewish history and has published extensively on Jews from Arab countries, ethnic relations, and migration. His many publications include *The Jews of Libya: Coexistence, Persecution, Resettlement* (Sussex Academic Press, 2008), lately translated into Italian as *Gli ebrei di Libia dalla coesistenza all'esodo* (Castelvecchi, 2015). He taught at American and Italian universities and serves on the editorial boards of Italian and Israeli journals.

Vivienne Roumani-Denn is an oral historian, writer, and documentary film director. She served as the Judaica Librarian at the University of California, Berkeley, where she created the website www.jewsoflibya.com in 1998, and as the executive director of the American Sephardi Federation. Her oral histories of Jews from Libya are in the collections of the Library of Congress and the National Library of Israel. Her chapter "Overall Vision of the History and Heritage of the Jews of Libya" will appear in *Juifs d'ailleurs*, ed. E. Bruder (Paris: Albin Michel, 2018). Roumani-Denn's documentaries *The Last Jews of Libya* (2007), narrated by Isabella Rossellini, and *Out of Print* (2013), narrated by Meryl Streep, both premiered at the Tribeca Film Festival and have been viewed worldwide.

Rachel Simon, PhD, is a historian studying the Jews of the modern Middle East and North Africa, with special reference to Libya, women, education, and Zionism. She is the author of *Change within Tradition among Jewish Women in Libya* (University of Washington Press, 1992); and "Between the Family and the Outside World: Jewish Girls in the Modern Middle East and North Africa," *Jewish Social Studies* 7, no. 1 (2000): 81–108, among other works.

Sumikazu Yoda is an associate professor of Linguistics at the University of Osaka, Japan, and author, among other works, of *A Description of the Arabic Dialect of the Jews of Tripoli (Libya): Grammar, Texts and Glossary* (Wiesbaden: Harrassowitz Verlag, 2005).

Index

Italic page number denotes illustration.

colonialism. *See* Italian colonialism

communal training camps (*hakhsha-rot*), 167

Compagnia Lavoro, *228*

concentration camps. *See* internment and concentration camps

condolences (*taazia*), 205

contact zones, 138–41, *139, 140, 141*

Coptic church, 119

couscous, 45–46, 54–55, 175, 198

culinary traditions. *See* food and cooking

cultural diversity, 189

cultural traditions, 9, 11, 43–44; Arab-Jew relations and, 81; for baths, 47–48; in Benghazi vs. Tripoli, 183–84; brides and, 45–47, *46*; *bsisa* preparation, 66–67; celebration of births, 62–63; coffee and tea rituals, 48, *49*; daily life and, 73, 82, 84; henna parties, 65–66; identity and, 1, 2; Italian culture and, 75; Jewish law and, 11, 68–69; memories of, 196–99; modernity and, 43, 75–80; Orthodoxy and, 82–83; for Passover, *53*, 56–58, *61*; preservation of, 8, 154, 208–9; for Purim, 52–53, 83; religious life and, 71–74, 84; for Shabbat, 54–56, 60–61; women in Italy on, 174, 179; for Yom Kippur, 64–65

Cyprus, 23, 26, 30, 31, 34–36

Cyrenaica: agriculture vs. nomadic pastoralism in, 19–20; Arab conquest of 642 and, 39–41; Arabization of, 85; Arab-Jew relations in, 205–6; archaeology of, 17–18, 34–36, 34n33; British administration of, 186; deportations to camps

from, 221; history of, 185–86, 208, 209; Italian colonial period in, 207–8, 246; Qaramanlis rule over, 41; Sanusi order in, 37. *See also* Jewish revolt of Cyrenaica (115–117 CE)

Cyrene: destruction of, 26, 29–30, 30n24, 34–36; Great Rebellion of 66–73 and, 20, 24, 32–33; inscription from, *35*

daily life: cultural traditions and, 73, 82, 84; historical perspective on, 80–82; Judeo-Arabic documents on, 105; spoken Arabic dialects for, 86–89; of women, 155

Dante Alighieri Italian high school, 269

Dar Al Serussi, 117, 126, 127, *129, 130*

Dar Barukh synagogue, 161

Dar Bibi synagogue, 117, *118*, 126

Dar Bishi synagogue, 114–15, *116, 117*

Dar Burta synagogue, 77–80

dati (religious), or nonreligious (*lo dati*), 74

Dear Film Company, 141

death: after emigration, 176; in Bergen-Belsen, 237, 238, 239–40; mourning period for, 264; songs and singing about, 159

Decebalus, 33

decision making, 43, 72, 175

decree of December 1958, 261–62

decuman, 110, 110n1

Degel Sion (newspaper), 103–4, *104*

DeMille, Cecil, 5

Derna synagogue, *121, 122*

dfina (Sephardic cholent), 55–56

ḥasidut (special piety), 75
Haskalah (Jewish Enlightenment), 42
Hassuna Pasha mansion, 136
"Ha Tikvah," 243
Ha-Tiqvah school, 163–64
ḥayyalenu (our soldiers), 216
Hazan, Efraim, 286
Hazan, Eliahu Bekhor, 42, 76, 78
ḥazzan, 264
head coverings, 75
Hebrew language: biblical texts in, 155–56; linguistic games with, 265, 266, 268, 278; loan words from, 88, 93–96; *Mi Khamokha piyyutim* in, 217; revival of, 163–64, 164n22; study of, 62, 255; women in Israel on, 180
Hebrew Memorbuch of Libyan Jewry, 224
Hebrew schools, 163–64, 165, 169
Hebrew script. *See* Tripolitanian Judeo-Arabic (written)
Hechalutz (youth organization), 255
Hellenism, 24n6, 34, 36
henna parties, 65–66
Higgid Mordekhay (Mordecai Related) (Ha-Kohen), 42, *88*, 97, 105
Hirbet Qumran, 20, 36–37
"Historicizing the Concept of Arab Jews in the *Mashriq*" (Levy), 6
history, memory and, 4, 4n5, 14–15
Hitler, Adolf, 3, 233
holidays. *See* Jewish holidays
Holocaust experiences, 192, 208, 222–23. *See also* internment and concentration camps
Holocaust literature, 14, 226–43; of Gini Alhadeff, 232–33, 233n11; of Albert Bensoussan, 230–32,

230n7; of Edmond Jabés, 229–30; of Albert Memmi, 227–28; of Nine Moati, 232, 232n10; of Yossi Sucary, 14, 27, 192, 208, 226, 233–43
Holocaust Memorial Day, 223–24
Holy Ark (*Aron Hakodesh*), 59, 247
homes. *See* dwellings
Homs synagogue, *122*
hospitality, 188
housing project, 124–25, *125, 126*
Hush Al-Harem mansion, 126
Hush Angelo, 126
Hush Bashagha, 126, *128*
Hush Rabbi Nissim, 126
Hussein (King of Jordan), 274
al-Husseini, Amin, 254
hymns. *See piyyutim* (hymns)

Ibn 'Awkal, Joseph, 40
Ibn Ezra, Abraham, 40, 213–14
Ibn Gabriol, 266
Ibn Jenah, Moshe, 70
Ibn Khaldun, 39
identity: Arab Jews and, 5–7; cultural heritage and, 1, 2; Libyan Jewish, 201; multiple overlapping, 8, 180; national, 259; politics of, 258; self-determination of, 233; sports fans and, 259; women in Italy on, 179
Idris (King), 2, 4, 183, 186, 207
illiteracy, 156, 157, 164
illnesses, home remedies for, 62, 247
images, pagan cultic, 24–26, 27
Independence Day (Israel), 61
industrial construction, 150–51, *151*
inheritance, 179
Innsbruck-Reichenau, 191

Muslim writers, 233n12
Mussolini, Benito, 79–80, 151, 191, 221, 250
mysticism, Jewish, 264, 269, 271

nāda ("to call"), 96, *96*
Nafusa Mountains, *246*
Nafusa tribe, 39
Nahum (Rabbi), 207
Nahum, Aldo, 148
Nahum, Halfalla, 144
Nahum mansion, 126, *127, 128*
Naim, Jojo, 190, 193, 200
Naím, Moisés, 1, 200
Napoleon, 250–51
Al-Nasr cinema, 142
Nasser, Gamal, 229, 274
national anthem, 207
national identity, 259
nationalism. *See* Arab nationalism
Nazis, 191, 211, 221. *See also* Holo-caust experiences; internment and concentration camps; World War II
nefilat apayyim, 216
Nemni, Gheula Canarutoo, 12–13, 153, 154, 172–79
Nero, 20
ner tamid (lamp), 119
Netanya, Israel, 180, 181
"New Month of the Girls" (*rosh ḥodesh 'banat*), 158
Nissan, year of, 67
nomadic pastoralism, 19–20
nonreligious (*lo dati*), or religious (*dati*), 74
North Africa: Arabization of, 85, 104–5, 186; Holocaust literature of, 226; refuge in, 231, 231n9; World War II in, 228

nukides (Tripolitanian gnocchi), 64
Nunes-Vais, Barolina, 162
nurses, 168
nusach (cantillation), Libyan, 196

Odeon Cinema, 141, *142, 143*
old people's hospice (*gherfa*), 117, 126
olim, 139, 139n3
oral education, 11, 42, 43
oral histories, 186, 187–88. *See also* interviews; memories
oral poetry, 157–58
Orosius, 26
Orthodoxy, 73, 82–83, 84
ostrich feather processing, 168
O There Descended (*Aha Yarad*) (ibn Ezra), 40
Othman Bank, 130
Ottoman rule, 2, 18, 41–42; *ḥakham bashi* (chief rabbi) and, 42, 78; history of, 186; Jewish quarters of Tripoli and, 108, 110; protec-tion of Jews during, 252; Purim celebrations and, 190; women and, 153–54
ovens, public, 58–59, 125, 195

pagan cultic images, 24–26, 27
Pagani, Alfonzo, 4, 4n6
Paggi, Giannetto, 162
Palazzi Nahum, *134*, 134
Palazzo Haddad, 134, *135*
Palazzo "Nafha," 134, *134*
Palestine: curriculum from, 165; Jewish revolt of Cyrenaica and, 17; kibbutz life in, 167; liberation of, 271; Yishuv and, 254, 254n3, 255; youth movements and, 166

wage earners: in Israel, 182; in Italy, 175–76, 179; in post–World War II period, 261; women as, 159, *160*, *161*, 167–69, 179, 182

Wahba, Yusuf, 207

War of Independence (Israel), 198, 215

"War of the Sons of Light with the Sons of Darkness, The" (scroll), 20

wedding ceremonies, 158–59

wells, without water, 57

Western lifestyle, 78–80, 81, 174

"What Makes Oral History Different" (Portelli), 187

Who Remembers the Sea (Qui se souvient de la mer) (Dib), 241, 242

women, 12–13; from Benghazi, 180–81, *188*; in *Benghazi— Bergen-Belsen* (Sucary), 234–35, 235n15, 238–39; communal training camps (*hakhsharot*) and, 167; community status of, 169–70; creativity of, 159–60; decision making and, 175; education for, 153–54, 157, 160–65, 170, 177; elderly, 174; in *Emiliyah u melah ha-Arets: Vidui* (Sucary), 233–34; gender roles and, 153, 155; in Israel, 153, 154, 179–82; Italian colonial period and, 153–54, 235; in Italy, 153, 154, 172–79; Jewish law and, 157; literature by, 157–58, 169–70; marginalization of, 12, 155–71; Ottoman rule and, 153–54; photographs of, 46, *166*, *173*; primary role of, 175, 176, 177, 178, 179; religious life and, 83–84, 153, 154, 157, 178;

in Sephardic society, 176, 197; socializing by, 158, 175; songs and singing by, 157–59, 170; spiritual life of, 157–58; as teachers, 165, *167*, 168, 169, 177; theater performances by, 166; as wage earners, 159, *160*, *161*, 167–69, 175–76, 179, 182; Zionism and, 154

wool, lamb's, 45–46

World Cup, 270, 271

World War II, 2; in Africa, 214, 228; deportations during, 82, 246–47; education during, 164–65, 177; El Alamein offensive and, 254; emigration during, 247; end of, 186; growing up during, 174; memories of, 191; racial laws during, 177; Sanusi brotherhood in, 246; traumatic events during, 211, 220–25. *See also* British administration and occupation; Holocaust literature; internment and concentration camps

yeshivas, 71, 117, 124, 124n2, 126

Yishuv, 254, 254n3, 255

Yizkor, 225

Yoda, Sumikazu, 12, 43–44, 85–106

Yom Hazikaron (Memorial Day), 234

Yom Kippur, 64–65, 264, 271

youth movements, 166–67, 169, 255

Yusuf ibn Ya'qub al-Itrabulsi, 40

Yusuf Pasha, 126

Zakhor, 215n2

zamzamat, 158